ADVANCED PLACEMENT
ECONOMICS
MICROECONOMICS

Student Resource Manual

4th Edition
Gary L. Stone

COUNCIL FOR
**Economic
Education**

Teaching Opportunity

Authors and Contributors

Author

Gary L. Stone is a professor of economics and director of the Center for Economic Education at Winthrop University. He has conducted numerous workshops for Advanced Placement Economics teachers and has been a reader and table leader for the AP Economics Examinations for over two decades. Gary received the Bessie B. Moore Service Award from the National Association of Economic Educators for his work in economic education with K–12 teachers in the United States and other countries.

Contributing Author

Margaret A. Ray, author of *Advanced Placement Economics Macroeconomics* and contributor to Unit 1, is a professor of economics and director of the Center for Economic Education at the University of Mary Washington. She taught AP Economics at Collegiate School in Richmond, Virginia, in 2002–2003 and was an economist and director of economic education at the Federal Reserve Bank of Richmond. Margaret has been a reader, table leader, and question leader for the AP Economic Examinations from 1993 to the present and she currently serves on the AP Microeconomics Test Development Committee.

Content Consultant

Dennis Placone is professor emeritus of economics and director of the Center for Economic Education at Clemson University. He has more than 35 years of teaching, research, and administrative experience at Clemson, and has conducted workshops for K–12 teachers including AP teachers since 1989. He served as chair of the AP Economics Test Development Committee from 1997–2003.

Project Director

Kevin Gotchet is the Director for the Excellence in Economic Education program. He has been with the Council for Economic Education for more than eight years and has taken a leading role in several CEE initiatives.

Funding

The Council for Economic Education gratefully acknowledges the funding of this publication by the U.S. Department of Education, Office of Innovation and Improvement, Excellence in Economic Education: Advancing K–12 Economic & Financial Education Nationwide grant award U215B100002. The contents of this book developed under the grant from the Department of Education do not necessarily represent the policy of the Department of Education, and you should not assume endorsement by the federal government.

ISBN: 978-156183-670-3

Contents

Unit 1 **Basic Economic Concepts   1**

Key Ideas   3

Activity 1-1   Do You Think Like an Economist?   5

Activity 1-2   Scarcity, Opportunity Cost, and Production Possibilities Curves   7

Activity 1-3   Determining Comparative Advantage   15

Activity 1-4   Demand Curves, Movements along Demand Curves, and Shifts in Demand Curves   23

Activity 1-5   Reasons for Changes in Demand   29

Activity 1-6   Supply Curves, Movements along Supply Curves, and Shifts in Supply Curves   31

Activity 1-7   Reasons for Changes in Supply   37

Activity 1-8   Equilibrium Price and Equilibrium Quantity   39

Activity 1-9   Shifts in Supply and Demand   43

Activity 1-10 Economic Systems   47

Activity 1-11 Anything Worth Doing Is Not Necessarily Worth Doing Well   49

Multiple-Choice Sample Questions   53

Unit 2 **The Nature and Functions of Product Markets   61**

Key Ideas   63

Activity 2-1   How Markets Allocate Resources   65

Activity 2-2   Why Is a Demand Curve Downward Sloping?   69

Activity 2-3   Elasticity: An Introduction   77

Activity 2-4   The Determinants of Price Elasticity of Demand   87

Activity 2-5   Elasticity and Total Revenue   91

Activity 2-6   Excise Taxes   93

Activity 2-7   Maximum and Minimum Price Controls   99

Activity 2-8   Property Rights and Market Failure   101

Activity 2-9   Deadweight Loss   103

Multiple-Choice Sample Questions   107

Unit 3 **The Theory of the Firm   111**

Key Ideas   113

Activity 3-1   Different Types of Market Structures   115

Activity 3-2   Mirror Images: Marginal Product and Marginal Cost   117

Activity 3-3   Understanding the Different Cost Measures of a Firm   127

Activity 3-4   A Firm's Long-Run Average Total Cost Curve   135

Activity 3-5   Revenue, Profit, and Rules to Maximize Total Profit   139

Activity 3-6   Profit Maximization by a Perfectly Competitive Firm   145

Activity 3-7   Short-Run Equilibrium and Short-Run Supply in Perfect Competition   157

Activity 3-8   Long-Run Equilibrium and Long-Run Supply
in Perfect Competition   163

Activity 3-9   Graphing Perfect Competition   171

Activity 3-10 The Revenue Functions of a Monopoly   175

Activity 3-11 Profit Maximization by a Monopoly   179

Activity 3-12 Equilibrium in a Monopolistic Market   183

Activity 3-13 Price Discrimination   187

Activity 3-14 Regulating a Monopoly   193

Activity 3-15 Comparing Perfect Competition and Monopoly   197

Activity 3-16 Monopolistic Competition   201

Activity 3-17 Game Theory   207

Multiple-Choice Sample Questions   213

Unit 4   Factor Markets   223

Key Ideas   225

Activity 4-1   How Many Workers Should a Firm Hire?   227

Activity 4-2   The Optimal Combination of Resources   235

Activity 4-3   The Only Game in Town   239

Activity 4-4   Factor Market Pricing   243

Activity 4-5   How Wages Are Determined in Labor Markets   249

Activity 4-6   Wages and Employment in Competitive and
Monopsonistic Labor Markets   253

Activity 4-7   Problems Dealing with Factor Markets   259

Multiple-Choice Sample Questions   263

Unit 5   The Role of Government   269

Key Ideas   271

Activity 5-1   Private or Public? Public Goods and Services   273

Activity 5-2   Externalities   277

Activity 5-3   Private or Public? The Coase Theorem   287

Activity 5-4   Economic Efficiency and the Optimum Amount of Pollution Cleanup   289

Activity 5-5   What Is a Fair Tax?   293

Activity 5-6   Who Pays the Income Tax?   295

Activity 5-7   The Lorenz Curve and Gini Coefficient   299

Multiple-Choice Sample Questions   303

MICROECONOMICS

Basic Economic Concepts

Unit 1

- Scarcity exists because we have limited resources and unlimited wants. No society has ever had enough resources to produce all the goods and services its members wanted.

- Goods and services are produced from resources. These resources—land, labor, capital, and entrepreneurship—are limited.

- Scarcity requires people to make choices. If we use scarce resources for one purpose, we cannot use them for another.

- Opportunity cost is the forgone benefit of the next best alternative when resources are used for one purpose rather than another.

- Because of scarcity, every decision has an opportunity cost.

- Economic costs take account of the opportunity cost of doing one thing rather than another.

- Economic costs include explicit costs and implicit costs. Explicit costs are expenditures for something. Implicit costs are the opportunity costs of using your own resources rather than selling them to someone else. Both implicit and explicit costs are opportunity costs.

- Using free goods does not involve opportunity cost because free goods are available in unlimited quantities.

- Economics is concerned with marginal decision making. In economics, "making decisions at the margin" is very important. Marginal choices involve the effects of additions and subtractions from the current situation. We compare the marginal benefit of an extra unit of an activity with that unit's marginal cost.

- A production possibilities curve can be used to illustrate scarcity, choice, and opportunity cost graphically.

- The slope of a production possibilities curve shows the opportunity cost of producing another unit of one good in terms of the amount of the other good that must be given up.

- Because resources are scarce, using them efficiently allows us to get the most from them. Efficiency is increased through specialization and trade. Economists use the concept of comparative advantage to explain why trade takes place between countries and between individuals. This concept is based on the differences in producers' opportunity costs of producing goods and services.

- Because of scarcity, people and societies use economic systems to determine what to produce, how to produce, and for whom to produce.

- Throughout history, nations have used tradition, command, and market systems to allocate resources.

- The law of comparative advantage shows how everyone can gain through trade.

- Economic theory is useful in analyzing and understanding the world around us.

- The test of an economic theory is its ability to predict correctly the future consequences of economic actions.

- The broad social goals of a society influence decisions about how best to use resources.

- A diagram of the circular flow of resources, goods and services, and money-income payments is a simplified way of illustrating how a market economy operates. Prices in the product market and prices in the factor, or resource, market are determined by the interaction of supply and demand. This diagram is also called the circular flow of income.

- Markets bring together buyers and sellers of a good or service.

- The law of demand states that buyers will want more of an item at a low price than at a high price, other things being equal.

- The law of supply states that sellers will provide more of an item at a high price than at a low price, other things being equal.

- The equilibrium price is the price at which the quantity demanded of an item equals the quantity supplied. That quantity is called the equilibrium quantity.

- Shifts in the market demand and supply curves result in new values of the equilibrium price and quantity. Understanding what causes shifts in the demand and supply curves is an important part of knowing how a market operates.

Do You Think Like an Economist?

Circle T for *true* or F for *false* in the statements that follow.

T F 1. Because it is desirable, sunshine is scarce.

T F 2. Because it is limited, polio is scarce.

T F 3. Because water covers three-fourths of the earth's surface and is renewable, it cannot be considered scarce.

T F 4. The main cost of going to college is tuition, room, and board.

T F 5. If mass transportation fares are raised, almost everyone will take the trains anyway.

T F 6. You get what you pay for.

T F 7. If someone makes an economic gain, someone else loses.

T F 8. If one nation produces everything better than another nation, there is no economic reason for these two nations to trade.

T F 9. A nonregulated monopoly tends to charge the highest possible price.

T F 10. A business owner's decision to show more care for consumers is a decision to accept lower levels of profits.

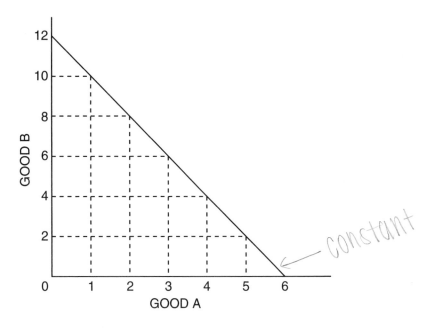
Scarcity, Opportunity Cost, and Production Possibilities Curves

The primary economic problem facing all individuals, families, businesses, and nations is the scarcity of resources: There simply are not enough resources to satisfy the unlimited wants for goods and services. Scarcity necessitates choice. Consuming or producing more of one thing means consuming or producing less of something else. The opportunity cost of using scarce resources for one thing instead of something else is often represented in graphical form as a *production possibilities curve* (PPC). A nation's PPC shows how many units of two goods or services the nation can produce in one year if it uses its resources fully and efficiently. This activity uses the PPC to illustrate how scarcity requires choices and the opportunity cost of those choices.

Part A: Basic Production Possibilities Curves

Figure 1-2.1 shows a basic PPC for the production of Goods A and B. Use Figure 1-2.1 to answer the questions that follow.

Figure 1-2.1
A Linear Production Possibilities Curve

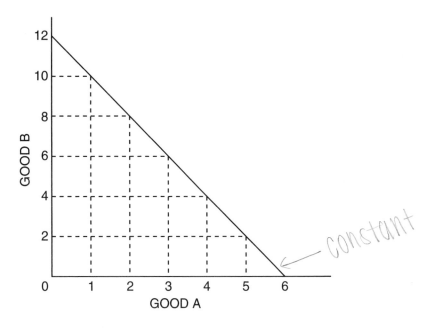

1. Assume the economy represented by Figure 1-2.1 is presently producing 12 units of Good B and 0 units of Good A:

   (A) The opportunity cost of increasing production of Good A from 0 units to 1 unit is the loss of _____2_____ unit(s) of Good B.

   (B) The opportunity cost of increasing production of Good A from 1 unit to 2 units is the loss of _____2_____ unit(s) of Good B.

   (C) The opportunity cost of increasing production of Good A from 2 units to 3 units is the loss of _____2_____ unit(s) of Good B.

   (D) This is an example of (*constant* / *increasing* / *decreasing* / *zero*) opportunity cost per unit for Good A.

Advanced Placement Economics Microeconomics: Student Resource Manual © Council for Economic Education, New York, N.Y.

Figure 1-2.2 contains a typical PPC often used by economists. This PPC is concave to the origin; it gets steeper as the country moves out along its horizontal axis. Use Figure 1-2.2 to answer the questions below it.

Figure 1-2.2
A Concave Production Possibilities Curve

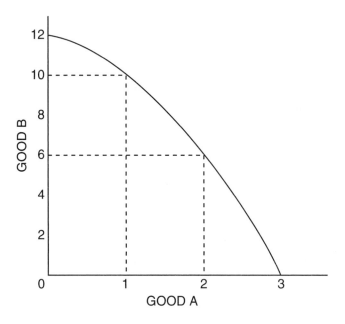

2. If the economy represented in Figure 1-2.2 is presently producing 12 units of Good B and 0 units of Good A:

   (A) The opportunity cost of increasing production of Good A from 0 units to 1 unit is the loss of _____2_____ unit(s) of Good B.

   (B) The opportunity cost of increasing production of Good A from 1 unit to 2 units is the loss of _____4_____ unit(s) of Good B.

   (C) The opportunity cost of increasing production of Good A from 2 units to 3 units is the loss of _____6_____ unit(s) of Good B.

   (D) This is an example of (*constant / increasing / decreasing / zero*) opportunity cost per unit for Good A.

Part B: Understanding the Shape of a Concave PPC

The "law of increasing opportunity cost" explains why the typical PPC is concave to the origin (bowed outward). Figure 1-2.3 shows the PPC for the country of Costica. The country currently operates at point A and produces 75 million units of civilian goods and 2 million units of military goods. If the country decides to increase its military provision to 3 million units, it must give up only 5 million units in civilian goods because certain factories are easily converted from civilian production to military production. However, if Costica decides it must continue to increase its military production, the opportunity cost of doing so increases because now it is more difficult to convert other factories to military production. Resources are not equally well suited to the production of all goods. The opportunity cost of increasing military output from 6 million units to 7 million units (point C to point D) has increased to 15 million units in civilian goods. This increasing opportunity cost is reflected in the steeper slope of the PPC as the country produces more military goods and fewer civilian goods.

Figure 1-2.3
Showing the Law of Increasing Opportunity Cost

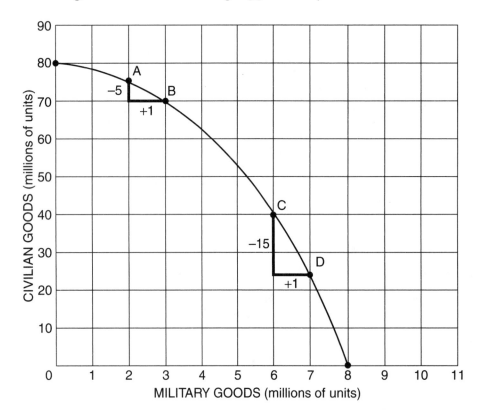

Part C: Drawing Various PPCs

Use the following axes to draw the type of curve that illustrates the label above each graph.

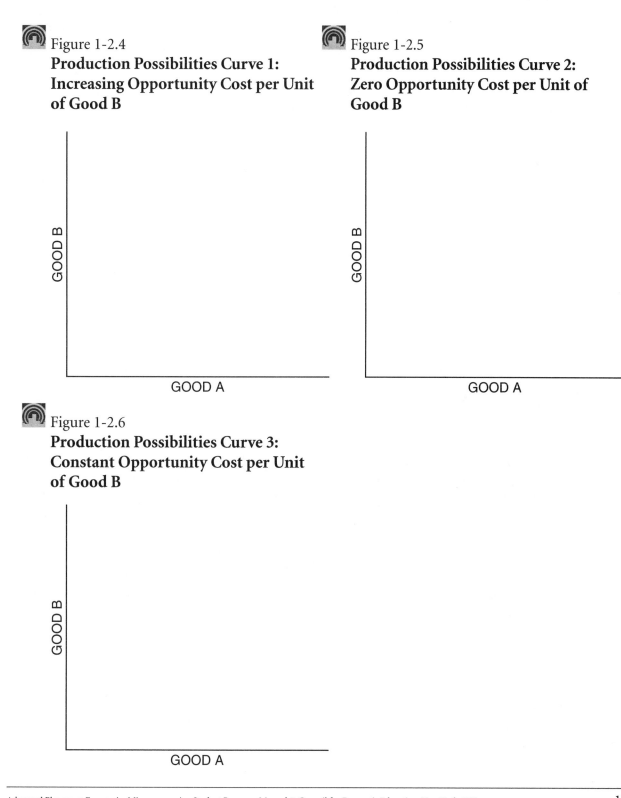

Figure 1-2.4
**Production Possibilities Curve 1:
Increasing Opportunity Cost per Unit
of Good B**

GOOD B

GOOD A

Figure 1-2.5
**Production Possibilities Curve 2:
Zero Opportunity Cost per Unit of
Good B**

GOOD B

GOOD A

Figure 1-2.6
**Production Possibilities Curve 3:
Constant Opportunity Cost per Unit
of Good B**

GOOD B

GOOD A

Part D: Economic Growth

Over time, most countries see an increase in their ability to produce goods and services. This "economic growth" is shown as an outward shift of the PPC and results from a variety of factors, including improved technology, better education, and the discovery of new resources. Use Figure 1-2.7 to answer the next five questions. Each question starts with Curve BE as a country's PPC.

Figure 1-2.7

Production Possibilities Curve: Capital Goods and Consumer Goods

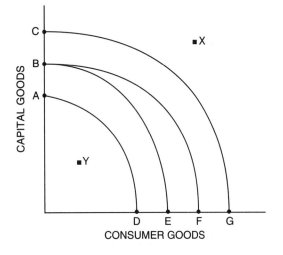

3. Suppose there is a major technological breakthrough in the consumer-goods industry, and the new technology is widely adopted. Which curve in the diagram would represent the new PPC? (Indicate the curve you choose with two letters.) _____ BF

4. Suppose a new government comes into power and forbids the use of automated machinery and modern production techniques in all industries. Which curve in the diagram would represent the new PPC? (Indicate the curve you choose with two letters.) _____ AD

5. Suppose massive new sources of oil and coal are found within the economy, and there are major technological innovations in both industries. Which curve in the diagram would represent the new PPC? (Indicate the curve you choose with two letters.) _____ CG

6. If BE represents a country's current PPC, what can you say about a point like X? (Write a brief statement.) Point X is unattainable

7. If BE represents a country's current PPC, what can you say about a point like Y? (Write a brief statement.) Point y is not using all of your resources.

Use Figure 1-2.8 to answer the next three questions.

Figure 1-2.8
Production Possibilities Curve: Economic Growth

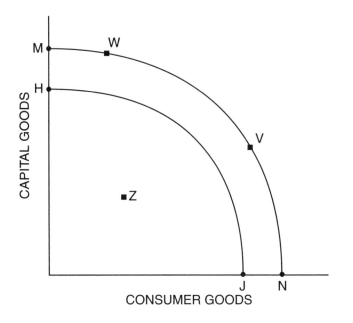

8. What change could cause the PPC to shift from the original curve (HJ) to the new curve (MN)?

9. Under what conditions might an economy be operating at Point Z?

10. Why might a government implement a policy to move the economy from Point V to Point W?

Determining Comparative Advantage

Voluntary trade between two individuals or two countries occurs if both parties feel that they will benefit. Producers have an incentive to make products for which they have a lower opportunity cost than other producers. When both producers specialize according to their *comparative advantage*, they increase the total amount of goods and services that are available for consumption. To determine who has a comparative advantage in producing a particular item, we need to calculate each producer's opportunity costs of creating the items. The way we calculate opportunity cost depends on how the productivity data are expressed.

There are two ways to measure productivity: the "input method" and the "output method." We can calculate the quantity of output produced from a given amount of inputs, or we can measure the amount of inputs necessary to create one unit of output. Examples of output are tons of wheat per acre, miles per gallon, words per minute, apples per tree, and televisions produced per hour. Examples of input are number of hours to do a job, number of gallons of paint to paint a house, and number of acres to feed a horse. We will work through an example that expresses productivity from the perspectives of an input measure and an output measure.

Part A: Two Approaches to Comparative Advantage

Student Alert: In using these models to determine the lower opportunity costs from both an input and output viewpoint, you must pay attention to the format of the chart. It makes a difference!

Input Method

The "input method" provides data on the amount of resources needed to produce one unit of output. Table 1-3.1 gives productivity information for Ted and Nancy.

Table 1-3.1
Productivity Data Using the Input Method

	Time required to produce one radio	Time required to produce one bushel of wheat
Ted	20 minutes	5 minutes
Nancy	30 minutes	15 minutes

Ted has an *absolute advantage* in the production of both radios and wheat because he uses fewer resources (time) to produce each item than does Nancy. Even though this might suggest that Ted cannot benefit from trade with Nancy, our examination of the opportunity costs of production will show that is not the case.

Table 1-3.2 shows the opportunity costs for each producer. To find the opportunity cost of producing one radio, the amount of resources it takes to produce a radio goes *above* the amount of resources that it takes to produce a bushel of wheat.

Table 1-3.2
Opportunity Cost of Producing Radios and Wheat

	Opportunity cost of producing one radio	Opportunity cost of producing one bushel of wheat
Ted	$1 \text{ radio} = \dfrac{20 \text{ minutes}}{5 \text{ minutes}} = 4 \text{ bushels}$	$1 \text{ wheat} = \dfrac{5 \text{ minutes}}{20 \text{ minutes}} = \text{¼ radio}$
Nancy	$1 \text{ radio} = \dfrac{30 \text{ minutes}}{15 \text{ minutes}} = 2 \text{ bushels}$	$1 \text{ wheat} = \dfrac{15 \text{ minutes}}{30 \text{ minutes}} = \text{½ radio}$

In the 20 minutes it takes Ted to produce one radio, he instead could have produced four bushels of wheat. Instead of producing one radio in 30 minutes, Nancy could have produced two bushels of wheat. The fact that Nancy has the lower opportunity cost of producing radios means she has the comparative advantage in radios.

In the five minutes he needs to produce one bushel of wheat, Ted could have made ¼ of a radio. Nancy's opportunity cost of producing one bushel of wheat is ½ of a radio. Because his sacrifice in producing one bushel of wheat is less than Nancy's, Ted has the comparative advantage in wheat production.

If Ted specializes in wheat production while Nancy specializes in radio production, their combined output of radios and wheat will be larger than it would be if each person produced both products.

Output Method

The "output method" gives data on the amount of output that can be produced with a given amount of an input. Now let's take this same set of productivity data and turn it into an output format. To do this, we ask how many units of an item the producers can create with a given amount of resources. Let's suppose that both producers have one hour to produce each product. Table 1-3.3 shows how many radios and how many bushels of wheat each producer can make in one hour. From this output viewpoint, you once again see that Ted has the absolute advantage in the production of both products. With the same amount of resources (one hour of labor), he can produce more radios and more wheat than Nancy.

Table 1-3.3
Productivity Data Using the Output Method

	Radios produced per hour	Wheat produced per hour
Ted	$\dfrac{60 \text{ minutes}}{20 \text{ minutes}} = 3 \text{ radios}$	$\dfrac{60 \text{ minutes}}{5 \text{ minutes}} = 12 \text{ bushels}$
Nancy	$\dfrac{60 \text{ minutes}}{30 \text{ minutes}} = 2 \text{ radios}$	$\dfrac{60 \text{ minutes}}{15 \text{ minutes}} = 4 \text{ bushels}$

But what about the opportunity cost to produce each item? Check out Table 1-3.4, which shows how to calculate each producer's opportunity cost of the two items. To find Ted's opportunity cost of producing one radio, the number of radios he can produce in one hour goes *under* the number of bushels of wheat he can produce in that same time frame.

Table 1-3.4

Opportunity Cost of Producing Radios and Wheat

	Opportunity cost of producing one radio	Opportunity cost of producing one bushel of wheat
Ted	3 radios = 1 hour = 12 bushels 1 radio = 12/3 = 4 bushels	12 bushels = 1 hour = 3 radios 1 bushel = 3/12 = ¼ radio
Nancy	2 radios = 1 hour = 4 bushels 1 radio = 4/2 = 2 bushels	4 bushels = 1 hour = 2 radios 1 bushel = 2/4 = ½ radio

Because Ted's cost per radio is four bushels of wheat, whereas Nancy's cost is only two bushels, we know Nancy has the comparative advantage in producing radios. Ted has the comparative advantage in wheat production since he has the lower opportunity cost of producing a bushel of wheat (¼ radio compared to Nancy's ½ radio). Does this sound familiar? This is the same result we reached using the input method.

The differences in opportunity costs define the limits of a trade in which both parties will benefit. If Nancy specializes in radio production, she will accept no less than two bushels of wheat for one radio. Ted will pay no more than four bushels of wheat per radio. Thus, the "terms of trade" acceptable to both producers must lie in the range between two bushels for one radio and four bushels for one radio. For example, suppose they agree to trade one radio for three bushels of wheat. By producing and trading one radio to Ted, Nancy will have a net gain of one bushel. Her opportunity cost of producing the radio is two bushels and she receives three bushels in return for the radio. Because his opportunity cost of producing one bushel is ¼ radio, Ted's opportunity cost of producing the three bushels, which he trades to Nancy, is ¾ radio. Thus, the trade gives Ted a net gain of ¼ radio. Both producers gain by specializing according to their comparative advantage.

When it comes to producing wheat, Ted would have to receive at least ¼ of a radio in trade for a bushel of wheat. Nancy would require at least ½ of a radio before she would trade a bushel of wheat. The acceptable terms of trade would be found between ¼ radio and ½ radio per bushel of wheat.

The output data in Table 1-3.3 can be used to create production possibility frontiers for Ted and Nancy to show the combinations of radios and wheat each can produce in one hour of work. See Figure 1-3.1.

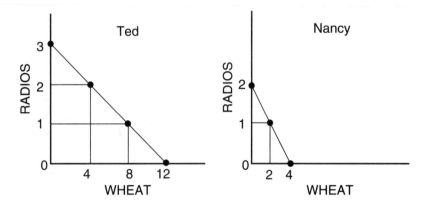

Figure 1-3.1
Production Possibilities Curves for Ted and Nancy

Part B: Comparative Advantage Exercises

For each of the following scenarios, answer the questions following the chart. The first problem is answered for you.

1. Anna and Barry can grow the following amounts of potatoes and cabbage with a week of labor.

	Potatoes per week	Cabbage per week
Anna	100 units	200 units
Barry	120 units	150 units

(A) Is this an example of an *input* problem or an *output* problem?

Output problem

(B) What is the opportunity cost for each producer in making these products?

   (1) Anna's opportunity cost of producing a unit of potatoes is __2__ units of cabbage.

   (2) Barry's opportunity cost of producing a unit of potatoes is __5/4__ units of cabbage.

(3) Anna's opportunity cost of producing a unit of cabbage is ___1/2___ units of potatoes.

(4) Barry's opportunity cost of producing a unit of cabbage is ___4/5___ units of potatoes.

(C) Who has the comparative advantage in producing potatoes? ___Barry___

(D) Who has the comparative advantage in producing cabbage? ___Anna___

Note: In this example, each producer has the absolute advantage in producing one item: Barry in potatoes and Anna in cabbage. That might not be the case in the other examples.

2. Henry and John are fishermen who catch bass and catfish. This chart shows how many of each type of fish they can catch in one day.

	Bass	Catfish
Henry	4 bass	6 catfish
John	24 bass	12 catfish

Henry
4B - 6C
1B - 3/2C
1C - 2/3B

John
24B - 12C
1B - 1/2C
1C - 2B

(A) Is this an example of an *input* problem or an *output* problem? output problem

(B) What is the opportunity cost for each person in catching these fish?
    (1) Henry's opportunity cost of catching 1 bass is ___3/2___ catfish.
    (2) John's opportunity cost of catching 1 bass is ___1/2___ catfish.
    (3) Henry's opportunity cost of catching 1 catfish is ___2/3___ bass.
    (4) John's opportunity cost of catching 1 catfish is ___2___ bass.

(C) Who has the comparative advantage in catching bass? ___John___

(D) Who has the comparative advantage in catching catfish? ___Henry___

3. This chart shows how many days it takes the ABC Corporation and the XYZ Corporation to produce one unit of cars and one unit of planes.

	Cars	Planes
ABC Corp.	8 days	10 days
XYZ Corp.	15 days	12 days

[handwritten: ABC corp 8DC–10DP 1C = 4/5P 1P = 5/4C   XYZ Corp 15DC–12DP 1C = 5/4P 1P = 4/5C]

(A) Is this an example of an *input* problem or an *output* problem?

[handwritten: input problem]

(B) What is the opportunity cost for each corporation in producing these goods?

   (1) ABC's opportunity cost of producing a unit of cars is ___4/5___ units of planes.

   (2) XYZ's opportunity cost of producing a unit of cars is ___5/4___ units of planes.

   (3) ABC's opportunity cost of producing a unit of planes is ___5/4___ units of cars.

   (4) XYZ's opportunity cost of producing a unit of planes is ___4/5___ units of cars.

(C) Who has the comparative advantage in producing cars? *[handwritten: ABC Corp]*

(D) Who has the comparative advantage in producing planes? *[handwritten: XYZ Corp]*

4. Here are the numbers of acres needed in India and China produce 100 bushels of corn or 100 bushels of rice each month.

	India	China
Corn	9 acres	8 acres
Rice	3 acres	2 acres

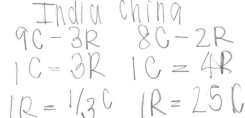

[handwritten: India China 9C–3R 8C–2R 1C=3R 1C=4R 1R=1/3C 1R=25C]

(A) Is this an example of an *input* problem or an *output* problem?

[handwritten: input problem]

(B) What is the opportunity cost for each country in producing these goods?

(1) India's opportunity cost of growing 100 bushels of corn is _300_ bushels of rice.

(2) China's opportunity cost of growing 100 bushels of corn is _400_ bushels of rice.

(3) India's opportunity cost of growing 100 bushels of rice is _33_ bushels of corn.

(4) China's opportunity cost of growing 100 bushels of rice is _25_ bushels of corn.

(C) Who has the comparative advantage in growing corn? _India_

(D) Who has the comparative advantage in growing rice? _China_

5. This chart shows how many cans of olives and bottles of olive oil can be produced in Zaire and Colombia from one ton of olives.

	Zaire	Colombia
Olives	60 cans	24 cans
Olive oil	10 bottles	8 bottles

Zaire   Columbia
60C - 10B   24C - 8B
1C - 1/6B   1C - 1/3B
1B - 6   1B - 3C

(A) Is this an example of an *input* problem or an *output* problem? _output problem_

(B) What is the opportunity cost for each country in producing these goods?

(1) Zaire's opportunity cost of producing 1 can of olives is _1/6_ bottles of olive oil.

(2) Colombia's opportunity cost of producing 1 can of olives is _1/3_ bottles of olive oil.

(3) Zaire's opportunity cost of producing 1 bottle of olive oil is _6_ cans of olives.

(4) Colombia's opportunity cost of producing 1 bottle of olive oil is _3_ cans of olives.

(C) Who has the comparative advantage in producing olives? _Zaire_

(D) Who has the comparative advantage in producing olive oil? _Colombia_

6. Here are the numbers of hours needed in Redland and Blueland to produce a unit of televisions and a unit of computers.

	Televisions	Computers
Redland	18 hours	6 hours
Blueland	16 hours	4 hours

Redland   Blueland
18 TV-6C   16TV-4C
1 TV - 3C   1 TV - 4C
1C - 1/3 TV   1C - 1/4 TV

(A) Is this an example of an *input* problem or an *output* problem?

input problem

(B) What is the opportunity cost for each country in producing these goods?

(1) Redland's opportunity cost of producing 1 unit of televisions is __3__ units of computers.

(2) Blueland's opportunity cost of producing 1 unit of televisions is __4__ units of computers.

(3) Redland's opportunity cost of producing 1 unit of computers is __1/3__ units of televisions.

(4) Blueland's opportunity cost of producing 1 unit of computers is __1/4__ units of televisions.

(C) Who has the comparative advantage in producing televisions? *Redland*

(D) Who has the comparative advantage in producing computers? *Blueland*

Demand Curves, Movements along Demand Curves, and Shifts in Demand Curves

Part A: A Change in Demand versus a Change in Quantity Demanded

Student Alert: The distinction between a "change in demand" and a "change in quantity demanded" is very important!

Table 1-4.1 shows the market demand for a hypothetical product: Greebes. Study the data and plot the demand for Greebes on the graph in Figure 1-4.1. Label the demand curve D, and answer the questions that follow.

Table 1-4.1
Demand for Greebes

Price (per Greebe)	Quantity demanded per week (millions of Greebes)
$0.10	350
$0.15	300
$0.20	250
$0.25	200
$0.30	150
$0.35	100
$0.40	50
$0.45	0

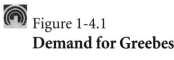

Figure 1-4.1
Demand for Greebes

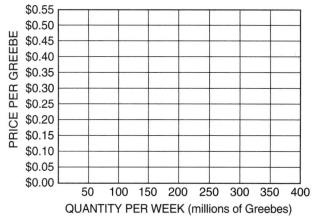

1. The data for demand curve D indicate that at a price of $0.30 per Greebe, buyers would be willing to buy _____ million Greebes. All other things held constant, if the price of Greebes increased to $0.40 per Greebe, buyers would be willing to buy _____ million Greebes. Such a change would be a decrease in (*demand / quantity demanded*). All other things held constant, if the price of Greebes decreased to $0.20, buyers would be willing to buy _____ million Greebes. Such a change would be called an increase in (*demand / quantity demanded*).

Now, let's suppose there is a change in federal income-tax rates that affects the disposable income of Greebe buyers. This change in the *ceteris paribus* (all else being equal) conditions underlying the original demand for Greebes will result in a new set of data, shown in Table 1-4.2. Study these new data, and add the new demand curve for Greebes to the graph in Figure 1-4.1. Label the new demand curve D_1 and answer the questions that follow.

Table 1-4.2
New Demand for Greebes

Price (per Greebe)	Quantity demanded per week (millions of Greebes)
$0.05	300
$0.10	250
$0.15	200
$0.20	150
$0.25	100
$0.30	50

2. Comparing the new demand curve (D_1) with the original demand curve (D), we can say that the change in the demand for Greebes results in a shift of the demand curve to the (*left / right*). Such a shift indicates that at each of the possible prices shown, buyers are now willing to buy a (*smaller / larger*) quantity; and at each of the possible quantities shown, buyers are willing to offer a (*higher / lower*) maximum price. The cause of this demand curve shift was a(n) (*increase / decrease*) in tax rates that (*increased / decreased*) the disposable income of Greebe buyers.

Now, let's suppose that there is a dramatic change in people's tastes and preferences for Greebes. This change in the *ceteris paribus* conditions underlying the original demand for Greebes will result in a new set of data, shown in Table 1-4.3. Study these new data, and add the new demand curve for Greebes to the graph in Figure 1-4.1. Label the new demand curve D_2 and answer the questions that follow.

Table 1-4.3
New Demand for Greebes

Price (per Greebe)	Quantity demanded per week (millions of Greebes)
$0.20	350
$0.25	300
$0.30	250
$0.35	200
$0.40	150
$0.45	100
$0.50	50

3. Comparing the new demand curve (D_2) with the original demand curve (D), we can say that the change in the demand for Greebes results in a shift of the demand curve to the (*left / right*). Such a shift indicates that at each of the possible prices shown, buyers are now willing to buy a (*smaller / larger*) quantity; and at each of the possible quantities shown, buyers are willing to offer a (*lower / higher*) maximum price. The cause of this shift in the demand curve was a(n) (*increase / decrease*) in people's tastes and preferences for Greebes.

Part B: Do You Get It?

Now, to test your understanding, choose the answer you think is the best in each of the following multiple-choice questions.

4. All other things held constant, which of the following would *not* cause a change in the demand (shift in the demand curve) for motorcycles?

   (A) A decrease in consumer incomes

   (B) A decrease in the price of motorcycles

   (C) An increase in the price of bicycles

   (D) An increase in people's tastes and preferences for motorcycles

5. "Rising oil prices have caused a sharp decrease in the demand for oil." Speaking precisely, and using terms as they are defined by economists, choose the statement that best describes this quotation.

   (A) The quotation is correct: an increase in price causes a decrease in demand.

   (B) The quotation is incorrect: an increase in price causes an increase in demand, not a decrease in demand.

   (C) The quotation is incorrect: an increase in price causes a decrease in the quantity demanded, not a decrease in demand.

   (D) The quotation is incorrect: an increase in price causes an increase in the quantity demanded, not a decrease in demand.

6. "As the price of domestic automobiles has risen, customers have found foreign autos to be a better bargain. Consequently, domestic auto sales have been decreasing, and foreign auto sales have been increasing." Using only the information in this quotation and assuming everything else remains constant, which of the following best describes this statement?

   (A) A shift in the demand curves for both domestic and foreign automobiles

   (B) A movement along the demand curves for both foreign and domestic automobiles

   (C) A movement along the demand curve for domestic autos, and a shift in the demand curve for foreign autos

   (D) A shift in the demand curve for domestic autos, and a movement along the demand curve for foreign autos

Part C: Consumer Surplus

Once we have the demand curve, we can define the concept of *consumer surplus*. Consumer surplus is the value a consumer receives from the purchase of a good in excess of the price paid for the good. Stated differently, consumer surplus is the difference between the amount a person is willing and able to pay for a unit of the good and the actual price paid for that unit. For example, if you are willing to pay $100 for a coat but are able to buy the coat for only $70, you have a consumer surplus of $30.

Refer again to the demand data from Table 1-4.1, and assume the price is $0.30. Some buyers will benefit because they are willing to pay prices higher than $0.30 for this good. Note that each time the price is reduced by $0.05, consumers will buy an additional 50 million units. Table 1-4.4 shows how to calculate the consumer surplus resulting from the price of $0.30.

Table 1-4.4
Finding the Consumer Surplus When the Price Is $0.30

Price willing to pay	Quantity demanded	Consumer surplus from the increments of 50 million units if P = $0.30
$0.40	50 million units	($0.10)(50 million units) = $5.0 million
$0.35	100 million units	($0.05)(50 million units) = $2.5 million
$0.30	150 million units	($0.00)(50 million units) = $0.0 million

For those consumers willing to buy 50 million units at a price of $0.40, the consumer surplus for each unit is $0.10 (= $0.40 – $0.30), making the consumer surplus for all these units equal to $5.0 million. If the price is reduced from $0.40 to $0.35, there are consumers willing to buy another 50 million units; the consumer surplus for these buyers is $0.05 per unit ($0.35 – $0.30) or a total of $2.5 million for all 50 million units. If the price is lowered another $0.05 to $0.30, an extra 50 million units will be demanded; the consumer surplus for these units is $0.00 since $0.30 is the highest price these consumers are willing to pay. Thus, if the price is $0.30, a total of 150 million units are demanded and the total consumer surplus is $7.5 million.

An approximation of the total consumer surplus from a given number of units of a good can be shown graphically as the area below the demand curve and above the price paid for those units. In Figure 1-4.2, redraw the demand curve (D) from the data in Table 1-4.1. We see that if the price is $0.30, the quantity demanded is 150 million units. Consumer surplus from these 150 million units is the shaded area between the demand curve D and the horizontal price line at $0.30. We can find the area of this triangle using the familiar rule of (½) × base × height.

Figure 1-4.2
Consumer Surplus

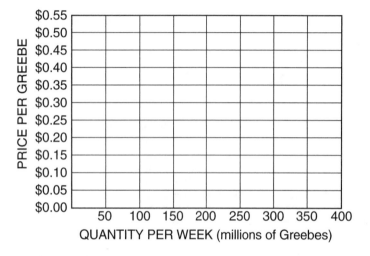

7. What is the value of consumer surplus in this market if the price is $0.30? $_____
   Show how you calculated the value of the area of the triangle representing consumer surplus.

8. Answer these questions based on the discussion of Figure 1-4.2.

   (A) If the price is increased from $0.30 to $0.35, consumer surplus will (*increase / decrease*). Why?

   (B) If the price is decreased from $0.30 to $0.25, consumer surplus will (*increase / decrease*). Why?

Reasons for Changes in Demand

Part A: Does the Demand Curve Shift?

Read the eight newspaper headlines in Table 1-5.1, and use the table to record the impact of each event on the demand for U.S.-made autos. In the second column, indicate whether the event in the headline will cause consumers to buy more or less U.S.-made autos. Use the third column to indicate whether there is a change in demand (ΔD) or a change in quantity demanded (ΔQd) for U.S.-made autos. In the third column, decide whether the demand curve shifts to the right or left or does not shift. Finally, indicate the letter for the new demand curve. Use Figure 1-5.1 to help you. **Always start at curve B**, and move only one curve at a time.

Table 1-5.1

Impact of Events on Demand for U.S.-Made Autos

Headline	Will consumers buy more or less U.S. autos?	Is there a change in demand (ΔD) or a change in quantity demanded (ΔQd)?	Does the demand curve for U.S. autos shift to the right or left or not shift?	What is the new demand curve for U.S. autos?
1. Consumers' Income Drops	More / Less	ΔD / ΔQd	Right / Left / No Shift	A / B / C
2. Millions of Immigrants Enter the U.S.	**More** / Less	ΔD / ΔQd	**Right** / Left / No Shift	A / B / **C**
3. Price of Foreign Autos Drop	More / **Less**	ΔD / ΔQd	Right / **Left** / No Shift	**A** / B / C
4. Major Cities Add Inexpensive Bus Lines	More / **Less**	ΔD / ΔQd	Right / **Left** / No Shift	**A** / B / C
5. Price of U.S. Autos Rises	More / **Less**	ΔD / **ΔQd**	Right / Left / **No Shift**	A / **B** / C
6. Price of U.S. Autos Expected to Rise Soon	More / Less	ΔD / ΔQd	Right / Left / No Shift	A / B / C
7. Families Look Forward to Summer Vacations	More / Less	ΔD / ΔQd	Right / Left / No Shift	A / B / C
8. U.S. Auto Firms Launch Effective Ad Campaigns	**More** / Less	**ΔD** / ΔQd	**Right** / Left / No Shift	A / B / **C**

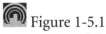

Figure 1-5.1
Demand for U.S.-Made Autos

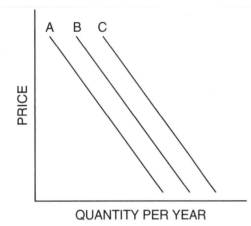

Part B: Why Does the Demand Curve Shift?

Categorize each change in demand in Part A according to the reason why demand changed. A given demand curve assumes that consumer expectations, consumer tastes, the number of consumers in the market, the income of consumers, and the prices of substitutes and complements are unchanged. In Table 1-5.2, place an X next to the reason that the event described in the headline caused a change in demand. One headline will have no answer because it will result in a change in quantity demanded rather than a change in demand.

Table 1-5.2
Reasons for a Change in Demand for U.S.-Made Autos

Reason	Headline number							
	1	2	3	4	5	6	7	8
9. A change in consumer expectations								
10. A change in consumer taste								
11. A change in the number of consumer in the market								
12. A change in income								
13. A change in the price of a substitute good								
14. A change in the price of a complementary good								

Supply Curves, Movements along Supply Curves, and Shifts in Supply Curves

In this activity, we will assume that the supply curve of Greebes is upward sloping.

Part A: A Change in Supply versus a Change in Quantity Supplied

Student Alert: The distinction between a "change in supply" and a "change in quantity supplied" is very important!

Study the data in Table 1-6.1 and plot the supply of Greebes on the graph in Figure 1-6.1. Label the supply curve S and answer the questions that follow.

Table 1-6.1
Supply of Greebes

Price (per Greebe)	Quantity supplied per week (millions of Greebes)
$0.05	0
$0.10	50
$0.15	100
$0.20	150
$0.25	200
$0.30	250
$0.35	300
$0.40	350

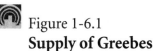

Figure 1-6.1
Supply of Greebes

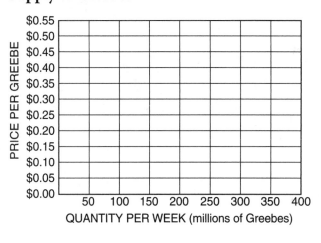

1. The data for supply curve S indicate that at a price of $0.25 per Greebe, suppliers would be willing to offer _____ million Greebes. All other things held constant, if the price of Greebes increased to $0.30 per Greebe, suppliers would be willing to offer _____ million Greebes. Such a change would be an increase in (*supply / quantity supplied*). All other things held constant, if the price of Greebes decreased to $0.20 per Greebe, suppliers would be willing to offer _____ million Greebes. Such a change would be called a decrease in (*supply / quantity supplied*).

Now, let's suppose that there is a change in the price of several of the raw materials used in making Greebes. This change in the *ceteris paribus* conditions underlying the original supply of Greebes will result in a new set of data, such as that shown in Table 1-6.2. Study the data, and plot this supply of Greebes on the graph in Figure 1-6.1. Label the new supply curve S₁ and answer the questions that follow.

Table 1-6.2
New Supply of Greebes

Price (per Greebe)	Quantity supplied per week (millions of Greebes)
$0.15	0
$0.20	50
$0.25	100
$0.30	150
$0.35	200
$0.40	250

2. Comparing the new supply curve (S₁) with the original supply curve (S), we can say that the change in the supply of Greebes results in a shift of the supply curve to the (*left / right*). Such a shift indicates that at each of the possible prices shown, suppliers are now willing to offer a (*smaller / larger*) quantity; and at each of the possible quantities shown, suppliers are willing to accept a (*higher / lower*) minimum price. The cause of this supply curve shift was a(n) (*increase / decrease*) in prices of several of the raw materials used in making Greebes.

Now, let's suppose that there is a dramatic change in the price of Silopanna, a resource used in the production of Greebes. This change in the *ceteris paribus* conditions underlying the original supply of Greebes will result in a new set of data shown in Table 1-6.3. Study the data, and plot this supply of Greebes on the graph in Figure 1-6.1. Label the new supply curve S₂ and answer the questions that follow.

Table 1-6.3
New Supply of Greebes

Price (per Greebe)	Quantity supplied per week (millions of Greebes)
$0.10	150
$0.15	200
$0.20	250
$0.25	300
$0.30	350
$0.35	400

3. Comparing the new supply curve (S₂) with the original supply curve (S), we can say that the change in the supply of Greebes results in a shift of the supply curve to the (*left / right*). Such a shift indicates that at each of the possible prices shown, suppliers are now willing to offer a (*smaller / larger*) quantity; and at each of the possible quantities shown, suppliers are willing to accept a (*lower / higher*) minimum price. The cause of this supply curve shift is a(n) (*increase / decrease*) in the price of Silopanna, a resource used in the production of Greebes.

Part B: Do You Get It?

Now, to check your understanding, choose the answer you think is the one best alternative in each of the following multiple-choice questions.

4. All other things held constant, which of the following would *not* cause a change in the supply of beef?

(A) A decrease in the price of beef

(B) A decrease in the price of cattle feed

(C) An increase in the price of cattle feed

(D) An increase in the cost of transporting cattle to market

5. "Falling oil prices have caused a sharp decrease in the supply of oil." Speaking precisely, and using terms as they are defined by economists, choose the statement that best describes this quotation.

   (A) The quotation is correct: decrease in price causes a decrease in supply.

   (B) The quotation is incorrect: decrease in price causes an increase in supply, not a decrease in supply.

   (C) The quotation is incorrect: decrease in price causes an increase in the quantity supplied, not a decrease in supply.

   (D) The quotation is incorrect: decrease in price causes a decrease in the quantity supplied, not a decrease in supply.

6. You overhear a fellow student say, "Economic markets are confusing. If supply increases, then price decreases; but if price decreases, then supply also will decrease. If supply falls, price will rise; but if price rises, supply also will rise." Dispel your friend's obvious confusion (in no more than one short paragraph) below.

Part C: Producer Surplus

Once we have the supply curve, we can define the concept of *producer surplus*. Producer surplus is the value a producer receives from the sale of a good in excess of the marginal cost of producing the good. Stated differently, producer surplus is the difference between the price a seller receives for a unit of the good and the cost to the seller of producing that unit. For example, if your cost of producing a coat is $50 but you are able to sell the coat for $70, you have a producer surplus of $20.

Refer again to the supply curve data from Table 1-6.1, and assume the price is $0.25. Some sellers will benefit because based on their low marginal costs of production, they are willing to accept prices lower than $0.25 for this good. Note that each time the price is increased by $0.05, sellers will provide an additional 50 million units. Table 1-6.4 shows how to calculate the producer surplus resulting from the price of $0.25.

Table 1-6.4
Finding the Producer Surplus When the Price Is $0.25

Price willing to accept	Quantity supplied	Producer surplus from the increments of 50 million units if P = $0.25
$0.10	50 million units	($0.15)(50 million units) = $7.5 million
$0.15	100 million units	($0.10)(50 million units) = $5.0 million
$0.20	150 million units	($0.05)(50 million units) = $2.5 million
$0.25	200 million units	($0.00)(50 million units) = $0.0 million

For those producers willing to sell 50 million units at a price of $0.10, the producer surplus for each unit is $0.15 (= $0.25 – $0.10), making the producer surplus for all these units equal to $7.5 million. There are other producers who will put an extra 50 million units on the market if the price is $0.15. The producer surplus for these sellers is $0.10 per unit (= $0.25 – $0.15) or a total of $5.0 million for all 50 million units. If the price is raised another $0.05 to $0.20, an extra 50 million units will be supplied; the producer surplus for these units is $2.5 million, or $0.05 per unit (= $0.25 – $0.20). If the price is $0.25, another 50 million units will be supplied. The producer surplus for these units, however, is $0.00 since $0.25 is the lowest price these producers are willing to accept. Thus, if the price is $0.25, a total of 200 million units are supplied and the total producer surplus is $15.0 million.

An approximation of the total producer surplus from a given number of units of a good can be shown graphically as the area above the supply curve and below the price paid for those units. In Figure 1-6.2, redraw the supply curve (S) from the data in Table 1-6.1. We see that if the price is $0.25, the quantity supplied is 200 million units. Consumer surplus from these 200 million units is the shaded area between the supply curve S and the horizontal price line at $0.25. We can find the area of this triangle using the familiar rule of (½) × base × height.

Figure 1-6.2
Producer Surplus

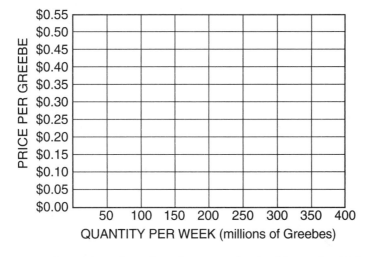

7. What is the value of producer surplus in this market if the price is $0.25? _____
   Show how you calculated the value of the area of the triangle representing producer surplus.

8. Answer these questions based on the discussion of Figure 1-6.2.

(A) If the price is increased from $0.25 to $0.30, producer surplus will (*increase / decrease*). Why?

(B) If the price is decreased from $0.25 to $0.20, producer surplus will (*increase / decrease*). Why?

Reasons for Changes in Supply

Part A: Does the Supply Curve Shift?

Read the eight newspaper headlines in Table 1-7.1, and use the table to record the impact of each event on the supply of cars from U.S. auto producers. In the second column, indicate whether the event in the headline will cause American auto producers to provide more or less cars. Use the third column to indicate whether there is a change in supply (ΔS) or a change in quantity supplied (ΔQs) of cars. In the third column, decide whether the supply curve shifts to the right or left or does not shift. Finally, indicate the letter for the new supply curve. Use Figure 1-7.1 to help you. **Always start at curve B**, and move only one curve at a time.

Table 1-7.1
Impact of Events on Supply of U.S.-Made Autos

Headline	Should U.S. auto firms produce more or less?	Is there a change in supply (ΔS) or a change in quantity supplied (ΔQs)?	Does the supply curve of cars shift to the right or left or not shift?	What is the new supply curve for cars?
1. Auto Workers' Union Agrees to Wage Cuts	*More* / Less	ΔS / ΔQs	Right / Left / No Shift	A / B / C
2. New Robot Technology Increases Efficiency	*More* / Less	ΔS / ΔQs	Right / Left / No Shift	A / B / C
3. Price of U.S. Cars Increases	*More* / Less	ΔS / ΔQs	Right / Left / No Shift	A / B / C
4. Nationwide Auto Workers Strike Begins	More / Less	ΔS / ΔQs	Right / Left / No Shift	A / B / C
5. Cost of Steel Decreases	More / Less	ΔS / ΔQs	Right / Left / No Shift	A / B / C
6. Major Auto Producer Goes Out of Business	More / Less	ΔS / ΔQs	Right / Left / No Shift	A / B / C
7. Buyers Reject New Car Models	More / Less	ΔS / ΔQs	Right / Left / No Shift	A / B / C
8. Government Gives Car Producers a Subsidy	More / Less	ΔS / ΔQs	Right / Left / No Shift	A / B / C

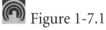
Figure 1-7.1
Supply of U.S.-Made Cars

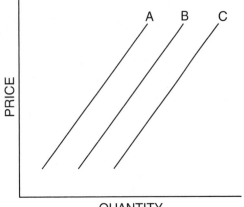

Part B: Why Does the Supply Curve Shift?

Categorize each change in supply in Part A according to the reason why supply changed. In Table 1-7.2, place an X next to the reason that the headline indicated a change in supply. In some cases, more than one headline could be matched to a reason. It is possible a headline does not indicate a shift in supply because it will result in a change in quantity supplied rather than a change in supply.

Table 1-7.2
Impact of Events on Supply of U.S.-Made Autos

Reason	Headline number							
	1	2	3	4	5	6	7	8
9. A change in costs of inputs to production process								
10. A change in technology								
11. A change in the number of producers in the market								
12. Government policies								

Equilibrium Price and Equilibrium Quantity

Table 1-8.1 below shows the demand for Greebes and the supply of Greebes. Plot these data on the axes in Figure 1-8.1. Label the demand curve D and label the supply curve S. Then answer the questions that follow.

 Student Alert: A "change in demand" or a "change in supply" results in a change in price, while a "change in quantity demanded" or a "change in quantity supplied" is the result of a change in price.

 Table 1-8.1
Demand for and Supply of Greebes

Price (per Greebe)	Quantity demanded (millions of Greebes)	Quantity supplied (millions of Greebes)
$0.05	400	0
$0.10	350	50
$0.15	300	100
$0.20	250	150
$0.25	200	200
$0.30	150	250
$0.35	100	300
$0.40	50	350
$0.45	0	400

Figure 1-8.1
Demand for and Supply of Greebes

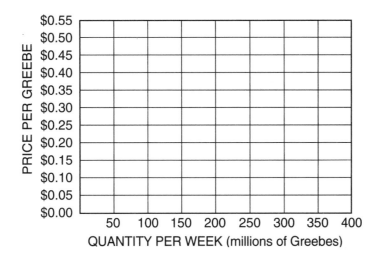

1. Under these conditions, competitive market forces would tend to establish an equilibrium price of _____ per Greebe and an equilibrium quantity of _____ million Greebes.

2. If the price currently prevailing in the market is $0.30 per Greebe, buyers would want to buy _____ million Greebes and sellers would want to sell _____ million Greebes. Under these conditions, there would be a (*shortage / surplus*) of _____ million Greebes. Competitive market forces would cause the price to (*increase / decrease*) to a price of _____ per Greebe. At this new price, buyers would now want to buy _____ million Greebes, and sellers now want to sell _____ million Greebes. Because of this change in (*price / underlying conditions*), the (*demand / quantity demanded*) (*increased / decreased*) by _____ million Greebes, and the (*supply / quantity supplied*) (*increased / decreased*) by _____ million Greebes.

3. If the price currently prevailing in the market is $0.20 per Greebe, buyers would want to buy _____ million Greebes, and sellers would want to sell _____ million Greebes. Under these conditions, there would be a (*shortage / surplus*) of _____ million Greebes. Competitive market forces would cause the price to (*increase / decrease*) to a price of _____ per Greebe. At this new price, buyers would now want to buy _____ million Greebes, and sellers now want to sell _____ million Greebes. Because of this change in (*price / underlying conditions*), the (*demand / quantity demanded*) (*increased / decreased*) by _____ million Greebes, and the (*supply / quantity supplied*) (*increased / decreased*) by _____ million Greebes.

4. At equilibrium, is each of the following true or false? Explain.

(A) The quantity demanded is equal to the quantity supplied.

(B) Demand equals supply.

5. Now, suppose a mysterious blight causes the supply schedule for Greebes to change as shown in Table 1-8.2:

Table 1-8.2
New Supply of Greebes

Price (per Greebe)	Quantity supplied (millions of Greebes)
$0.15	0
$0.20	50
$0.25	100
$0.30	150
$0.35	200

Plot the new supply schedule on the axes in Figure 1-8.1 and label it S_1. Label the new equilibrium E_1. Under these conditions, competitive market forces would tend to establish an equilibrium price of _____ per Greebe and an equilibrium quantity of _____ million Greebes.

Compared with the equilibrium price in Question 1, we say that because of this change in (*price / underlying conditions*), the (*supply / quantity supplied*) changed; and both the equilibrium price and the equilibrium quantity changed. The equilibrium price (*increased / decreased*), and the equilibrium quantity (*increased / decreased*).

Compared with the consumer and producer surpluses in Question 4, consumer surplus has (*increased / decreased*), and producer surplus has (*increased / decreased*).

6. Now, with the supply schedule at S_1, suppose further that a sharp drop in people's incomes as the result of a prolonged recession causes the demand schedule to change as shown in Table 1-8.3.

Table 1-8.3
New Demand for Greebes

Price (per Greebe)	Quantity demanded (millions of Greebes)
$0.15	200
$0.20	150
$0.25	100
$0.30	50
$0.35	0

Plot the new demand schedule on the axes in Figure 1-8.1 and label it D$_1$. Label the new equilibrium E$_2$. Under these conditions, with the supply schedule at S$_1$, competitive market forces would establish an equilibrium price of _____ per Greebe and an equilibrium quantity of _____ million Greebes. Compared with the equilibrium price in Question 5, because of this change in (*price / underlying conditions*), the (*demand / quantity demanded*) changed. The equilibrium price (*increased / decreased*), and the equilibrium quantity (*increased / decreased*).

Shifts in Supply and Demand

Part A: The Market for Jelly Beans

Fill in the blanks with the letter of the graph that illustrates each situation. You may use a graph more than once.

Figure 1-9.1
The Supply and Demand for Jelly Beans

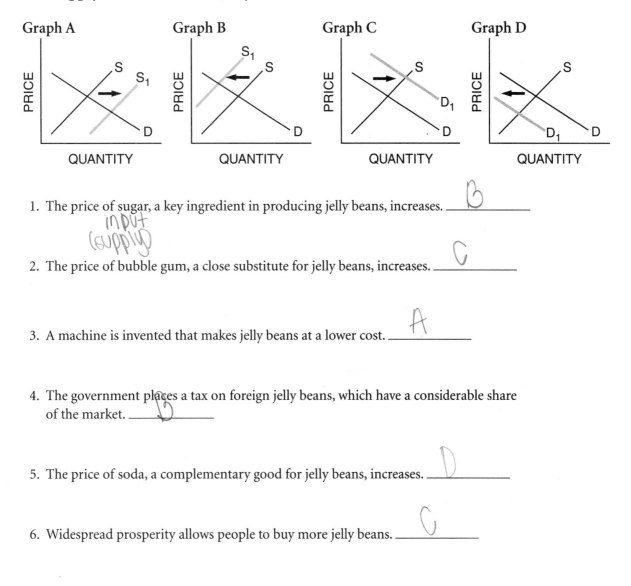

1. The price of sugar, a key ingredient in producing jelly beans, increases. _____B_____

   input (supply)

2. The price of bubble gum, a close substitute for jelly beans, increases. _____C_____

3. A machine is invented that makes jelly beans at a lower cost. _____A_____

4. The government places a tax on foreign jelly beans, which have a considerable share of the market. _____D_____

5. The price of soda, a complementary good for jelly beans, increases. _____D_____

6. Widespread prosperity allows people to buy more jelly beans. _____C_____

Part B: Apples, Pears, and Pies

Connecticut ships large amounts of apples to all parts of the United States by rail. Circle the words that show the effects on price and quantity for each situation, and complete the graphs below, showing how a hurricane that destroys apples before they are picked in Connecticut might affect the price and quantity of each commodity. Then provide your reasoning.

7. **Apples in Boston**

    Price: *Rises / Unchanged / Falls*

    Quantity: *Rises / Unchanged / Falls*

    Reason:

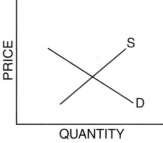

8. **Land devoted to apple orchards in the state of Washington**

    Price: *Rises / Unchanged / Falls*

    Quantity: *Rises / Unchanged / Falls*

    Reason:

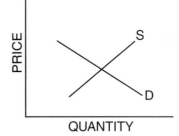

9. **Apples grown in the state of Washington**

    Price: *Rises / Unchanged / Falls*

    Quantity: *Rises / Unchanged / Falls*

    Reason:

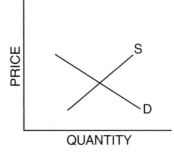

10. **Pears**

Price: *Rises / Unchanged / Falls*
Quantity: *Rises / Unchanged / Falls*
Reason:

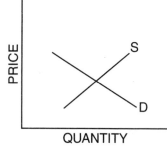

11. **Apple pies**

Price: *Rises / Unchanged / Falls*
Quantity: *Rises / Unchanged / Falls*
Reason:

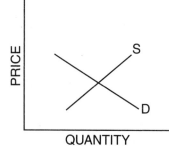

Economic Systems

Read the following description of economic systems, answer the review questions, and then complete the table.

It's a fact: our needs and wants are always greater than the available resources necessary to satisfy us. We all face scarcity, which forces us to choose how best to use the limited resources that are available. Ultimately, society has to make three very important economic decisions: what do we produce, how do we produce, and for whom do we produce? To answer these three questions, a society develops an economic system, or organized way of answering the three questions. Because people do not all share the same values, beliefs, geographic circumstances, and climates, different societies have developed very different economic systems to deal with scarcity. Figure 1-10.1 shows a continuum of the economic systems that have been developed throughout history based on the amount of freedom individuals have to answer the three economic questions.

Figure 1-10.1
Economic Systems

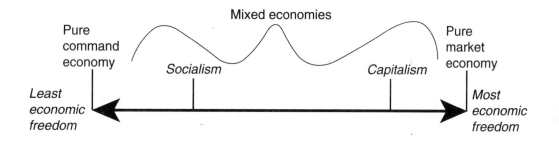

In a pure command economy, all economic decisions are made by the government or even a single leader. Ancient Egypt under the pharaohs and present-day North Korea are close, if not perfect, examples of pure command economies. The leaders decide what is to be produced, how it is produced, and for whom it is produced. Private property is nonexistent in the pure command model, and only the needs of the government are addressed.

In a pure market economy, all economic decisions are left to the individuals in the society. These individuals, motivated by their own self-interest and their desire for private property, answer the three economic questions. To get what they need or want, individuals come together in markets and trade for mutual benefit.

Although pure market economies are nonexistent, something close to the pure market model called *capitalism* does exist. The United States and a number of other countries can be described as capitalistic economies. Capitalism is an example of a mixed economy. Mixed economies are the reality of today's world. In a mixed economy, both individuals and government answer the three basic economic questions. If most decisions and property are under the control of individuals in the society, then the system can be described as capitalistic. If most decisions and property are under state control, then the system can be described as socialist.

1. What three basic questions must all societies answer?

2. Define economic system.

3. What is a market?

4. Complete the following table:

	Pure command economy	Mixed economy	Pure market economy
Who answers the three basic economic questions?			
What degree of economic freedom exists for individuals?			
Under which type of economic system would you prefer to live and why? Be prepared to discuss your answers with your classmates.			

Anything Worth Doing Is Not Necessarily Worth Doing Well

Student Alert: Should you do all you can to earn a perfect grade of 100 on your next economics exam?

Bartlett's Familiar Quotations contains wisdom from writers separated by more than a millennium. Whose wisdom best fits today's world?

> *Always take the short cut; and that is the rational one. Therefore say and do everything according to soundest reason.*
>
> Meditations iv.51
> Marcus Aurelius
> A.D. 120 to 181

> *Whatever is worth doing at all is worth doing well.*
>
> Philip Dormer Stanhope
> Earl of Chesterfield
> 1694 to 1773

Between these two extremes, one discovers the economic way of thinking. We know that productive resources are limited, so we cannot have everything we want. We must economize by choosing among alternatives.

We may want the very best product available, but we settle on a product with fewer features or less durability because the extra benefit of the product we would most like to have is simply not worth the extra cost. Resources that aren't devoted to making a good product perfect can be allocated to making other products.

Few choices we make in life are all-or-nothing decisions. We decide on the number of assigned chapters to read today based on alternative uses of our time. We frequently adjust the number of hours we study for each subject because of tests and nonschool uses of our day. Epidemic doses of "senioritis"—severely curtailing work for grades after college-acceptance letters are received—may suggest that the majority of students agree with Marcus Aurelius rather than the Earl of Chesterfield. Even the most severe victims of senioritis may admit that they are incurring a very different cost: the lost opportunities to learn the cultural and scientific knowledge that will be required in college.

An excellent academic record in high school expands the array of college choices for the graduating high school senior. "A" grades are preferred to "C" grades for reasons that don't warrant an explanation: the extra benefits of the explanation are not worth the extra costs of reading it.

This comparison of additional, or marginal, benefits and costs applies to production decisions, too. Of course, auto companies can make cars that work for a quarter century, but would the extra manufacturing cost be worthwhile over the product lifetime? Technical advances frequently lead to superior products at lower cost. Because of blindingly rapid changes in computer technology, the concept of an "old" computer is measured in months; so building a computer case that lasts for 50 years would be wasteful. Can you suggest services or products that are satisfactory, but not superior?

Thinking about the future requires that we acknowledge what we have and then make incremental changes so the marginal benefits of the changes exceed the marginal costs. Mechanical equipment in an aircraft must meet higher quality standards than the same product in a car. If the alternator fails in a car, one typically has enough time to pull off the road before the car stops. In an airplane, safe landing options are fewer than those available to the motorist. Both quality decisions are correct because the added benefits from avoiding failure in a plane greatly exceed the marginal benefits from avoiding mechanical failure in a car.

1. After reading in *Bartlett's Familiar Quotations* that "knowledge is power," a student decides to be as knowledgeable as possible by devoting the next 20 years, without interruption, to college. From the hypothetical data below, would you advise this person to reconsider a career as a professional student? Answer the questions that follow.

Table 1-11.1

Degree Earned and Expected Lifetime Earnings and Costs

Highest degree earned	Expected lifetime earnings (total benefit) by degree	Marginal benefit of additional degree	Expected lifetime costs (total cost) by degree	Marginal cost of additional degree
High school	$600,000	+$600,000	$0	+$0
Associate	$1,200,000		$200,000	
Bachelor's	$1,700,000		$500,000	+$300,000
Master's	$2,100,000	+$400,000	$900,000	
Doctorate	$2,400,000		$2,400,000	

(A) Complete Table 1-11.1 with the missing values of the marginal benefit and marginal cost of earning an additional degree.

(B) Would a master's degree and a doctorate degree increase the human capital of the student? (*Yes / No*)

(C) In the process of building knowledge, would the doctorate degree be the best example of doing a job well? (*Yes / No*)

(D) Assuming that inflation and interest rates have been taken into account in these data, what is the optimal degree for this person to earn?

(E) Which criterion did you use to determine the optimal degree this person should obtain? (*Total Benefit = Total Cost / Marginal Benefit = Marginal Cost*)

(F) Since inflation is already factored into the data, what is the most likely reason that the costs of a doctorate degree rise to such a high level?

2. Wrapping garbage neatly before taking it to the trash can, raking leaves on a windy day, hand-drying dishes after they have been run through a dishwasher's dry cycle, and similar tasks seem to push the credibility of any value in doing a job well. Give examples of jobs with highly diminishing marginal benefits.

3. Consider an electronic item that you have thought about buying. Do you always choose the highest-priced good? Explain your answer.

4. If you wanted to eliminate "senioritis," how would you change the college acceptance process and/or the incentives offered by high school instructors?

Circle the letter of each correct answer.

1. The crucial problem of economics is
   (A) establishing a fair tax system.
   (B) providing social goods and services.
   (C) developing a price mechanism that reflects the relative scarcities of products and resources.
   (D) allocating scarce productive resources to satisfy unlimited wants.
   (E) enacting a set of laws that protects resources from overuse.

2. When one decision is made, the next best alternative not selected is called
   (A) economic resource.
   (B) opportunity cost.
   (C) scarcity.
   (D) comparative disadvantage.
   (E) production.

3. Which of the following is true if the production possibilities curve is a curved line concave to the origin?
   (A) Resources are perfectly substitutable between the production of the two goods.
   (B) It is possible to produce more of both products.
   (C) Both products are equally capable of satisfying consumer wants.
   (D) The prices of the two products are the same.
   (E) As more of one good is produced, increasing amounts of the other good must be given up.

4. Which of the following will *not* change the demand for oranges?
   (A) A change in consumers' incomes
   (B) A change in the price of grapefruits, a substitute for oranges
   (C) A change in the price of oranges
   (D) A change in consumers' taste for oranges
   (E) An expectation that the price of oranges will change in the future

5. To be considered scarce, an economic resource must be
   (A) limited but not free or desirable.
   (B) limited and free, but not desirable.
   (C) limited and desirable, but not free.
   (D) limited, free, and desirable.
   (E) free and desirable, but not limited.

6. If there is an increase in demand for a good, what will most likely happen to the price and quantity of the good exchanged?

	Price	Quantity
(A)	No change	No change
(B)	Increase	Increase
(C)	Increase	Decrease
(D)	Decrease	Increase
(E)	Decrease	Decrease

7. Which of the following items would be considered scarce?
   (A) Education
   (B) Gold
   (C) Time
   (D) Education and gold
   (E) Education, gold, and time

8. An increase in the price of gasoline will cause the demand curve for tires to shift in which direction?

(A) To the left, because gasoline and tires are substitutes

(B) To the left, because gasoline and tires are complements

(C) To the right, because gasoline and tires are substitutes

(D) To the right, because gasoline and tires are complements

(E) To the right, because an increase in the price of gasoline makes consumers poorer and thus not willing to pay as much for tires

9. Which of the following problems do all economic systems face?

I. How to allocate scarce resources among unlimited wants

II. How to distribute income equally among all the citizens

III. How to decentralize markets

IV. How to decide what to produce, how to produce, and for whom to produce

(A) I only

(B) I and IV only

(C) II and III only

(D) I, II, and III only

(E) I, II, III, and IV

10. In which way does a straight-line production possibilities curve differ from a concave production possibilities curve?

(A) A straight-line production possibilities curve has a decreasing opportunity cost.

(B) A straight-line production possibilities curve has a constant opportunity cost.

(C) A straight-line production possibilities curve has an increasing opportunity cost.

(D) A straight-line production possibilities curve does not show opportunity cost.

(E) There is no difference between the two production possibilities curves.

11. The law of increasing opportunity cost is reflected in the shape of the

(A) production possibilities curve concave to the origin.

(B) production possibilities curve convex to the origin.

(C) horizontal production possibilities curve.

(D) straight-line production possibilities curve.

(E) upward-sloping production possibilities curve.

The figure below is used for questions 12 through 15. It shows the production possibilities curve for a country with full employment of a given-size labor force.

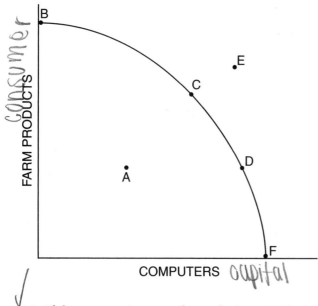

12. If the country is currently producing at Point C, it can produce more computers by doing which of the following?

   (A) Moving to Point A

   (B) Moving to Point B

   (C) Moving to Point D

   (D) Moving to Point E

   (E) Remaining at Point C

13. Which of the following statements about the production possibilities curve is true?

   (A) Point A is not attainable in a developed society.

   (B) Point D is not attainable given the society's resources.

   (C) The relative position of Points C and D reflect production alternatives rather than relative prices.

   (D) Elimination of unemployment will move the production possibilities curve to the right, closer to Point E.

   (E) Point E lies outside the production possibilities curve because it represents a combination of resources not desired by the citizens of the country.

14. How might Point E be attained?

   (A) If the country's resources were more fully employed

   (B) If the country's resources were shifted to encourage more efficient use of scarce resources

   (C) If improvements in technology occurred in either the computer sector or the farm products sector

   (D) If firms decreased their output of computers

   (E) If the nation used more of its scarce resources to produce farm products

15. The production possibilities curve of the country would be most likely to shift to the right if the country were currently producing at which of the following points?

   (A) Point A

   (B) Point B

   (C) Point C

   (D) Point D

   (E) Point E

The figure below is used for questions 16, 17, and 18. It shows the production possibilities curve for two types of goods for a country with full employment of a given-size labor force.

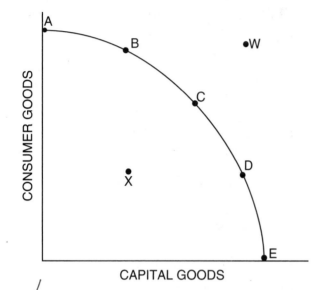

16. If the country is currently producing at Point C, it can produce more capital goods by moving in the direction of
    (A) Point A.
    (B) Point B.
    (C) Point D.
    (D) Point W.
    (E) Point X.

17. If the country moves from Point C to Point D, future economic growth will
    (A) decrease.
    (B) increase.
    (C) not change, but consumer satisfaction will increase.
    (D) not change, but unemployment will increase.
    (E) not change, but inflation will increase.

18. Which of the following is most likely to cause the production possibilities curve to shift outward toward Point W?
    (A) Employing the country's resources more fully
    (B) Shifting the country's resources to encourage more efficient use of scarce resources
    (C) Improving the technology for the production of either consumer or capital goods
    (D) Decreasing production of capital goods
    (E) Shifting some scarce resources to produce consumer goods in the current period

19. The opportunity cost of producing an additional unit of product J is
    (A) the dollar value of resources used to make the extra unit of product J.
    (B) the retail price paid for product J.
    (C) the wholesale price of product J.
    (D) the amount of product K that could have been produced with the resources used to make the unit of J.
    (E) the profit that was earned from producing product J.

20. Which of the following would cause a leftward shift of the production possibilities curve?
    (A) An increase in unemployment
    (B) An increase in inflation
    (C) An increase in capital equipment
    (D) A decrease in consumer demand
    (E) A decrease in working-age population

21. Which of the following would cause an outward or rightward shift in the production possibilities curve?
    (A) An increase in unemployment
    (B) An increase in inflation
    (C) An increase in capital equipment
    (D) A decrease in natural resources
    (E) A decrease in the number of workers

Use the following table for questions 22, 23, and 24.

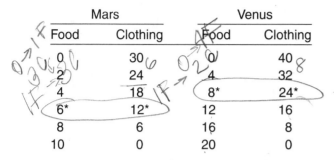

Mars		Venus	
Food	Clothing	Food	Clothing
0	30	0	40
2	24	4	32
4	18	8*	24*
6*	12*	12	16
8	6	16	8
10	0	20	0

Two nations, Mars and Venus, each produce food and clothing. The table above gives points on each nation's production possibilities curve. The asterisks indicate their current point of production.

22. In Mars, the opportunity cost of obtaining the first two units of food is how many units of clothing?

(A) 2   (D) 8

(B) 3   (E) 12

(C) 6

23. In Venus, the opportunity cost of the first unit of

(A) food is two units of clothing.

(B) food is eight units of clothing.

(C) clothing is two units of food.

(D) clothing is four units of food.

(E) clothing is eight units of food.

24. Which of the following statements is correct based on the concept of comparative advantage?

(A) Mars and Venus should continue producing the quantities indicated by the asterisks.

(B) Mars should specialize in the production of food.

(C) Mars should specialize in the production of clothing.

(D) Venus has the comparative advantage in clothing.

(E) Mars has an absolute advantage in the production of food.

25. The table below shows the number of hours needed to produce one bushel of soybeans and one bushel of rice in each of two countries.

Country	One bushel of soybeans	One bushel of rice
U.S.	5 hours	7 hours
Japan	15 hours	10 hours

Which of the following statements must be true?

(A) The U.S. has both the absolute and comparative advantage in producing soybeans.

(B) Japan has both the absolute and comparative advantage in producing soybeans.

(C) The U.S. has both the absolute and comparative advantage in producing rice.

(D) Japan has both the absolute and comparative advantage in producing rice.

(E) Japan has the absolute advantage in producing soybeans and the comparative advantage in producing rice.

26. A rational decision maker will choose to act only if

(A) the marginal benefit of the action is greater than the average cost of that action.

(B) the marginal benefit of the action is greater than the marginal cost of that action.

(C) the marginal benefit of the action is less than the average cost of that action.

(D) the average benefit of the action is less than the average cost of that action.

(E) the average benefit of the action is greater than the marginal cost of that action.

27. According to the theory of comparative advantage, a good should be produced where

    (A) its explicit costs are least.

    (B) its opportunity costs are least.

    (C) the cost of real resources used is least.

    (D) production can occur with the greatest increase in employment.

    (E) production can occur with the lowest increase in employment.

28. Which of the following statements violates the economic concept of matching marginal benefits with marginal costs in test taking?

    (A) "My grade in this course is already an A and the final examination is optional, so I'm not taking the final examination in this class."

    (B) "My grade going into the final examination for math is B-plus. The final exam constitutes half of the course grade, so I'm going to study more for the final in this class than in solid-state genetics, where I have a solid A."

    (C) "Most of my grades are B-minus, but in fluid dynamics I have an A. I'm going to study only for the final exam in fluid dynamics."

    (D) "If I spend two extra hours a week reading English literature, my scores on standardized tests of verbal skills will improve by 20 percent. Since my verbal skills are average, I'm going to reallocate my time into reading more literature."

    (E) All the statements violate the concept of matching marginal benefits with marginal costs in test taking.

29. "If you want to have anything done correctly, you have to do it yourself." This quote violates the principle of which of the following economic concepts?

    (A) Scarcity

    (B) Supply

    (C) Comparative advantage

    (D) Diminishing marginal returns

    (E) Demand

30. Which of the following will *not* cause the demand curve for athletic shoes to shift?

    (A) A change in tastes for athletic shoes

    (B) Widespread advertising campaign for athletic shoes

    (C) Increase in money incomes of athletic-shoe consumers

    (D) Expectations that the price of athletic shoes will decrease in the future

    (E) A decrease in the price of athletic shoes

31. Assume that the demand for apples is downward sloping. If the price of apples falls from $0.80 per pound to $0.65 per pound, which of the following will occur?

    (A) A smaller quantity of apples will be demanded.

    (B) A larger quantity of apples will be demanded.

    (C) Demand for apples will decrease.

    (D) Demand for apples will increase.

    (E) Supply of apples will decrease.

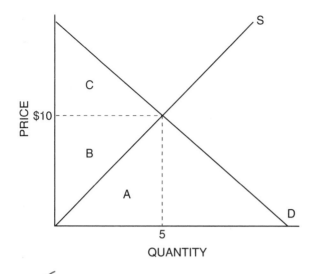

33. Producer surplus is the

    (A) area under the supply curve to the left of the amount sold.

    (B) area under the supply curve to the right of the amount sold.

    (C) amount the seller is paid plus the cost of production.

    (D) amount the seller is paid less the cost of production. *(minus)*

    (E) cost to sellers of participating in a market.

32. On the graph above, what area represents consumer surplus when the price is $10?

    (A) A   (D) A and B

    (B) B   (E) B and C

    (C) C

MICROECONOMICS

The Nature and Functions of Product Markets

Unit 2

- Demand is the relationship between price and the amount of a good or service that consumers are willing and able to purchase at various prices in a given period of time. The law of demand states that consumers buy more at lower prices and less at higher prices, all other things being equal.

- There is a difference between a "change in demand" and a "change in quantity demanded." A change in the quantity demanded of Good X can be caused only by a change in the price of Good X. It is a movement along the demand curve. At a lower price, a greater quantity is demanded.

- The reason the price of Good X is treated differently from the other factors which influence consumers is that the price of Good X is on the vertical axis of the graph.

- A change in demand means that more or less is demanded at every price; it is caused by changes in preferences, incomes, expectations, population, and the prices of complementary or substitute goods.

- The income effect, the substitution effect, and the law of diminishing marginal utility explain why a demand curve is downward sloping.

- The law of diminishing marginal utility states that as more of a good or service is consumed in a given period of time, the additional benefit or satisfaction from an extra unit declines.

- Supply is the relationship between price and the amount of a good or service that producers are willing and able to sell at various prices in a given period of time. Producers are willing to sell more at higher prices and less at lower prices, all other things being equal.

- There is a difference between a "change in supply" and a "change in quantity supplied."

- A change in the quantity supplied of Good X can be caused only by a change in the price of Good X. It is a movement along the supply curve. A change in supply is a shift of the curve where more or less is supplied at every price. Changes in technology, production costs, taxes, subsidies, and expectations will cause a shift in supply.

- In competitive markets, supply and demand constitute the sum of many individual decisions to sell and to buy. The interaction of supply and demand determines the price and quantity that will clear the market. The price where quantity supplied and quantity demanded are equal is called the equilibrium or market-clearing price.

- At a price higher than equilibrium, there is a surplus and pressure on sellers to lower their prices. At a price lower than equilibrium, there is a shortage and pressure on buyers to offer higher prices.

- An administered maximum price is called a price ceiling. A price ceiling below the equilibrium price causes a shortage. A price ceiling set at or above the equilibrium price has no effect on the market.

- An administered minimum price is called a price floor. A price floor above the equilibrium price causes a surplus. A price floor set at or below the equilibrium price has no effect on the market.

- Market prices promote economic progress because at the equilibrium price there is both consumer surplus and producer surplus. In other words, buyers and sellers are both better off at the equilibrium price.

- Consumer surplus is the difference between the highest price consumers are willing to pay for a good or service and the price that they actually have to pay.

■ Producer surplus is the difference between the lowest price businesses would be willing to accept for a good or service and the price they actually receive.

■ Price elasticity of demand refers to how strongly the quantity demanded changes in response to a given change in price. If the percentage change in quantity demanded is greater than the percentage change in price, the demand for the good is considered elastic. If the percentage change in quantity demanded is less than the percentage change in price, the demand for the good is considered inelastic. If the percentage change in price is equal to the percentage change in quantity demanded, the demand for the good is considered unit elastic.

■ Luxuries have a more elastic demand than necessities. High-priced goods have a more elastic demand than low-priced goods. Goods that are habit-forming tend to have an inelastic demand. Demand is more elastic in the long run than in the short run.

■ Price elasticity of demand can be determined by comparing the value of total revenue before and after the price change and by using the arc method to calculate the percentage changes in price and quantity demanded.

■ Price elasticity of supply refers to how strongly quantity supplied changes in relation to a change in price. Supply is more elastic in the long run than in the short run.

■ In a market economy, prices provide information to buyers and sellers, allocate resources, and act as rationing devices. It is important to know how to illustrate a wide range of situations with supply and demand graphs.

■ When property rights are not established, a market will fail to provide an efficient allocation of resources.

■ The presence of an externality results in a market failure with the market output not being the socially efficient level.

How Markets Allocate Resources

Markets use prices as signals to allocate resources to their highest valued uses. Consumers will pay higher prices for goods and services that they value more highly. Producers will devote more resources to the production of goods and services that have higher prices, other things being equal. And other things being equal, workers will provide more hours of labor to jobs that pay higher salaries.

This allocation principle applies both to product markets for items such as cars, houses, and haircuts and to resource markets for items such as labor, land, and equipment. Households play two important roles in an economy—they demand goods and services and supply resources. Businesses also have dual roles—they supply goods and services and demand resources. The interaction of demand and supply in product and resource markets generates prices that serve to allocate items to their highest valued alternatives. Factors that interfere with the workings of a competitive market result in an inefficient allocation of resources, causing a reduction in society's overall well-being.

Figures 2-1.1 and 2-1.2 illustrate how markets can be interrelated. Assume the markets are perfectly competitive and that the supply and demand model is completely applicable. The graphs show the supply and demand in each market *before* the assumed change occurs. Trace through the effects of the assumed change, all other things held constant. Work your way from left to right. Shift no more than one curve in each market. In each market graph, show any shift in the demand or supply curve, labeling each new curve D_1 or S_1. Then circle the correct symbol under each graph ($\uparrow$ for increase, — for unchanged, and $\downarrow$ for decrease).

1. Assume that a new fertilizer dramatically increases the number of potatoes that can be harvested with no additional labor or machinery. Also assume that this fertilizer does not affect wheat farming and that people are satisfied to eat either potatoes or bread made from wheat flour.

Figure 2-1.1
Effects of a New Fertilizer

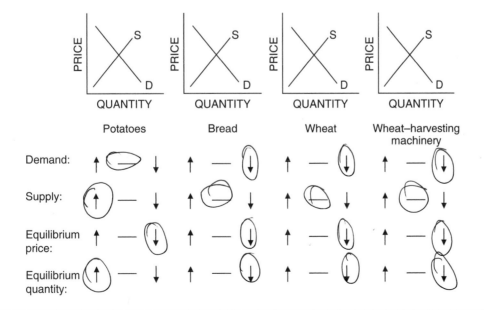

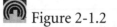
2. Assume new studies show that coffee is worse for people's health than tea and that more people use cream in coffee than in tea.

Figure 2-1.2
Effects of New Health Studies

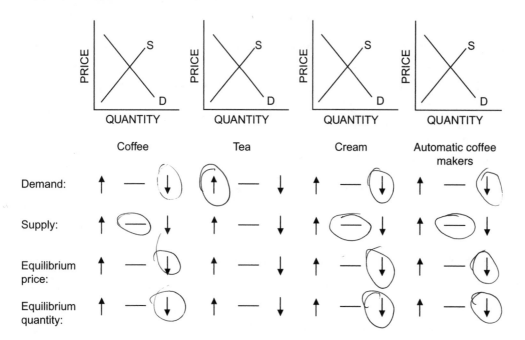

3. Examine Figure 2-1.3, which shows an increase in demand in the housing market in the country of Pajotte.

Figure 2-1.3
Increase in Housing Demand in Pajotte

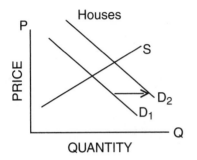

(A) Which of the following factors would cause an increase in the demand for houses in Pajotte?

(1) An increase in the annual income of many Pajottians

(2) A reduced rate of immigration into Pajotte

(3) Lower interest rates on loans to buy houses

(B) The demand for lumber in Pajotte would (*increase*/ *decrease*), which would result in (*higher* / *lower*) lumber prices.

(C) Employment of workers who build houses would (*increase* / *decrease*) and their wages would (*increase* / *decrease*).

Why Is a Demand Curve Downward Sloping?

To most people, the law of demand is obvious: consumers buy more of a good at a lower price and less at a higher price. Economics goes beyond describing the combined demand of all consumers in a market. To explain why a demand curve is downward sloping, or negatively sloped, economists focus on the demand curve of a single consumer.

The total utility of a quantity of goods and services to a consumer can be represented by the maximum amount of money he or she is willing to give in exchange for that quantity. The marginal utility of a good or service to a consumer (measured in monetary terms) is the maximum amount of money he or she is willing to pay for one more unit of the good or service. With these definitions, we can now state a simple idea about consumer tastes: the more of a good a consumer has, the less will be the marginal utility of an additional unit.

Part A: Total Utility and Marginal Utility

Table 2-2.1 presents data on Dolores's evaluation of different quantities of polo shirts and different quantities of steak.

1. Use the data to compute the marginal utility of each polo shirt and each steak. The total utility numbers in the figure represent the total satisfaction in dollars Dolores receives from a given quantity of shirts or steaks. The marginal utility numbers represent the amount of dollars Dolores is willing to pay for an additional shirt or steak.

Table 2-2.1
Marginal Utility of Polo Shirts and Steaks

Number of polo shirts	Total utility	Marginal utility	Number of steaks	Total utility	Marginal utility
0	$0		0	$0	
1	$60	$60	1	$20	$20
2	$100	$40	2	$36	$16
3	$130	30	3	$51	15
4	$150	20	4	$65	14
5	$165	15	5	$78	13
6	$175	10	6	$90	12

2. Using Figure 2-2.1, plot Dolores's total utility and marginal utility for polo shirts and steaks. Each graph has two points to get you started.

Figure 2-2.1

Total and Marginal Utility of Polo Shirts and Steaks

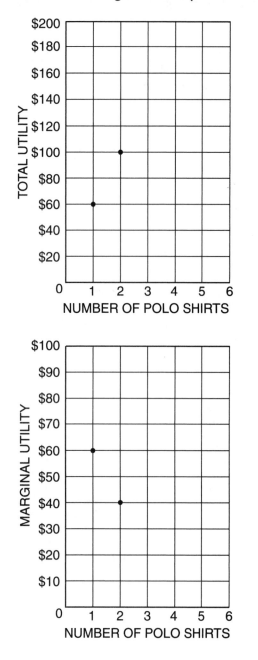

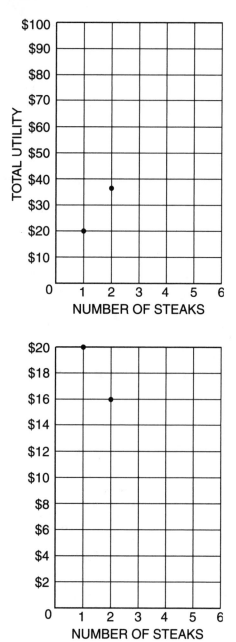

Advanced Placement Economics Microeconomics: Student Resource Manual © Council for Economic Education, New York, N.Y.

3. Looking at the table and graphs, you can conclude for both goods that as she consumes more units:

(A) total utility is always (*increasing* / *decreasing*).

(B) marginal utility always (*increases* / *decreases*).

Because your graphs show that Dolores receives less and less marginal utility, you have demonstrated the law of *diminishing marginal utility*.

Part B: The Marginal Utility per Dollar

Student Alert: **In spending your income wisely, it is the marginal utility per dollar (MU per $1) that matters, and not the marginal utility (MU) by itself.**

If Dolores has a given budget and must choose between polo shirts and steaks, she will make her choice so that the marginal utility per dollar spent of each good is the same. Using the data in Table 2-2.1 and assuming that the price of both goods is $30, let's see what happens if Dolores spends her entire budget of $150 dollars and buys five polo shirts and zero steaks. Her marginal utility from the fifth polo shirt is $15, and her marginal utility from the first steak is $20. So if she buys only four polo shirts and one steak, her total utility drops by $15 on the polo shirt, but it increases by $20 on the steak. Dolores is better off because her total utility has increased by $5 and her total budget is unchanged.

Suppose Dolores spends her $150 and buys four polo shirts and one steak. Her marginal utility from the fourth polo shirt is $20, and her marginal utility from the first steak is also $20. She will not want to switch. To buy the next steak gives her an increase in total utility of $16, but she would have to give up a polo shirt, which would reduce her utility by $20. Conversely, to buy an additional polo shirt would increase her total utility by $15, but she would lose $20 from giving up the steak. Dolores should not change her purchases. Note that this example assumes both the shirt and steak have the same price.

If the prices (P) of the two goods differ, then Dolores will adjust her consumption until the MU of the two goods, *per dollar spent*, are equal. Or, stated in another way,

$$\frac{MU_x}{P_x} = \frac{MU_y}{P_y}.$$

4. Use the information in Table 2-2.2 to analyze Callie's choice between gasoline and food.

Callie has an income of $55, the price of a unit of gasoline is $5, and the price of a unit of food is $10. Complete the table.

Table 2-2.2

Callie Buys Gasoline and Food

Gasoline (G)	MU_G	MU_G/P_G	Food (F)	MU_F	MU_F/P_F
1 unit	+$60	12	1 unit	+$120	12
2 units	+$30	6	2 units	+$80	+8.0
3 units	+$15	+3.0	3 units	+$60	6
4 units	+$5	1	4 units	+$30	+3.0
5 units	+$3	+0.6	5 units	+$10	1
6 units	+$1	.2	6 units	+$5	+0.5

(A) What is the meaning of the value "+3" when Callie consumes the fourth unit of food?

extra 3 dollar in extra utility

(B) How much income would Callie have to spend to purchase the combination of 1 G and 5 F?

$ 55

(C) Will the combination of 1 G and 5 F maximize Callie's total utility? Why?

No

(D) If the combination of 1 G and 5 F will not maximize her total utility from her income of $55, Callie should

(1) buy more units of G and fewer units of F.

(2) buy more units of F and fewer units of G.

(E) Callie will maximize her total utility from her budget of $55 if she buys ___3___ units of G and ___4___ units of F. This combination will give her a total utility of $___345___.

Part C: Consumer Surplus

Assume you go into a store to buy a bottle of water. The bottle of water costs you $1. You would have been willing to pay $2. The difference between what you paid and what you would have been willing to pay is *consumer surplus.*

We can calculate Dolores's consumer surplus from buying steak by looking at her demand curve. Refer back to Table 2-2.1 and look at her marginal utility values for steak. If she has two steaks, Dolores is willing to pay $15 for one more steak; if she has three steaks, she is willing to pay $14 for a fourth steak. Dolores will buy steak until the point where the price is equal to the marginal utility of the last steak. Dolores will pay the same price for each of the steaks she buys. Thus, if the price of steak is $14, she will buy four steaks; the marginal utility of the fourth steak is $14. Dolores would have been willing to pay more for the first three steaks. She has gotten a bargain buying four steaks at $14 apiece for a total expenditure of $56. She would have been willing to pay $20 for the first steak, $16 for the second, $15 for the third, and $14 for the fourth, for a total outlay of $65. The consumer surplus is the difference between what she was willing to pay ($65) and what she actually paid ($56). Her total consumer surplus from buying four steaks at a price of $14 is $9.

Consider the information in Table 2-2.3 on Joel's total utility for CD purchases, and then answer the questions that follow.

Table 2-2.3
Total Utility of CDs

Number of CDs	Total utility	
1	$25	25
2	$45	20
3	$63	18
4	$78	15
5	$90	12
6	$100	10
7	$106	6
8	$110	4

5. What marginal utility is associated with the purchase of the third CD?

(A) $18   (B) $21   (C) $45   (D) $63

6. What is Joel's consumer surplus if he purchases three CDs at $11 apiece?

   (A) $30   (B) $33   (C) $63   (D) $96

7. What would happen to Joel's consumer surplus if he purchased an additional CD at $11?

   (A) Consumer surplus declines by $11.

   (B) Consumer surplus increases by $11.

   (C) Consumer surplus increases by $15.

   (D) Consumer surplus increases by $4.

8. How many CDs should Joel buy when they cost $11 apiece?

   (A) 0   (B) 3   (C) 5   (D) 7

9. What is Joel's consumer surplus at the optimal number of CD purchases?

   (A) $35   (B) $55   (C) $79   (D) $100

10. If CDs go on sale and their price drops to $8, how many CDs do you expect Joel to buy?

    (A) 5   (B) 6   (C) 7   (D) 8

11. Why is consumer surplus important? How does it help explain the law of demand?

Part D: Income and Substitution Effects

Another way of explaining the downward sloping demand curve is through the *income* and *substitution effects*.

Income effect: When the price of a good falls, consumers experience an increase in purchasing power from a given income level. When the price of a good increases, consumers experience a decrease in purchasing power.

Substitution effect: When the price of a good falls, consumers will substitute toward that good and away from other goods.

Here's an example. Suppose you go to your favorite burger place. The price of a burger has increased, but the price of the chicken sandwich stays the same. Over the course of a week, you generally buy both burgers and chicken sandwiches.

12. How will the increase in the price of a burger affect your purchase of burgers? Explain.

13. Describe how the substitution effect changes your purchases of hamburgers and chicken sandwiches.

14. Describe how the income effect changes your purchases.

Elasticity: An Introduction

🛈 *Student Alert:* Elasticity measures the *strength* of your response to a change in a variable.

In many circumstances, it is not enough for an economist, policymaker, firm, or consumer to simply know the direction in which a variable will be moving. For example, if I am a producer, the law of demand tells me that if I increase the price of my good, the quantity demanded by consumers will decrease. The law of demand tells me the *direction* of the consumer response to the price change, but it does not tell me the *strength* of the consumer response. The law of demand doesn't tell me what will happen to my total revenue (the price of the good times the number of units sold). Whether total revenue increases or decreases depends on how responsive the quantity demanded is to the price change. Will total revenue increase or decrease by a little or a lot? Throughout the discipline of economics, in fact, the responsiveness of one variable to changes in another variable is an important piece of information. In general, *elasticity* is a measurement of how responsive one variable is to a change in another variable, *ceteris paribus* (holding all other variables constant).

Because elasticity measures responsiveness, changes in the variables are measured relative to some base or starting point. Each variable's change is measured as a percentage change. Consider the following elasticity measurements:

The price elasticity of demand, ε_d

$$\varepsilon_d = \frac{\text{percentage change in quantity demanded of Good X}}{\text{percentage change in price of Good X}}.$$

The income elasticity of demand, ε_I

$$\varepsilon_I = \frac{\text{percentage change in quantity demanded of Good X}}{\text{percentage change in income}}.$$

The cross-price elasticity of demand, ε_{CP}

$$\varepsilon_{CP} = \frac{\text{percentage change in quantity demanded of Good X}}{\text{percentage change in price of Good W}}.$$

The price elasticity of supply, ε_S

$$\varepsilon_S = \frac{\text{percentage change in quantity supplied of Good X}}{\text{percentage change in price of Good X}}.$$

Part A: Bonus Pay at Work

1. You have a job stocking items on the shelves at the local home improvement store. To increase productivity, your boss says a bonus will be paid based on how many items you put on the shelves each hour. Write the equation of the "elasticity of productivity" for this situation:

$$\varepsilon_{\text{productivity}} = \frac{percentage\ change\ in}{percentage\ change\ in}.$$

2. Assume your boss wants you to double your output, which would be a 100 percent increase in the number of items you shelve each hour. Underline the correct answer in each of these statements.

   (A) If your productivity is very responsive to a pay increase, then a given increase in your pay results in a large increase in your hourly output. In this case, your boss will need to increase the bonus pay by (*more than / less than / exactly*) 100 percent.

   (B) If your productivity is not very responsive to a pay increase, then a given increase in your pay results in a small increase in your hourly output. In this case, your boss will need to increase the bonus pay by (*more than / less than / exactly*) 100 percent.

Part B: The Price Elasticity of Demand

It's easy to imagine that there are many applications for the elasticity concept. Here we will concentrate on the price elasticity of demand for goods and services. For convenience, the measure is repeated here:

$$\varepsilon_{\text{d}} = \frac{percentage\ change\ in\ quantity\ demanded\ of\ Good\ X}{percentage\ change\ in\ price\ of\ Good\ X}.$$

Note the following points:

- Price elasticity of demand is always measured *along* a demand curve. When measuring the responsiveness of quantity demanded to a change in price, all other variables must be held constant.

- Because of the law of demand, which states that price and quantity demanded move in opposite directions, when you calculate the value of the price elasticity of demand, expect it to be a negative number. When we interpret that value, we consider the absolute value of ε_{d}.

- Along a linear, downward sloping demand curve, there are price ranges over which demand is elastic, unit elastic, and inelastic.

Advanced Placement Economics Microeconomics: Student Resource Manual © Council for Economic Education, New York, N.Y.

Table 2-3.1

Relationship between Changes in Quantity Demanded and Price

%ΔQd compared to %ΔP	Absolute value of ε_d	Interpretation
%ΔQd > %ΔP	> 1	Elastic
%ΔQd = %ΔP	= 1	Unit elastic
%ΔQd < %ΔP	< 1	Inelastic

Part C: Calculating the Arc Elasticity Coefficient

The arc elasticity calculation method is obtained when the midpoint or average price and quantity are used in the calculation. This is reflected in the formula below.

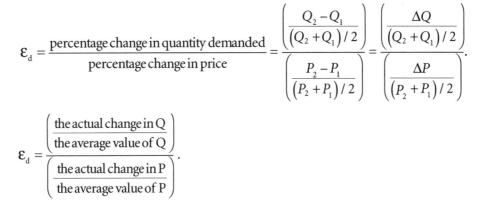

$$\varepsilon_d = \frac{\text{percentage change in quantity demanded}}{\text{percentage change in price}} = \frac{\left(\dfrac{Q_2 - Q_1}{(Q_2 + Q_1)/2}\right)}{\left(\dfrac{P_2 - P_1}{(P_2 + P_1)/2}\right)} = \frac{\left(\dfrac{\Delta Q}{(Q_2 + Q_1)/2}\right)}{\left(\dfrac{\Delta P}{(P_2 + P_1)/2}\right)}.$$

$$\varepsilon_d = \frac{\left(\dfrac{\text{the actual change in Q}}{\text{the average value of Q}}\right)}{\left(\dfrac{\text{the actual change in P}}{\text{the average value of P}}\right)}.$$

Suppose in Figure 2-3.1 that price is decreased from P_1 to P_2 and so quantity demanded increases from Q_1 to Q_2.

Figure 2-3.1

Calculating the Arc Elasticity Coefficient

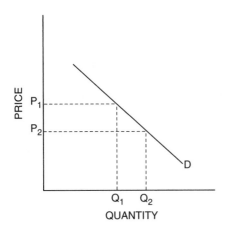

Because price decreased, our calculations will show the percentage change in price is negative. Because quantity demanded increased, the percentage change in quantity demanded is positive. The ratio of the two percentage changes thus will have a negative value. When we interpret the calculated value of ε_d, we consider its absolute value in deciding whether demand over this price range is elastic, unit elastic, or inelastic. Note that we have used the average of the two prices and the two quantities. We have done this so that the elasticity measured will be the same whether we are moving from Q_1 to Q_2 or the other way around.

Part D: Coffee Problems

Suppose Moonbucks, a national coffee-house franchise, finally moves into the little town of Middleofnowhere. Moonbucks is the only supplier of coffee in town and faces the weekly demand schedule as shown in Table 2-3.2. Answer the questions that follow.

Table 2-3.2
Cups of Coffee Demanded per Week

Price (per cup)	Quantity demanded	Price (per cup)	Quantity demanded
$10	0	$4	120
$9	20	$3	140
$8	40	$2	160
$7	60	$1	180
$6	80	$0	200
$5	100		

3. What is the arc price elasticity of demand when the price changes from $1 to $2? _____

$$\varepsilon_d = \frac{\left(\dfrac{\Delta Q}{(Q_2 + Q_1)/2}\right)}{\left(\dfrac{\Delta P}{(P_2 + P_1)/2}\right)} \quad = \quad \frac{\rule{2cm}{0.4pt}}{\rule{2cm}{0.4pt}} \quad = \quad \frac{\%}{\%} \quad = \quad \rule{2cm}{0.4pt}.$$

So, over this range of prices, demand is (*elastic / unit elastic / inelastic*).

4. What is the arc price elasticity of demand when the price changes from $5 to $6? _____

$$\varepsilon_d = \frac{\dfrac{\Delta Q}{(Q_2 + Q_1)/2}}{\dfrac{\Delta P_1}{(P_2 + P_1)/2}} \quad = \quad \frac{\rule{2cm}{0.4pt}}{\rule{2cm}{0.4pt}} \quad = \quad \frac{\%}{\%} \quad = \quad \rule{2cm}{0.4pt}.$$

So, over this range of prices, demand is (*elastic / unit elastic / inelastic*).

Part E: Comparing Slope and Price Elasticity of Demand

Now, consider Figure 2-3.2, which graphs the demand schedule given in Table 2-3.2.

Recall that the slope of a line is measured by the rise over the run: slope = rise / run = $\Delta P / \Delta Q$.

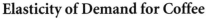 Figure 2-3.2
Elasticity of Demand for Coffee

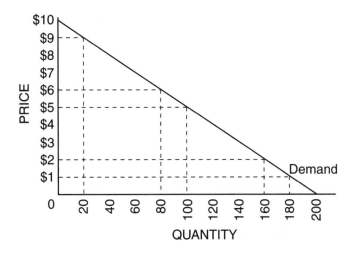

5. Using your calculations of ΔP and ΔQ from Question 3, calculate the slope of the demand curve between the prices of $1 and $2.

6. Using your calculations of ΔP and ΔQ from Question 4, calculate the slope of the demand curve between the prices of $5 and $6.

7. The law of demand tells us that an increase in price results in a decrease in the quantity demanded. Questions 5 and 6 remind us that the slope of a straight line is *constant everywhere along the line.* Anywhere along this demand curve, a change in price of $1 generates a change in quantity demanded of 20 cups of coffee a week.

   You've now shown mathematically that while the slope of the demand curve is related to the price elasticity of demand, the two concepts are not the same thing. Briefly discuss the relationship between where you are along the demand curve and the price elasticity of demand. How does this tie into the notion of *responsiveness*?

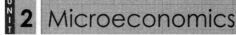

Part F: Two Extreme Cases of Price Elasticity of Demand

8. A horizontal demand curve is *perfectly elastic* because consumers will completely stop buying the good if the price is increased even by a small amount. This extreme case is shown by the demand curve facing a perfectly competitive firm. Such a firm can sell all it wants at the current market price (P_1), but if it raises its price it will lose all of its customers to other firms selling the same product at price P_1.

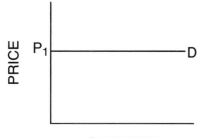 Figure 2-3.3
Perfectly Elastic Demand

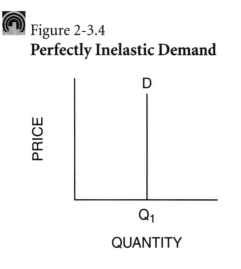

9. A vertical demand curve is *perfectly inelastic* because consumers want to buy the same amount (Q_1) of the good, no matter what the price. If the price increases, there is no response by consumers. This extreme case is approximated by the demand for a life-saving drug for which there are no acceptable substitutes.

Figure 2-3.4
Perfectly Inelastic Demand

Advanced Placement Economics Microeconomics: Student Resource Manual © Council for Economic Education, New York, N.Y.

Part G: Other Types of Elasticities

While the concept of price elasticity of demand captures most of the attention, an economist can create a measure of the elasticity that exists between any two variables. Three other elasticities that merit examination are income elasticity of demand, cross-price elasticity of demand, and price elasticity of supply.

The *income elasticity of demand* shows how responsive consumers are to a change in their income.

$$\varepsilon_I = \frac{\text{percentage change in quantity demanded of Good X}}{\text{percentage change in income}}.$$

Table 2-3.3 shows how economists interpret the value of ε_I:

Table 2-3.3

Income Elasticity of Demand

Value of ε_I	Interpretation
$\varepsilon_I > 0$	Good X is a normal (superior) good.
$\varepsilon_I < 0$	Good X is an inferior good.

A *normal good* is one for which income and demand move in the same direction. If income and demand move in opposite directions, the good is an *inferior good*.

10. Example: When income increases by 5 percent, the amount demanded of Tasty Cola increases by 3 percent and the amount demanded of Crusty Cola decreases by 2 percent. Answer these questions:

   (A) The value of ε_I for Tasty Cola is _____.

   (B) The value of ε_I for Crusty Cola is _____.

   (C) Tasty Cola is considered a(n) (*normal / inferior*) good.

   (D) Crusty Cola is considered a(n) (*normal / inferior*) good.

The *cross-price elasticity of demand* shows how responsive consumers of Good X are to a change in the price of some other good.

$$\varepsilon_{CP} = \frac{\text{percentage change in quantity demanded of Good X}}{\text{percentage change in price of Good W}}.$$

Table 2-3.4 shows how economists interpret the value of ε_{CP}:

Table 2-3.4

Cross-Price Elasticity of Demand

Value of ε_{CP}	Interpretation
$\varepsilon_{CP} > 0$	X and W are substitute goods.
$\varepsilon_{CP} = 0$	X and W are unrelated goods.
$\varepsilon_{CP} < 0$	X and W are complementary goods.

Hamburgers and pizzas are *substitute goods*; if the price of pizza rises, the amount of hamburgers demanded also rises. Ice cream and ice cream cones are *complementary goods*; if the price of ice cream falls, the amount of cones demanded rises.

11. Example: When the price of Good W increases by 4 percent, the amount demanded of Good A increases by 3 percent, the amount demanded of Good B falls by 2 percent, and the amount demanded of Good C is unchanged. Answer these questions:

(A) The value of ε_{CP} between Good A and Good W is _____.

(B) The value of ε_{CP} between Good B and Good W is _____.

(C) The value of ε_{CP} between Good C and Good W is _____.

(D) Good A and Good W are (*substitute / unrelated / complementary*) goods.

(E) Good B and Good W are (*substitute / unrelated / complementary*) goods.

(F) Good C and Good W are (*substitute / unrelated / complementary*) goods.

The *price elasticity of supply* shows how responsive producers of Good X are to a change in the price of Good X. The law of supply tells us that the sign of ε_S will be positive because price and quantity supplied move in the same direction.

$$\varepsilon_S = \frac{\text{percentage change in quantity supplied of Good X}}{\text{percentage change in price of Good X}}.$$

Table 2-3.5 shows how economists interpret the value of ε_S:

Table 2-3.5

Price Elasticity of Supply

Value of ε_S	Interpretation
$\varepsilon_S > 1$	Supply is elastic over this price range.
$\varepsilon_S = 1$	Supply is unit elastic over this price range.
$\varepsilon_S < 1$	Supply is inelastic over this price range.

12. Example: Assume the price of bookcases increases by 5 percent.

(A) If the quantity supplied of bookcases increases by 8 percent, the value of ε_S is _____ and the supply is (*elastic / unit elastic / inelastic*) over this price range.

(B) If the quantity supplied of bookcases increases by 5 percent, the value of ε_S is _____ and the supply is (*elastic / unit elastic / inelastic*) over this price range.

(C) If the quantity supplied of bookcases increases by 3 percent, the value of ε_S is _____ and the supply is (*elastic / unit elastic / inelastic*) over this price range.

The Determinants of Price Elasticity of Demand

Suppose we don't know the precise demand schedule for electricity and there is a 20 percent increase in the price of a kilowatt hour of electricity. We know that quantity demanded will decrease, but will it be by less than 20 percent (inelastic demand), exactly 20 percent (unit elastic demand), or more than 20 percent (elastic demand)? What factors influence the price elasticity of demand? (Remember, *ceteris paribus*!)

Part A: Presence of a Substitute Good or Service

Consider the following representative households in our market for electricity: Household A uses electricity for lighting, appliances, and heating. Household B uses electricity for lighting, appliances, and heating. It also has a heating system that can be switched to burn natural gas.

1. Household _____ will have the more elastic demand for electricity because of the presence of a _____ good.

2. Because Household A has no available substitutes, should we assume that the quantity demanded of electricity will remain unchanged given the increase in price? _____

   Do you think Household A's response will be relatively more elastic or inelastic than that of Household B? _____

3. Rate the following items in terms of their price elasticity of demand. Put a 1 in front of the good with the most elastic demand, a 3 in front of the item with the least elastic demand, and a 2 in front of the other good. Explain your reasoning.

   _____ Demand for insulin

   _____ Demand for Granny Smith apples

   _____ Demand for running shoes

   Rationale:

4. To summarize: demand is (*more / less*) elastic for goods with many available substitutes.

Part B: Proportion of Income Spent on a Good or Service

Consider the following representative households in the electricity market: Household A has income of $1,200 per month and spends $300 a month on electricity. Household B has income of $3,600 per month and spends $300 a month on electricity.

5. Household _____ will have the more elastic demand for electricity because the expenditures on this good account for a (*smaller / larger*) proportion of its income.

6. Illustrate your understanding of price elasticity of demand by placing a 1, 2, or 3 by each item below, denoting the most elastic (1) to the least elastic (3). Explain your reasoning.

_____ Demand for chewing gum

_____ Demand for automobiles

_____ Demand for clothing

Rationale:

7. To summarize: goods that command a (*small / large*) proportion of a consumer's income tend to be more price elastic.

Part C: Nature of the Good or Service

We expect that the price elasticity of demand will also vary with the nature of the good being considered. Is it a necessity? Is it a durable good? Are we considering the short run or the long run? Consider the following alternatives, and choose the option that correctly completes each statement.

8. The price elasticity of demand for cigarettes: a product that is considered to be a necessity will have a relatively price (*elastic / inelastic*) demand.

9. The price elasticity of demand for automobiles: in the short run, consumers can postpone the purchase of durable goods, and so the demand for such goods will be relatively (*more / less*) price elastic.

10. Briefly summarize how the nature of the good—necessity, durable good, or luxury good—and the time frame over which demand is measured affect the price elasticity of demand for a good or a service.

Part D: Income Elasticity of Demand

Now, suppose that prices in the market for electricity remain constant, but consumers' income increases by 30 percent. Even though we may not know the precise demand schedule, we are able to use the concept of income elasticity of demand to speculate about what will happen to demand.

Recall the income elasticity of demand, ε_I:

$$\varepsilon_I = \frac{\text{percentage change in quantity demanded}}{\text{percentage change in income}}.$$

Note in this case, income and quantity demanded are the relevant variables. All other variables, including the price of electricity, are held constant.

11. In measurements of income elasticity, if income and quantity demanded move in opposite directions—that is, if one increases while the other decreases—then the income elasticity coefficient will be (*positive / negative*).

12. Remember that if income increases, the demand for a normal good increases and the demand for an inferior good decreases. If the good is a normal good, income elasticity will be (*negative / positive*). If it is an inferior good, income elasticity will be (*negative / positive*).

Elasticity and Total Revenue

The income a firm receives from selling its good or services is called its *total revenue*. It also can be thought of as total consumer expenditure on that good or service.

$$\text{Total revenue (TR)} = \text{Price (P)} \times \text{quantity demanded (Qd)}.$$

Since price and quantity demanded were involved in our discussion of price elasticity of demand, it makes sense that total revenue somehow is related to the demand elasticity of the good or service the firm is selling. How strongly quantity demanded responds to a change in price will determine whether that price change leads to an increase or decrease in the firm's total revenue.

The law of demand tells us that a price increase will result in a decrease in quantity demanded. By itself, the higher price increases total revenue because the firm gets a higher price for each unit sold. But total revenue also is decreased because the firm will sell fewer units at the higher price. What happens to total revenue when price increases is determined by whether the effect of the higher price dominates the effect of the lower quantity demanded. Knowing the price elasticity of demand allows us to answer this important question. Table 2-5.1 presents the "total revenue test" related to the price elasticity of demand.

Table 2-5.1
Price Elasticity of Demand and Total Revenue

Category of price elasticity of demand	Relationship between price and total revenue
Elastic	P and TR move in opposite directions.
Inelastic	P and TR move in the same direction.
Unit elastic	TR is unaffected by a change in P.

1. Choose the correct answers in Table 2-5.2 to test your understanding of the "total revenue test."

Table 2-5.2
Price Elasticity of Demand and Total Revenue

	%ΔP	%ΔQd	Over this price range, demand is:	As a result of the ΔP, TR will:
(A)	+5%	−2%	elastic / unit elastic / inelastic	rise / fall / not change
(B)	+5%	−5%	elastic / unit elastic / inelastic	rise / fall / not change
(C)	+5%	−8%	elastic / unit elastic / inelastic	rise / fall / not change
(D)	−4%	+6%	elastic / unit elastic / inelastic	rise / fall / not change
(E)	−4%	+3%	elastic / unit elastic / inelastic	rise / fall / not change
(F)	−4%	+4%	elastic / unit elastic / inelastic	rise / fall / not change

You can use the total revenue test to determine the nature of price elasticity of demand without using percentage change values or calculating the value of the price elasticity of demand. Suppose when the price of calculators is increased from $15 to $17, the quantity demanded decreases from 10 million to 6 million calculators.

2. Complete Table 2-5.3 by determining the value of TR before and after the price change, then answer the questions that follow.

Table 2-5.3
Using Changes in TR to Identify Elasticity

	P	Qd	TR
(A) Old value	$15	10 million	$ million
(B) New value	$17	6 million	$ million

(C) How did TR change when P increased?

(D) This indicates that demand over this price range is (*elastic / unit elastic / inelastic*).

Note: The total revenue test in Table 2-5.1 is based on the price elasticity of demand. It is not related to the price elasticity of supply because if suppliers produce a lot more of their product when its price increases, that does not tell us how much of the product consumers are buying.

Excise Taxes

Table 2-6.1 and Figure 2-6.1 show the current supply of Greebes.

Table 2-6.1
Supply Schedule of Greebes

Quantity (millions)	Supply price before tax (per Greebe)	Supply price after tax (per Greebe)
50	$0.10	
100	$0.15	
150	$0.20	
200	$0.25	
250	$0.30	
300	$0.35	

Figure 2-6.1
Current Supply Schedule of Greebes

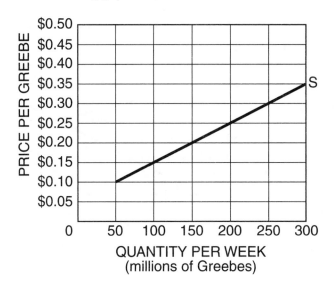

Now, suppose that in order to raise revenue for higher education, the government enacts an excise (sales) tax on sellers of $0.15 per Greebe. *This tax will result in a new supply curve for Greebes.* Since sellers will view this tax as an additional cost to them, there will be a decrease in supply. To determine where this new supply curve lies, reason as follows. Firms will try to pass the tax on to consumers through a higher price. If before the tax, firms were willing to supply 50 million Greebes at a price of $0.10, they would now be willing to supply 50 million Greebes only if the price were $0.25. (Remember: $0.15 of the price of each Greebe sold is now going to go to the government. So, if the price is $0.25 and the government is getting $0.15 of this price, then the seller is receiving the remaining $0.10.)

1. Fill in the blank spaces in Table 2-6.1. In Figure 2-6.1 draw the new supply curve that results from the tax. Label the new supply curve S_T.

What will be the result of this excise tax on the equilibrium quantity of Greebes? On the equilibrium price paid by buyers? On the equilibrium price received by sellers? On the tax revenue received by the government? On the revenue kept by sellers after they give the government its tax revenue?

The answers to these important questions will depend on the price elasticity of demand for Greebes. The next section of this activity will help you determine the effects of a $0.15 per unit excise tax on Greebes under four different demand conditions.

Part A: Relatively Elastic and Relatively Inelastic Demand

Compare the demand curves in Figures 2-6.2 and 2-6.3. Demand curve D_1 is relatively more inelastic than demand curve D_2. Put another way, D_2 is relatively more elastic than D_1.

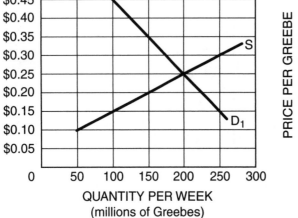

Figure 2-6.2
Relatively Inelastic Demand for Greebes

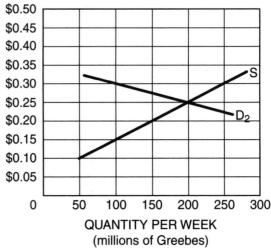

Figure 2-6.3
Relatively Elastic Demand for Greebes

2. Complete Table 2-6.2, which compares conditions before the tax and after the tax based on demand curves D_1 and D_2. Remember, the government is placing a $0.15 per unit excise tax on the sellers of the good. You will need to add the new supply curve S_T to Figures 2-6.2 and 2-6.3.

 Table 2-6.2

Comparing Effects of Tax Based on Price Elasticity of Demand

	Relatively inelastic demand D_1 Figure 2-6.2		Relatively elastic demand D_2 Figure 2-6.3	
	Before tax	After tax	Before tax	After tax
Equilibrium quantity	200 million			100 million
Equilibrium price	$0.25			$0.30
Total expenditure by consumers		$52.5 million	$50.0 million	
Total revenue sellers get to keep	$50.0 million			$15.0 million
Total tax revenue to government	$0.0 million		$0.0 million	

The incidence or burden of the excise tax refers to how the $0.15 per unit excise tax is shared between the buyers and the sellers. The incidence on the consumer is the increase in the equilibrium price resulting from the tax. The seller's incidence is that part of the tax not paid by consumers.

3. Under demand curve D_1, the incidence of the tax is $ _____ per unit on consumers and $ _____ per unit on sellers. Remember, these two values must add up to the per unit excise tax of $0.15.

4. Under demand curve D_2, the incidence of the tax is $ _____ per unit on consumers and $_____ per unit on sellers. Remember, these two values must add up to the per unit excise tax of $0.15.

5. The incidence of the tax is greater on buyers if demand is relatively (*more / less*) inelastic.

6. The incidence of the tax is greater on sellers if demand is relatively (*more / less*) inelastic.

Part B: Perfectly Elastic and Perfectly Inelastic Demand

Figure 2-6.4
Perfectly Inelastic Demand for Greebes

Figure 2-6.5
Perfectly Elastic Demand for Greebes

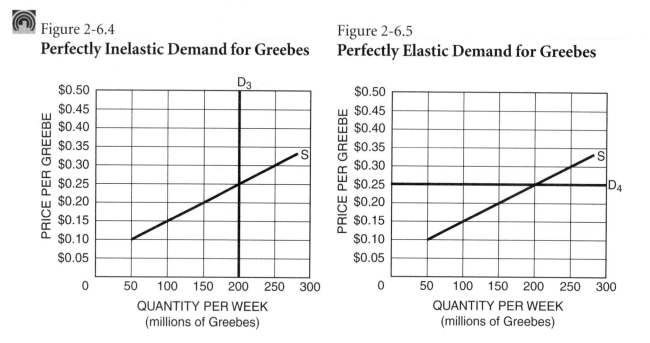

7. In the extreme cases of perfectly inelastic or perfectly elastic demand, the burden of the excise tax is not shared by consumers and sellers—one party will pay the entire tax. Compare Figures 2-6.4 and 2-6.5 and complete Table 2-6.3. Then answer the questions following the table. Remember, the government is placing a $0.15 per unit excise tax on the sellers of the good. You will need to add the new supply curve S_T to Figures 2-6.4 and 2-6.5.

Table 2-6.3
Comparing Effects of Tax Based on Perfectly Inelastic or Perfectly Elastic Demand

	Perfectly inelastic demand D₃ Figure 2-6.4		Perfectly elastic demand D₄ Figure 2-6.5	
	Before tax	After tax	Before tax	After tax
Equilibrium quantity	200 million			50 million
Equilibrium price	$0.25			$0.25
Total expenditure by consumers		$80.0 million	$50.0 million	
Total revenue sellers get to keep	$50.0 million			$5.0 million
Total tax revenue to government	$0.0 million		$0.0 million	

8. Under demand curve D_3, the incidence of the tax is $ _____ per unit on consumers and $ _____ per unit on sellers. Remember, these two values must add up to the per unit excise tax of $0.15.

9. Under demand curve D_4, the incidence of the tax is $ _____ per unit on consumers and $ _____ per unit on sellers. Remember, these two values must add up to the per unit excise tax of $0.15.

10. The incidence of the tax is totally on buyers if demand is perfectly (*elastic / inelastic*).

11. The incidence of the tax is totally on sellers if demand is perfectly (*elastic / inelastic*).

Part C: Excise Tax Examples

12. A famous Supreme Court justice once said, "The power to tax is the power to destroy." This is more likely to be true regarding sellers if the demand for the product taxed is relatively (*elastic / inelastic*).

13. If you were a government revenue agent interested in getting the most tax revenue possible, you would suggest putting excise taxes on goods whose demand is (*elastic / unit elastic / inelastic*).

14. Think of some real-world goods on which the government places excise taxes: liquor, cigarettes, gasoline. Do you think that the demand for these goods is relatively elastic or relatively inelastic? How does this affect the amount of tax revenue the government receives from taxes on these goods?

Maximum and Minimum Price Controls

Prices send signals and provide incentives to buyers and sellers. When supply or demand changes, market prices adjust, affecting incentives. High prices induce extra production while they discourage consumption.

In this exercise, we discover how the imposition of price controls (maximum or minimum prices) interrupts the process that matches production with consumption. *Price ceilings* (maximum prices) sometimes appear in the form of rent control, utility prices, and other caps on upward price pressure. *Price floors* (minimum prices) occur in the form of agricultural price supports and minimum wages.

When the government imposes price controls, citizens should understand that some people gain and some people lose from every policy change. By understanding the consequences of legal price regulations, citizens are able to weigh the costs and benefits of the change.

As a general rule, price floors create a *surplus* of goods or services, or *excess supply*, since the quantity demanded of goods is less than the quantity supplied. Conversely, price ceilings generate *excess quantity demanded*, causing *shortages*.

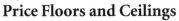 Figure 2-7.1
Price Floors and Ceilings

Price floors and ceilings can be plotted with supply and demand curves. Use Figure 2-7.1 to answer the questions.

1. What is the market price? __$50__

---

2. What quantity is demanded and what quantity is supplied at the market price?

(A) Quantity demanded _____ 120

(B) Quantity supplied _____ 120

3. What quantity is demanded and what quantity is supplied if the government passes a law requiring the price to be no higher than $30 (a price ceiling)?

(A) Quantity demanded _____160_____

(B) Quantity supplied _____60_____

(C) There is a ((shortage)/ surplus) of _____100_____.

4. What quantity is demanded and what quantity is supplied if the government passes a law requiring the price to be no lower than $80 (a price floor)?

(A) Quantity demanded _____60_____

(B) Quantity supplied _____210_____

(C) There is a (shortage /(surplus)) of _____150_____

(D) What happens to total consumer surplus? _____decrease_____

(E) Is society better or worse off after the price floor is imposed? _____

(F) Who gains from the price floor? _____producers_____

Property Rights and Market Failure

A key requirement of a well-functioning market economy is the establishment and enforcement of well-defined property rights. When individuals, rather than central governments, own the land and physical capital, many important economic incentives are created. When a person owns property, he or she has the right to use, sell, or trade with another person for mutual gain. For example, a homeowner has an incentive to keep that home in nice condition whether he wants to continue to live in the home or if he thinks that the home might eventually be sold. If the person living in that home doesn't own the home, he may not have a very strong incentive to keep the home in tip-top condition.

If the owner of a restaurant owns the capital used by the firm, she has a profit incentive to produce a high-quality product that is demanded by consumers. After all, if the firm is not profitable, the firm will go bankrupt and the owner's physical capital may be lost.

In the case of the homeowner and the restaurateur, property rights allow for the housing and restaurant markets to exist and to function reasonably well. This of course begs the question: what would happen to a market if property rights were not very well established or were absent altogether?

Many cities and towns are located along a river for two reasons: the river proved to be an excellent source of water for residential and industrial usage, and it was an excellent way of disposing of residential and industrial wastes. A river is an example of a nation's natural resources, but it is owned by nobody. As a result of the absence of property rights to the water (either for consumption or for disposal purposes), it tends to be overused and polluted. We can see this with another example of a negative externality.

Suppose that many chemical companies are located on the banks of the lovely Bohio River. The Bohio is a source of drinking water for many cities, it is a source of recreation for swimmers and boaters, a fishing industry exists on the Bohio, and the river serves a pivotal role in the ecosystem throughout the watershed.

Like all firms, these companies incur marginal production costs for each ton of chemicals that is produced. These marginal costs that accrue to the chemical companies are referred to as *marginal private costs* (*MPC*) of production and are assumed to increase as more tons of chemicals are produced. In fact, it is the marginal private cost curve that represents the market supply of chemicals. Suppose that the chemical companies can discharge toxic waste into the Bohio River, a common resource that is critical to everyone but owned by no one. This toxic waste requires cities to install additional water purification equipment, causes swimmers to develop skin rashes, hurts the profitability of the firms in the fishing industry, and threatens the viability of the ecosystem. These negative by-products of producing another ton of chemicals are additional *external costs* to society. When we add the marginal private cost to the external cost of producing chemicals, we get a higher dollar amount, the *marginal social cost* (*MSC*). Figure 2-8.1 shows both the MSC and MPC curves in the market for chemicals. The vertical distance between the two represents the external costs, or negative externality, imposed upon society because nobody owns the Bohio River.

The graph also shows the downward sloping *marginal social benefit* (*MSB*) curve that represents the demand for chemicals in this market. Assuming that all the benefits of the chemicals are received by the buyers of the chemicals, the demand curve also represents the *marginal private benefit* (*MPB*) curve.

1. The market for chemicals will ignore the external costs to society. Businesses seeking to maximize their total profit will produce the output level where their marginal private benefit equals their marginal private cost (MPB = MPC). In Figure 2-8.1, label the market equilibrium quantity of chemicals and the equilibrium price of chemicals as Q_M and P_M.

Figure 2-8.1
The Market for Chemicals

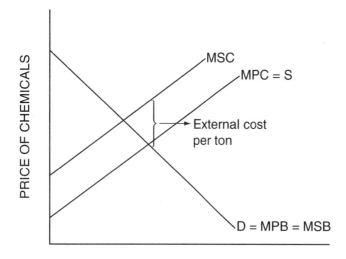

2. From society's perspective, the optimal or socially efficient output level of chemicals is the one where marginal social benefit equals marginal social cost (MSB = MSC). In the graph, label the socially efficient quantity of chemicals and socially efficient price of chemicals as Q_E and P_E.

3. Which output level is greater: the one produced by firms in the market or the one desired by society? Does this indicate that the negative externality caused by pollution results in an over-allocation or an under-allocation of society's scarce resources to the chemical market? Explain.

4. What impact did the absence of property rights for the Bohio River have on the outcome of the chemical market?

Deadweight Loss

When a market transaction is made between a buyer and a seller, both parties expect to benefit from that transaction: Buyers will receive consumer surplus, and sellers will receive producer surplus. If the market is competitive and free of externalities, the equilibrium price and quantity are such that the sum of consumer surplus and producer surplus (total surplus or total welfare) is maximized. There is no other outcome that can generate more total welfare than the competitive outcome. However, when something prevents the market from reaching that equilibrium outcome, total welfare falls, and the decline in total welfare is called *deadweight loss*. Deadweight loss really just represents the value of transactions that *could have* been made, but are not made. In the activities below you will see deadweight loss can emerge in a couple of different ways but common sources of deadweight loss include: price and quantity controls, excise taxes, monopoly power, and externalities.

Part A: The Market for Hamburgers

Table 2-9.1 shows the demand and supply schedules for hamburgers, a good that is currently exchanged in a competitive market. We can see that consumers have diminishing marginal benefit from hamburgers as more are consumed. We can also see that suppliers have increasing marginal cost of producing hamburgers as more are produced. Use the table to answer the questions that follow.

Table 2-9.1
The Market for Hamburgers

Demand			Supply		
Quantity of hamburgers demanded	Marginal benefit from a hamburger	Consumer surplus (CS)	Quantity of hamburgers supplied	Marginal cost of a hamburger	Producer surplus (PS)
1	$10	$4	1	$2	
2	$9		2	$3	$3
3	$8		3	$4	
4	$7		4	$5	
5	$6		5	$6	
6	$5		6	$7	
7	$4		7	$8	
8	$3		8	$9	
9	$2	-$4	9	$10	
10	$1		10	$11	-$5

1. What is the equilibrium quantity of hamburgers exchanged in the market, and what is the equilibrium price in the market?

2. At the equilibrium quantity, complete the columns of consumer and producer surplus. Remember that each hamburger is sold at the equilibrium price.

3. What is the total welfare generated by the competitive equilibrium in the hamburger market?

4. Now suppose the government decides that too many hamburgers are being exchanged in the competitive market and requires that only three hamburgers be bought and sold at the equilibrium price found in Question 1. How does this regulation affect total welfare?

Part B: The Market for Textbooks

This activity will use a little bit of algebra and graphical analysis to see how deadweight loss is created with a price ceiling.

Suppose that the market for textbooks can be described with the following demand and supply equations.

$$\text{Market Demand: } P = 300 - Q_d$$

$$\text{Market Supply: } P = 100 + Q_s$$

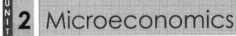

5. Sketch a graph of this market and solve for the equilibrium price and quantity.

 Figure 2-9.1
The Market for Textbooks

PRICE

QUANTITY

6. Show the area of CS and PS in the graph.

7. Compute the dollar value of CS and PS.

8. Now suppose a benevolent college president has decided that the price of textbooks is "too high" and successfully imposes a price ceiling of $150. Show the impact of a price ceiling in the graph.

9. Recalculate the CS and PS and determine the amount of deadweight loss (DWL) that is created by this policy.

Circle the letter of each correct answer.

1. A downward sloping demand curve can be explained by

   I.   diminishing marginal utility.

   II. diminishing marginal returns.

   III. the substitution effect.

   IV. the income effect.

   (A) I only

   (B) II only

   (C) I and III only

   (D) I and IV only

   (E) I, III, and IV only

2. If hot dogs are an inferior good, an increase in income will result in

   (A) an increase in the quantity demanded for hot dogs.

   (B) an increase in the demand for hot dogs.

   (C) a decrease in the quantity demanded for hot dogs.

   (D) a decrease in the demand for hot dogs.

   (E) no change in the demand for hot dogs.

3. Assume that coal is a normal good. If the price of coal increases and the quantity sold increases, which of the following is consistent with these observations?

   (A) The price of oil, a substitute for coal, increased.

   (B) A wage increase was given to coal miners.

   (C) New machinery made coal mining more efficient.

   (D) Consumers' incomes fell.

   (E) The demand curve is inelastic.

4. During a football game, it starts to rain and the temperature drops. The senior class, which runs the concession stand and is studying economics, raises the price of coffee from 50 cents to 75 cents a cup. They sell more than ever before. Which answer explains this?

   (A) The supply of coffee increased.

   (B) The demand curve for coffee was elastic.

   (C) The supply of coffee decreased.

   (D) The demand for coffee increased.

   (E) The demand curve for coffee was inelastic.

5. Which of the following statements best reflects the law of *diminishing marginal utility*?

   (A) "I have to have a scoop of ice cream on my pie."

   (B) "I'll never get tired of your cooking."

   (C) "The last bite tastes just as good as the first."

   (D) "I couldn't eat another doughnut if you paid me."

   (E) "I prefer to eat several small meals a day, rather than three large ones."

6. If the cost of producing automobiles increases, the price, equilibrium quantity, and consumer surplus will most likely change in which of the following ways?

	Price	Quantity	Consumer surplus
(A)	Increase	Increase	Increase
(B)	Increase	Decrease	Increase
(C)	Increase	Decrease	Decrease
(D)	Decrease	Increase	Decrease
(E)	Decrease	Decrease	Decrease

7. Compare 2011 with 2012. Which of the following statements is (are) true?

Year	Quantity sold	Price
2011	30,000	$10
2012	50,000	$20

   I.   Demand has increased.

   II. Quantity demanded has increased.

   III. Supply has increased.

   IV. Quantity supplied has increased.

   V.   Supply has decreased.

   (A) I only

   (B) V only

   (C) I and IV only

   (D) I and V only

   (E) I, II, and III only

8. During the 1990s, the price of VCRs fell by about 30 percent, and quantity sold decreased by the same amount. The demand for VCRs must

   (A) be inelastic.

   (B) be elastic.

   (C) be unit elastic.

   (D) have shifted to the right.

   (E) have shifted to the left.

9. Which of the following will occur if a legal price floor is placed on a good below its free-market equilibrium?

   (A) Surpluses will develop.

   (B) Shortages will develop.

   (C) Underground markets will develop.

   (D) The equilibrium price will ration the good.

   (E) The quantity sold will increase.

10. A marketing survey shows that gate receipts would increase if the price of tickets to a summer rock concert increased, even though the number of tickets sold would fall. What does this imply about the price elasticity of demand for concert tickets?

   (A) Demand is inelastic.

   (B) Demand is elastic.

   (C) Demand is unit elastic.

   (D) Demand is perfectly inelastic.

   (E) Demand is perfectly elastic.

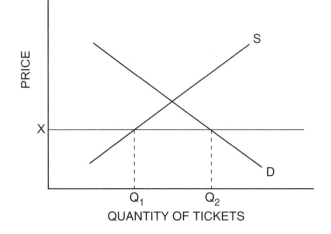

11. According to the graph above, which of the following will occur if a legal price ceiling is imposed at price X?

   (A) Shortages will occur.

   (B) Surpluses will occur.

   (C) Demand will increase.

   (D) Q_2 will be purchased.

   (E) Supply will decrease.

12. Which of the following statements about price controls is true?

    (A) A price ceiling causes a shortage if the ceiling price is above the equilibrium price.

    (B) A price floor causes a surplus if the price floor is below the equilibrium price.

    (C) A price ceiling causes an increase in demand if the ceiling price is set below the equilibrium price.

    (D) A price ceiling causes a decrease in demand if the price floor is set above the equilibrium price.

    (E) Price ceilings and price floors result in a misallocation of resources.

13. If the price of lunch at the school cafeteria increases and cafeteria revenue remains constant, the price elasticity of demand for a school lunch must be

    (A) elastic.

    (B) perfectly elastic.

    (C) unit elastic.

    (D) inelastic.

    (E) perfectly inelastic.

14. If an excise tax is imposed on a product, consumer surplus and producer surplus for this good will most likely change in which of the following ways?

	Consumer surplus	Producer surplus
(A)	Decrease	Decrease
(B)	Decrease	Increase
(C)	Decrease	Not change
(D)	Not change	Increase
(E)	Not change	Not change

15. If the price of paperback books increases and consumer expenditures on paperback books also increase, which of the following is necessarily true?

    (A) Paperback books are normal goods.

    (B) Paperback books are inferior goods.

    (C) The demand for paperback books is unit elastic.

    (D) The demand for paperback books is elastic.

    (E) The demand for paperback books is inelastic.

16. The substitution effect causes a consumer to buy less of a product when the price increases because the

    (A) product is now less expensive compared to similar products.

    (B) product is now more expensive compared to similar products.

    (C) consumer's real income has decreased.

    (D) consumer's real income has increased.

    (E) consumer will buy more inferior goods and fewer normal goods.

Product	% Change in income	% Change in quantity
A	+5	+5
B	+5	−5
C	−10	−5
D	−10	+10

17. Based on the information in the table above, which product(s) is/are inferior?

    (A) Product A only

    (B) Product B only

    (C) Product D only

    (D) Product A and C only

    (E) Product B and D only

18. Brooke is spending all of her income consuming products X and Y. If $MU_x/P_x = 10$ and $MU_y/P_y = 6$, what should Brooke do to maximize her satisfaction?

    (A) Buy more X and more Y.

    (B) Buy more X and less Y.

    (C) Buy less X and less Y.

    (D) Buy less X and more Y.

    (E) Make no changes.

19. If the price of a good decreases by 3 percent and total revenue increases, the absolute value of the price elasticity of demand for the good could possibly be

    (A) 1.3   (D) 0.2

    (B) 1   (E) 0

    (C) 0.8

20. Advocates of higher minimum wages for unskilled labor defend their position by arguing that

    (A) low-income workers deserve to earn incomes above the poverty level.

    (B) higher wages boost worker productivity and efficiency.

    (C) higher wages will cause employers to reduce the payroll, but the total wages of remaining workers will be higher.

    (D) higher wages induce more workers into the labor market and thus reduce unemployment.

    (E) it is more efficient for the private sector to provide a higher wage than for the government to provide transfer payments to low-income workers.

21. A paper mill located on a scenic river decides to dump its untreated waste products into the river. Which of the following is the likely result of this action?

    (A) The marginal private cost and marginal social cost of paper production will be equal.

    (B) The marginal private cost will be greater than the marginal social cost of paper production.

    (C) The price of paper produced by the mill will increase.

    (D) The mill will produce more paper than society would like it to produce.

    (E) The mill will produce the socially optimal amount of paper.

Answer Questions 22 and 23 based on this graph of the market for Good X.

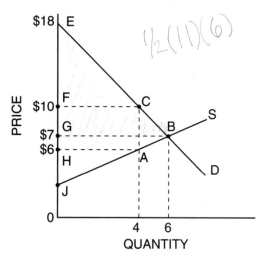

22. In a competitive market the value of consumer surplus is

    (A) $0.   (D) $33.

    (B) $11.   (E) $42.

    (C) $18.

23. If the government decided that only 4 units of Good X could be sold, the deadweight loss of this policy would be shown by area

    (A) ABC.   (D) CFE.

    (B) ACEJ.   (E) BGJ.

    (C) AHJ.

MICROECONOMICS

The Theory of the Firm

Unit 3

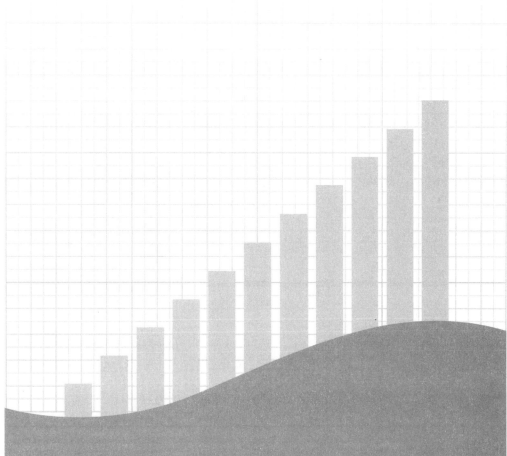

- All firms have costs. It is important to be able to define and plot graphically these costs.

- Explicit costs are monetary payments a firm must make to an outsider to obtain a resource.

- Implicit costs are income a firm sacrifices when it employs a resource it owns to produce a product instead of selling the resource to someone else.

- Total fixed costs do not change with a change in output. There are fixed costs only in the short run. The long run is defined as a period in which there are no fixed costs, and firms are free to allocate their resources as they please.

- Total variable costs change with a change in output. Total costs equal total fixed costs plus total variable costs. Marginal cost is the additional cost of producing an additional unit of output. Marginal cost is very important in determining at what price and output a firm will operate.

- Marginal cost eventually rises because of the law of diminishing marginal returns. The law of diminishing marginal returns is based on evidence that marginal product eventually declines when equal amounts of a variable factor of production are added to fixed factors of production.

- Average total cost and average variable cost are total cost and total variable cost divided by output.

- Average total cost and average variable cost fall when marginal cost is below them and rise when marginal cost is above them.

- The marginal cost curve crosses the average variable cost curve and the average total cost curve at their lowest points.

- If a firm has total revenue that just covers its total cost, it breaks even.

- An economist views total cost as the sum of explicit cost and implicit cost.

- If a firm has more total revenue than total costs, it makes a positive economic profit.

- If a firm has more total costs than total revenue, it operates at an economic loss.

- In the long run, a firm must cover all its implicit and explicit costs, including a normal rate of profit.

- A normal profit represents the opportunity cost of an entrepreneur using her/his own resources in the firm. It is the return needed to keep those resources in their current use.

- In the short run, a firm can operate at a loss as long as its total revenue covers its total variable costs.

- Economic profits are profits over and above the normal rate of profit at which a firm just covers its total costs. A firm makes an accounting profit when its total revenue exceeds its explicit costs.

- A firm makes an economic profit if its total revenue is greater than the sum of its explicit and implicit costs.

- The objective of a firm is to maximize total economic profit or minimize loss.

- Firms maximize total profit when they produce the level of output where marginal revenue equals marginal cost.

- Perfect competition exists when there are many small producers and many small consumers of a homogeneous product.

- For a perfectly competitive firm, marginal revenue is equal to price. A perfectly competitive firm produces where price equals marginal cost. A perfectly competitive firm breaks even in the long run and earns a normal profit.

■ Other things being constant, the most efficient allocation of resources occurs when a firm produces at the level of output where price is equal to marginal cost.

■ A monopoly occurs when one firm controls the market. It faces the market demand for the good or service it is selling.

■ Barriers to entry allow a monopoly to keep out competing firms and maintain a positive economic profit in the long run.

■ Allocative efficiency means a firm operates at the point where price equals marginal cost. Productive efficiency means a firm operates at the point where price equals the minimum value of average total cost.

■ A perfectly competitive firm is allocatively and productively efficient in the long run.

■ For a monopoly firm or any other firm under imperfect competition, marginal revenue is less than price.

■ A monopoly firm maximizes profits by producing at the quantity where marginal

revenue equals marginal cost and by setting price according to the demand curve at that quantity.

■ A monopoly firm can make economic profits in the long run. However, a long-run economic profit is not guaranteed.

■ In the long run, a monopoly firm charges a higher price and produces at a lower output than a perfectly competitive market with the same cost curves.

■ A monopoly firm will operate where price is greater than marginal cost, causing it to produce too little of its good or service from society's perspective.

■ A monopoly is neither productively efficient nor allocatively efficient.

■ Oligopoly occurs when a few large firms control the market.

■ Monopolistic competition is close to pure or perfect competition except that there is product differentiation.

■ A monopolistically competitive firm will break even in the long run. It will be neither productively efficient nor allocatively efficient.

Different Types of Market Structures

Firms sell goods and services in an attempt to maximize their total economic profit. It is important to understand the nature of the four types of product markets in which a firm can sell its good or service. At one end of the spectrum is a perfectly competitive market in which there are many small firms selling the identical product. At the other end of the market spectrum is a monopoly in which only one firm supplies the product. In between these two market formats are monopolistic competition and oligopoly. Although all firms have the common goal of profit maximization, the characteristics of the product markets influence a firm's decisions about how much output to produce and what price to charge.

After you have learned about the four types of market structures, complete Table 3-1.1.

Table 3-1.1
Market Structures

Characteristics			
Market structure	Number of firms	Differentiated or homogeneous product	Ease of entry
Perfect competition			
Monopolistic competition			
Oligopoly			
Monopoly			

Results					
Market structure	Price-setting power	Nonprice competition	Allocative and productive efficiency	Long-run profits	Examples
Perfect competition					
Monopolistic competition					
Oligopoly					
Monopoly					

Mirror Images: Marginal Product and Marginal Cost

Most of the activities in this unit concern a firm's costs of production. You will learn about a firm's costs of producing a given amount of its product—*total fixed cost (TFC)*, *total variable cost (TVC)*, and *total cost (TC)*. You also will work with the firm's costs of a typical (average) unit of output—*average fixed cost (AFC)*, *average variable cost (AVC)*, and *average total cost (ATC)*. The most important measure of a firm's cost is *marginal cost (MC)* because it shows the change in the firm's total cost when it produces one more unit of output. You will not be surprised to find that the cost of producing output is based on the productivity of the firm. If a firm is highly productive, that means it is producing a lot of output from a given amount of resources, thus reducing its costs of production. Firms that are inefficient will have high production costs and be at a competitive disadvantage. Because high productivity implies low cost, economists treat a firm's cost measures as mirror images of its productivity measures.

A firm makes production decisions in two time horizons. The "short run" is a period of time in which the amount of some key factor of production, often capital, is fixed. Other factors, such as labor, are variable because the firm can increase or decrease the amount of these resources in the short run. In the "long run," all resources are variable and can be increased or decreased by the firm.

There are three measures of the productivity of a firm.

1. The firm's *total physical product* or *total output* (Q) is how many units of its good or service the firm produces in a specified period of time. If a firm produces 100 units per week, we express this as Q = 100.

2. The firm's *average physical product* (APP) shows how many units of output are produced by an average unit of labor (the variable resource). If the firm uses five units of labor (L) to produce 100 units of output each week, we say APP = Q/L = 100/5 = 20 units of output.

3. The firm's *marginal physical product* (MPP) tells us the change in total product when the firm adds an extra unit of labor to its fixed stock of capital. If, as a result of adding a sixth unit of labor the firm's total output increases from 100 units to 114 units, then the MPP of the sixth labor unit is +14 units: MPP = $\Delta Q/\Delta L$ = +14/+1 = +14.

🛈 *Student Alert*: **The terms *average physical product* and *average product* mean the same thing. Also, *marginal physical product* is the same as *marginal product*. Some textbooks use APP and MPP, while others use AP and MP. But you cannot use "average" terms interchangeably with "marginal" terms!**

The key productivity principle in the short run is the "law of diminishing marginal productivity" (also called the law of diminishing marginal returns). Assume a firm operates in the short run with a fixed amount of capital and with labor as its variable resource. The law of diminishing marginal productivity states that as the firm adds more labor units to its fixed stock of capital, eventually the MPP from an extra unit of labor will diminish.

Part A: The Productivity Measures of a Firm

Table 3-2.1 is a short-run production chart showing how the productivity of the firm changes as it adds additional units of labor to its fixed stock of capital. Assume the data refer to the firm's productivity in a one-week period.

1. Complete Table 3-2.1. Some data are already included in the chart. Put the values of MPP at the new labor level. For example, when the firm increases its labor from one to two units per week, its total output increases by 15 units. Write "+15" at $L = 2$ in the MPP column.

Table 3-2.1
The Three Productivity Measures of a Firm

L	Q	MPP = $\Delta Q/\Delta L$	APP = Q/L
0	0	–	–
1	10		10.0
2	25	+15	
3	36		
4	46		11.5
5	55	+9	
6	63		
7	63		9.0
8	60	–3	

Advanced Placement Economics Microeconomics: Student Resource Manual © Council for Economic Education, New York, N.Y.

2. When you have completed Table 3-2.1, plot the L and Q data in Figure 3-2.1. (The first two combinations are plotted for you already.) This Q curve shows how much total output the firm produces with different amounts of labor. Note that the firm's total product increases as it adds more labor, but eventually the total product declines if the firm adds too many labor units on its limited amount of equipment.

Figure 3-2.1
Total Product

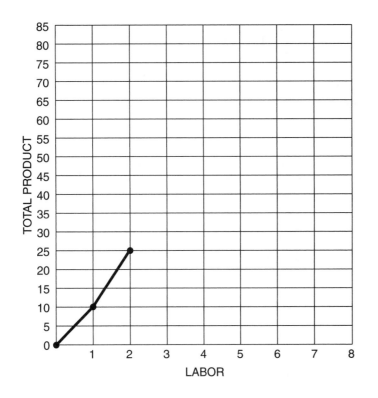

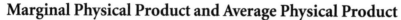
3. Now plot the L, MPP, and APP data in Figure 3-2.2. You can connect the MPP points with a solid line and the APP points with a dotted line. (Some combinations are plotted for you already.) Plot the values of MPP at the new labor level. For example, put a dot on the graph at the combination of L = 2 and MPP = +15 since the MPP resulting from adding the second labor unit is 15 units of output. Note that both MPP and APP increase initially but then decrease as the firm adds more units of labor.

Figure 3-2.2
Marginal Physical Product and Average Physical Product

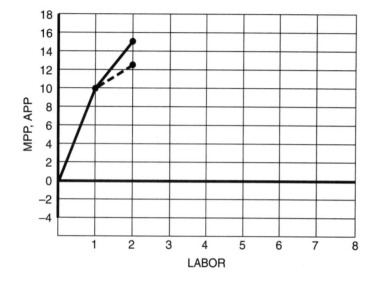

4. Diminishing marginal productivity sets in with the addition of the _____ labor unit.

5. The average physical product continues to increase as long as the marginal physical product is (*greater than / equal to / less than*) the average physical product.

6. Can the average physical product of labor be negative? Why?

7. Can the marginal physical product of labor be negative? Why?

8. Total product increases as the firm adds units of labor as long as the marginal physical product is (*positive / zero / negative*).

9. Although our graphs have no information about the price of the good or the price of labor, we can conclude that the firm will not want to hire a unit of labor for which marginal physical product is (*diminishing / negative*). Explain your answer.

10. What is the relationship between marginal physical product and total product?

11. What is the relationship between marginal physical product and average physical product?

Part B: Productivity and Cost: A Mirror View of Each Other

As you work with productivity and cost graphs, note how the axes are labeled. The productivity graphs typically have L on the horizontal axis because that is the variable resource that the firm changes in order to alter its level of total output. The vertical axis has some measure of productivity (such as Q or APP). There are no dollar signs on a productivity graph because such graphs are not dealing with revenue or cost. The cost graphs always have total output or total physical product (Q) on the horizontal axis because costs are expressed in relation to the Q of the firm. Cost graphs always have a dollar-measured concept on the vertical axis (such as total cost [TC] or marginal cost [MC]).

Figure 3-2.3 shows the relationship between a firm's MPP and APP. The graph assumes MPP initially increases as the firm adds labor units due to specialization of labor on the firm's equipment. Eventually diminishing marginal productivity sets in, which means that at some point APP also will decline as more labor units are added.

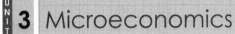

Figure 3-2.3
Marginal Physical Product and Average Physical Product

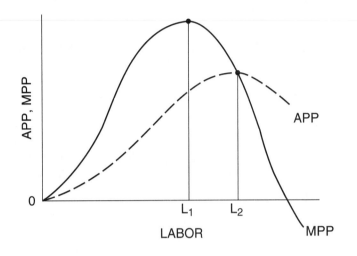

12. Diminishing marginal productivity sets in at (L_1 / L_2) labor units.

13. APP increases as long as MPP is (*greater than / equal to / less than*) APP.

14. APP decreases as long as MPP is (*greater than / equal to / less than*) APP.

15. Why is APP maximized at L_2 labor units?

16. "If MPP is diminishing, then APP must also be diminishing." Is this a correct statement? Why?

Figure 3-2.4 shows the relationship between a firm's MC and AVC: AVC = TVC/Q. If the firm has L as its only variable resource, then AVC represents the labor cost per unit of output. Suppose a firm pays each of its 10 workers a daily wage of $80 and produces a Q of 400 units. Its TVC is $800 = (10)($80), and its AVC is $2 = $800/400. Each of its 400 units has a labor cost component of $2.

Figure 3-2.4
Marginal Cost and Average Variable Cost

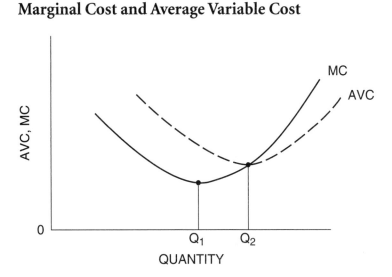

17. AVC decreases as long as MC is (*greater than / equal to / less than*) AVC.

18. AVC increases as long as MC is (*greater than / equal to / less than*) AVC.

19. Why is AVC minimized at Q_2 units of output?

20. "If MC is increasing, then AVC must also be increasing." Is this a correct statement? Why?

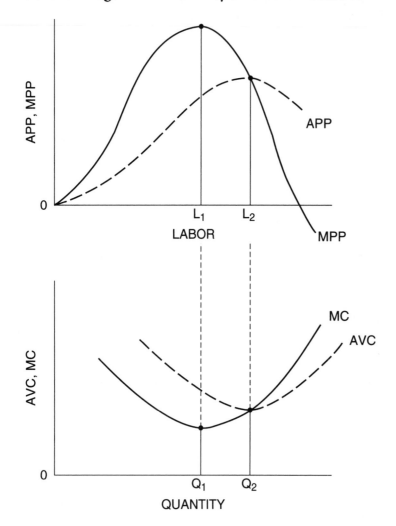

Figure 3-2.5

Mirror Image of Productivity and Cost Measures

The productivity of a firm is the basis of its cost. A firm wants to be highly productive in order to keep its costs low. Refer to Figure 3-2.5 to answer the following questions based on a firm's productivity and cost measures. Assume outputs Q_1 and Q_2 are produced by this firm when it uses L_1 and L_2 labor units, respectively.

21. As long as the MPP of labor is increasing, the MC of producing extra units of output will (*increase / not change / decrease*).

22. As long as the MPP of labor is decreasing, the MC of producing extra units of output will (*increase / not change / decrease*).

23. The MC of producing extra units of output will be minimized when the MPP of labor is

    _____.

24. As long as the APP of labor is increasing, the AVC of producing output will (*increase / not change / decrease*).

25. As long as the APP of labor is decreasing, the AVC of producing output will (*increase / not change / decrease*).

26. The AVC of producing output will be minimized when the APP of labor is _____.

Understanding the Different Cost Measures of a Firm

Part A: Different Meanings of the Word "Profit"

Economists assume the goal of a firm is to maximize its total profit. This sounds like an easy goal to understand, but the economist's view of profit is different from that of an accountant. Let's use a short story about Pat to illustrate the differences. First, we must define two categories of cost. An *explicit cost* is an expenditure by the firm; it could be a payment for items such as wages, rent, or advertising. An *implicit cost* is the opportunity cost of an entrepreneur using his/her own resource in the company.

An economic short story: Pat is a banker who earned an annual salary of $50,000 last year. She invested a total of $100,000 of her own money in various savings assets, which gave her interest income of $6,000. Pat also owns a small building, which she leased to someone last year for $14,000. But now Pat decides she wants to leave banking and set up her own landscaping company. Rather than borrowing money to buy new equipment, she uses her $100,000 in savings to buy it. She also decides to stop leasing her building so she can use it for her new enterprise. In her first year of landscaping, Pat brings in total revenue of $300,000. She spends $220,000 for such things as her equipment, workers, supplies, and insurance.

1. An accountant defines total profit to be total revenue minus explicit costs. Pat's *accounting profit* from her landscaping company is $_____ this year.

2. In addition to explicit costs, an economist considers implicit costs as well. This year, Pat's *economic profit* from her landscaping business is $_____.

3. Another type of profit is called *normal profit*. It recognizes that Pat should "pay herself" for using her resources in her own company. Her normal profit, which is equal to her implicit costs, indicates the income Pat's resources would have earned had they been used in their best alternative occupations. Pat's normal profit is $_____.

4. If Pat's total revenue from her landscaping business is only $280,000, what would be the values of the different measures of profit?

   (A) Accounting profit = $_____

   (B) Economic profit = $_____

   (C) Normal profit = $_____

Part B: The Seven Measures of a Firm's Short-Run Costs

The Morton Boat Company produces the very popular Jazzy Johnboat, which is desired by many fishermen and fisherwomen. Assume the firm operates in the short run with a fixed amount of equipment (capital) and views labor as its only variable resource. If it wants to produce more output, it will add more units of labor to its stock of equipment. Of course, the firm will have to pay its workers and also the owners of its capital, which means its total cost will increase as it produces more boats. Table 3-3.1 defines the seven cost measures the Morton Boat Company must consider.

 Table 3-3.1

The Seven Short-Run Cost Measures of a Firm

Cost measure	What it means	How to calculate it
Total fixed cost (TFC)	All costs that do not change when output changes. TFC is a constant amount at all Q levels.	TFC = total cost of all fixed factors of production TFC = Q × AFC
Total variable cost (TVC)	All costs that do change when output changes. TVC gets bigger as Q increases because the firm needs more labor to make more output.	TVC = total cost of all variable factors of production TVC = Q × AVC
Total cost (TC)	All costs at a given output level. TC is the sum of TFC and TVC. TC increases as the level of output increases.	TC = TFC + TVC TC = Q × ATC
Average fixed cost (AFC)	Fixed cost (capital cost) per unit of output. AFC always falls as Q rises since TFC is a constant value.	AFC = TFC/Q
Average variable cost (AVC)	Variable cost (labor cost) per unit of output. AVC falls at first, and then rises as Q increases.	AVC = TVC/Q
Average total cost (ATC)	Total cost per unit of output. It is the sum of AFC and AVC. ATC falls at first, and then rises as Q increases.	ATC = TC/Q ATC = AFC + AVC
Marginal cost (MC)	Change in the firm's TC when it produces another unit of output. Also shows change in TVC from an extra unit of output. MC falls at first, and then rises as Q increases.	MC = ΔTC/ΔQ MC = ΔTVC/ΔQ because the only part of TC that changes when more Q is produced is TVC.

Reminder: The AVC curve is U-shaped (falls, then rises as Q increases) because its shape is the mirror image of the APP curve as shown in Activity 3-2. The MC curve also is U-shaped because it is the mirror image of the MPP curve. Refer back to Figure 3-2.5.

Table 3-3.2 is the cost spreadsheet for the Morton Boat Company. It has information on all seven short-run cost measures based on different Q levels of the firm.

5. Complete Table 3-3.2. Some of the data have been posted for you already.

Table 3-3.2

The Seven Short-Run Cost Measures of the Morton Boat Company (daily data)

Q boats per day	(1) TFC	(2) TVC	(3) TC = TFC + TVC	(4) AFC = TFC/Q	(5) AVC = TVC/Q	(6) ATC = TC/Q = AFC + AVC	(7) MC = ΔTC/ΔQ = ΔTVC/ΔQ
0				–	–	–	–
1	$300		$1,000				
2					$650		$600
3		$1,800					
4				$75			$600
5	$300					$680	
6							$740

6. What trend do you observe in the value of TFC as the level of Q is increased? How do you explain this trend?

7. What trend do you observe in the value of TVC as the level of Q is increased? How do you explain this trend?

8. Compare the ATC value at any Q level with the MC value at the next Q level. What relationship do you see between ATC and MC?

9. Compare the AVC value at any Q level with the MC value at the next Q level. What relationship do you see between AVC and MC?

10. Compare the AFC value at any Q level with the MC value at the next Q level. What relationship do you see between AFC and MC?

Part C: Graphing the Cost Functions of a Firm

The relationships that exist among the firm's cost functions can be illustrated by plotting the data in Table 3-3.1 in cost graphs. Figure 3-3.1 is the "total" cost graph because it contains information about the firm's TC, TVC, and TFC functions. Figure 3-3.2 is the "marginal-average" cost graph because it shows the data for the firm's MC, ATC, AVC, and AFC functions.

11. Plot the data from Table 3-3.1 in the appropriate graphs. Two observations of TC and AVC have already been plotted for you.

12. Plot the values of MC at the new output level. For example, put a dot on the graph at the combination of Q = 4 and MC = $600 since the MC resulting from producing the fourth boat is $600. Connect the MC dots in your graph with a dotted line.

Figure 3-3.1
The Firm's "Total" Cost Graph

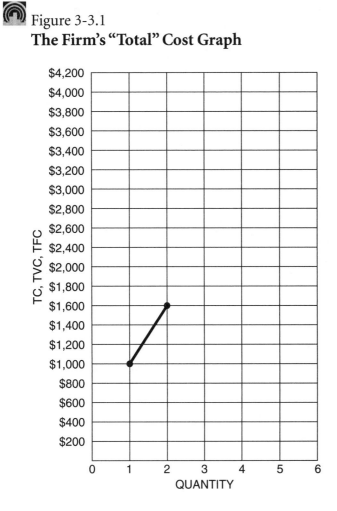

13. Why is the vertical gap between the TC and TVC curves the same at all Q levels?

14. The slope of the TC curve can be expressed as rise/run = $\Delta TC/\Delta Q$. Do you know another cost function that is found using the ratio $\Delta TC/\Delta Q$?

15. Why do both the TC and TVC curves keep climbing higher and higher as the Morton Boat Company increases the number of boats it produces?

16. Why does the TC curve not begin at the origin?

Figure 3-3.2
The Firm's "Marginal-Average" Cost Graph

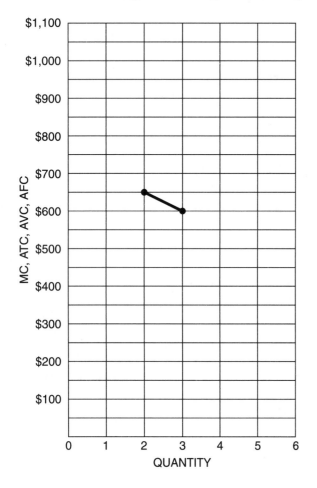

17. AVC continues to decrease as long as MC is (*greater than / equal to / less than*) AVC.

18. AVC continues to increase as long as MC is (*greater than / equal to / less than*) AVC.

19. ATC continues to decrease as long as MC is (*greater than / equal to / less than*) ATC.

20. ATC continues to increase as long as MC is (*greater than / equal to / less than*) ATC.

21. Mr. Burpin, your AP teacher, asks you to explain the following statement: "Average fixed cost falls as long as marginal cost is less than average fixed cost." What is your response?

22. Do you agree with the following statement? "Average variable cost is minimized at the output level where marginal cost is equal to average variable cost." Explain.

23. What do you say to someone who says, "Fixed cost is the same at all output levels"?

24. Can you tell from Table 3-3.1 how many boats the Morton Boat Company should produce to maximize its total profit? Explain.

A Firm's Long-Run Average Total Cost Curve

The cost curves that we used in previous activities were the short-run cost curves of a firm. In the short run, a firm can vary its output by changing its variable resources, but it cannot change its plant capacity. In this activity we turn to the long run, defined as a time period in which all resources, including plant capacity, can be changed. In the short run, the shapes of the firm's average total cost (ATC) and marginal cost (MC) curves result from the principle of diminishing marginal productivity of resources. In the long run, the shape of the firm's long-run average total cost (LRATC) curve results from *economies of scale* and *diseconomies of scale*. Economies of scale explain why the firm's ATC decreases as it expands its scale of operations. Sources of economies of scale include specialization of resources, more efficient use of equipment, a reduction in per-unit costs of factor inputs, an effective use of production by-products, and an increase in shared facilities. Diseconomies of scale explain why the firm's ATC can increase as it increases its level of production. Sources of diseconomies of scale include limitations on effective management decision making and competition for factor inputs.

Part A: A Firm's Long-Run Average Total Cost Curve

A firm's LRATC curve shows the lowest ATC at which a firm can produce different levels of output when all inputs are variable. The LRATC is derived from a set of the firm's short-run average total cost (SRATC) curves. Figure 3-4.1 shows four SRATC curves for the Goodman Company, which is considering which of four different plant sizes it should use to produce various levels of output. Each SRATC curve represents the ATC of the firm as it produces output in the short run with a fixed plant size. As the firm increases its level of output, at some point it will need to increase its plant size. As it does so, we see that its SRATC falls as it moves from Plant Size 1 to Plant Size 2, and it falls again as it moves to Plant Size 3. As it moves to the larger Plant Size 4 to produce even larger output levels, its SRATC curve shifts upward. Note that the graph shows four SRATC curves of one firm, not one SRATC for each of four different firms.

Figure 3-4.1

A Firm's Long-Run Average Total Cost Curve

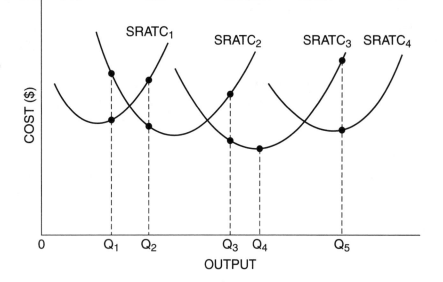

1. What does each of the SRATC curves represent?

2. At what output level in the long run will the firm minimize its ATC? Does this mean the firm will maximize its total profit if it produces this output level? Why?

3. The Goodman Company can produce output Q_1 with either Plant Size 1 or Plant Size 2. If the demand facing the firm is for this level of output, which plant size should the firm use? Why?

4. As the long-run demand for the company's product increases, it must decide which plant size is best as it tries to produce an output level at the lowest possible ATC. In the following chart, circle the firm's best plant size for these output levels.

Output level	Optimal plant size
Q_1	1 2 3 4
Q_2	1 2 3 4
Q_3	1 2 3 4
Q_5	1 2 3 4

5. Since the LRATC curve shows the lowest ATC at which different output levels can be produced, we can show it on Figure 3-4.1. Mark heavily the portions of each SRATC curve that will minimize the firm's ATC as the firm increases it scale of production. Label this heavily shaded curve as "LRATC."

Part B: Economies and Diseconomies of Scale

The opening section of this activity explained the concepts of economies and diseconomies of scale. They explain why the firm's LRATC curve slopes downward and then upward as the firm increases the scale of its production.

6. In Figure 3-4.1, as the firm increases its level of output from 0 to Q_4, it is experiencing (*economies of scale / diseconomies of scale*).

7. As the firm increases its production level beyond Q_4, it is experiencing (*economies of scale / diseconomies of scale*).

Part C: Returns to Scale

There are three concepts that are special cases of economies and diseconomies of scale where a firm increases all its inputs by the same percentage. A firm has *increasing returns to scale* if a proportionate increase in all resources results in an increase in output that is larger than the increase in resources. For example, if a firm increases all of its resources by 10 percent, and output increases by 14 percent, the firm experiences increasing returns to scale. *Decreasing returns to scale* are present if the increase in output is less than the proportionate increase in all resources. If output increases by only 7 percent when all inputs are increased by 10 percent, the firm has decreasing returns to scale. If output increases by the same proportion as all inputs were increased, the firm has *constant returns to scale*.

If we know the nature of the firm's returns to scale, we can determine what happens to the firm's ATC in the long run when it increases all resources by the same proportion. Since ATC = TC/Q, whether the firm's ATC increases, decreases, or stays the same depends on the resulting increase in output.

8. Assume the Goodman Company increases all of its inputs by 15 percent.

   (A) Its total cost will increase by (*more than / exactly / less than*) 15 percent.

   (B) If it has increasing returns to scale, its output will increase by (*more than / exactly / less than*) 15 percent, and its ATC will (*increase / not change / decrease*).

   (C) If it has decreasing returns to scale, its output will increase by (*more than / exactly / less than*) 15 percent, and its ATC will (*increase / not change / decrease*).

   (D) If it has constant returns to scale, its output will increase by (*more than / exactly / less than*) 15 percent, and its ATC will (*increase / not change / decrease*).

9. In Figure 3-4.2, draw the LRATC curve for a firm that experiences increasing returns to scale between output levels Q_1 and Q_2, constant returns to scale between Q_2 and Q_3, and decreasing returns to scale between Q_3 and Q_4. Label the curve as "LRATC." Be sure to label the axes.

Figure 3-4.2
Returns to Scale

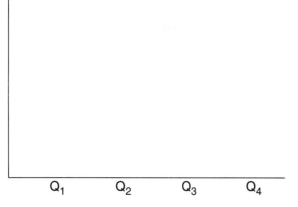

Revenue, Profit, and Rules to Maximize Total Profit

Now that you have explored the productivity and cost functions of a firm, you are ready to learn about its revenue and profit functions. It is important to note that the productivity and cost graphs look the same for any firm, regardless of whether the firm sells its output in a perfectly competitive, monopolistic, monopolistically competitive, or oligopolistic product market. Think of it this way: suppose you run a firm that produces computers. The productivity of your workers in your factory will determine your cost of producing computers. But now you are ready to take your computers from the factory and transport them to the product market to sell them. As we will see in subsequent activities, the shapes of your revenue functions will depend on how much competition you face in the product market. So although your productivity and cost functions are not affected by the product market, your revenue and profit functions will be. (We will see in Unit 4 that the factor markets for your resources will affect the prices you pay for inputs and thus will affect your cost functions.)

Part A: Revenue Terms

Student Alert: **The distinction between total, marginal, and average measures is important!**

There are three revenue terms you need to understand before you can answer questions about profit maximization. When a firm sells its product, the revenue it receives can be described in the three ways shown in Table 3-5.1.

Table 3-5.1
Three Measures of Revenue

Measure of revenue	Meaning	How to calculate
Total revenue (TR)	The total income the firm receives from selling a given level of output (Q) at a particular price (P)	$TR = P \times Q$
Average revenue (AR)	The revenue the firm receives from one unit at a given level of output	$AR = TR/Q$
Marginal revenue (MR)	The change in total revenue resulting from the firm selling one more unit of output	$MR = \Delta TR/\Delta Q$

The shapes of these revenue functions will depend on the type of product market in which a firm sells its good or service. The key point to watch for is whether a firm has to lower its price to sell more of its product. You will calculate values of these revenue measures and draw graphs of them in other activities where the type of product market is specified.

Part B: Profit Terms

In Activity 3-3 you learned the difference between accounting profit and economic profit. Since this book is preparing you to succeed on the AP Microeconomics Exam, it is time to focus on how a firm maximizes its total *economic* profit. A good habit to learn now is always to use the correct adjective in front of the word "profit": total, average, or marginal. Accuracy counts when you are answering exam questions. (The same habit also should be applied to measures of productivity, cost, and revenue!)

There are three profit (Π) terms you need to master so you will understand the decisions made by a firm as it tries to maximize its *total* profit. When a firm sells its product, the profit (or loss) it receives can be described in the three ways shown in Table 3-5.2.

Table 3-5.2
Three Measures of (Economic) Profit

Measure of profit	Meaning	How to calculate
Total profit (TΠ)	The difference between the firm's total revenue (TR) and total cost (TC) at a given level of output (Q)	$T\Pi = TR - TC$ $T\Pi = Q \times A\Pi$
Average profit (AΠ)	The profit the firm receives from one unit at a given level of output (= per-unit profit)	$A\Pi = T\Pi/Q$ $A\Pi = AR - ATC$ $A\Pi = P - ATC$
Marginal profit (MΠ)	The change in total profit resulting from the firm selling one more unit of output	$M\Pi = \Delta T\Pi/\Delta Q$ $M\Pi = MR - MC$

Note: While some college textbooks do not introduce the concept of marginal profit, it is a useful concept as you explain why a firm should (or should not) sell an extra unit of output.

Here's another useful hint: Be careful about mixing "totals," "averages," and "marginals." Look again at the three basic ways to calculate the measures of profit:

■ Total profit = *total* revenue – *total* cost.

■ Average profit = *average* revenue – *average* total cost.

■ Marginal profit = *marginal* revenue – *marginal* cost.

Part C: Key Rules for Any Firm to Follow

Economists assume firms try to maximize their total profit. This means a firm must decide how many units of its good or service to produce and what price to charge for that product. Fortunately, there are several basic rules that apply to any firm as it makes these decisions. At this point, we will give a general overview of the rules. You will work in detail with each rule as you move through other activities for firms in different types of product markets. Although the basic rules apply to all firms, the different levels of competition in the various markets will require that you stay focused to help the firm make the correct decisions.

Rule 1: A firm should produce the output level at which MR = MC.

This rule sounds so simple, but many students never really understand it (although many memorize it). How can producing a unit for which MR = MC maximize total profit? After all, doesn't MΠ = $0 for that unit? Yes, and ironically, that is why the rule works. Look at Table 3-5.3 which has information about the Sosin Company.

Table 3-5.3
The Sosin Company

Output units	MR compared to MC	MΠ	TΠ
1–499	MR > MC	MΠ > $0	TΠ increases.
500	MR = MC	MΠ = $0	TΠ has reached its peak.
501 and beyond	MR < MC	MΠ < $0	TΠ decreases.

If MR > MC for the first 499 units, the firm certainly wants to produce all of them. These units create positive MΠ, which means TΠ increases with each additional unit. What does the 500th unit do for the firm's TΠ? Nothing at all. The MΠ of the 500th unit is $0 because its MR is equal to its MC. But check out units beyond 500. Each of these units adds less to TR than it adds to TC (or, MR < MC). If the Sosin Company produces these units, each unit will have a negative MΠ, which means TΠ will decrease, and the firm does not want that to happen.

So what is so special about the 500th unit where MR = MC? The answer is surprisingly simple. If the firm produces 500 units, it has produced all the units that increased its TΠ (MΠ > $0) and stopped before it produced any units that would decrease its TΠ (MΠ < $0). The 500th unit itself had no effect on TΠ, but economists like the simple "MR = MC" rule as an efficient way to locate the output level that will maximize a firm's TΠ.

Rule 2: A firm should charge the price on the demand curve for its optimal output level.

Suppose your boss offers you a $5 per hour pay raise. Are you going to decline that offer? Of course not! You want to get the highest pay you can for your labor. A firm is no different. Once it decides on the optimal number of units of its product (where MR = MC), it wants to receive the highest possible price for that output level. And that is exactly the information the firm gets from its demand curve. Basically, it will go up to the demand curve at its optimal output level and hang a direct left to the vertical price axis.

Rule 3: A firm should shut down and produce zero output if TR is less than total variable cost (TVC).

Unfortunately, there are times when a firm cannot earn a positive total profit. Perhaps the high prices of resources have made the firm's production costs unprofitably high. Or perhaps a downturn in the economy has so reduced demand that the firm cannot get a profitable price for its product. When a firm earns a negative total profit at its best output level, it has two choices in the short-run: It can go ahead and produce that output and accept the loss, or it can produce no output at all (shut down).

Here is the rule the firm should follow: If its TR is greater than its TVC, it should produce its optimal output (where MR = MC) rather than shut down.

Here's the logic behind this rule:

■ If the firm shuts down (Q = 0), it will have no TR or TVC, but it will still have its total fixed cost (TFC). Thus, by shutting down, the firm is committed to a loss equal to its TFC (loss = TFC).

■ If the firm produces its best output and has *TR that is less than TVC*, then the firm will make a loss on its variable resources and still have all of its TFC. Its loss will be larger if it produces than if it shuts down (loss > TFC).

■ If the firm produces its best output and has *TR that exceeds TVC*, then after it pays all its TVC the firm has some leftover TR to apply toward its TFC. This will makes its loss less than its TFC (loss < TFC).

Part D: Do You Get It?

Here are some questions to see if you understand the revenue and profit terms and the three key rules to maximize total profit. Circle "T" if you feel the statement is true and "F" if you think it is false. Explain your answer for each statement.

T   F   1.   If a firm sells 200 units of its product at a price of $8, its total profit will be $1,600.

T   F   2.   If the average revenue from 150 units is $20, the firm's total revenue is $3,000.

T F 3. If the marginal revenue from the twenty-first unit is $30, then the total revenue from 22 units is $30 greater than the total revenue from 21 units.

T F 4. As long as MR is greater than MC, a firm's TΠ will increase if it increases its level of output.

T F 5. When MΠ is $0, we know TΠ also is $0.

T F 6. If MΠ is negative, a firm's TΠ will increase if the firm produces fewer units of output.

T F 7. At its current output level, the Placone Firm has AR = $12 and MC = $10, which means its AΠ = $2.

T F 8. A firm determines it will maximize its total profit by producing 800 units per week because at that output both MR and MC are $600. The price the firm should charge for its output also is $600.

Answer Questions 9 and 10 based on this information: The Wright Company estimates the following values at its optimal level of output: TR = $20,000, TVC = $18,000, and TFC = $5,000.

T F 9. This firm should shut down rather than produce its optimal level of output.

T F 10. If its optimal output is 5,000 units, the price it charges for its good is $4.00.

Profit Maximization by a Perfectly Competitive Firm

A perfectly competitive firm will maximize its total profit by producing the output level at which marginal revenue equals marginal cost. You need to understand how economists find these two important "marginal" measures.

Part A: Revenue Measures of a Perfectly Competitive Firm

A perfectly competitive firm is a "price taker." This means it has no control over price and will charge the market-determined price for its product. In fact, because it is such a small participant in the market, a perfectly competitive firm can sell all the output it wants at the market price. It does not have to reduce its price to sell additional units. This makes the revenue measures of a perfectly competitive firm easy to calculate and to graph.

1. Assume the market for yo-yos is perfectly competitive and that the market price currently is $17 per box of yo-yos. Complete Table 3-6.1, which has the three revenue measures of a typical firm in this market. Put the MR values at the new output level. For example, when the firm increases output from four to five units, its total revenue increases by $17, so put "+$17" in the MR column for Q = 5.

 Table 3-6.1

Revenue Measures of a Perfectly Competitive Firm

(1) Output (Q) [boxes of yo-yos]	(2) Price (P) [per box]	(3) Total revenue TR = P × Q	(4) Marginal revenue MR = ΔTR/ΔQ	(5) Average revenue AR = TR/Q
0	$17		–	–
1	$17			
2	$17			$17
3	$17	$51		
4	$17			
5	$17		+$17	
6	$17			
7	$17			$17
8	$17	$136		
9	$17			
10	$17			

2. What happens to the value of MR as more output is sold? Why?

3. What is the relationship between MR and AR at every output level? Why?

4. What happens to the value of TR each time the firm sells one more unit of its good? Why?

5. Why is P equal to $17 at every level of Q?

6. What is the relationship between P, MR, and AR? Why?

7. Plot the firm's total revenue data in Figure 3-6.1.

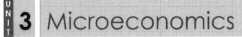 Figure 3-6.1
Total Revenue Function of a Perfectly Competitive Firm

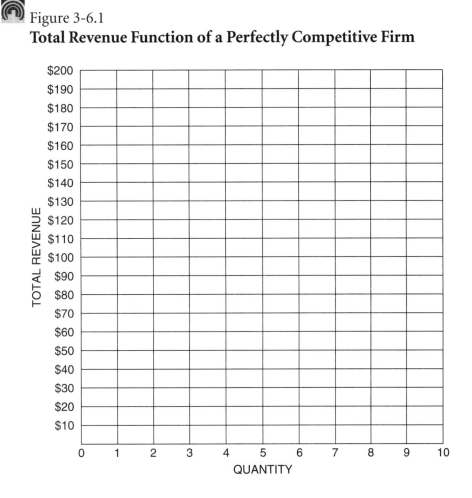

8. The slope of the total revenue function is ΔTR/ΔQ. What economic function does this ratio represent? Why is the TR curve a straight line?

9. If the market price increases, what will happen to the slope of the firm's TR curve? Will the TR curve still begin at the origin?

10. Plot the firm's marginal revenue, average revenue, and demand data in Figure 3-6.2.

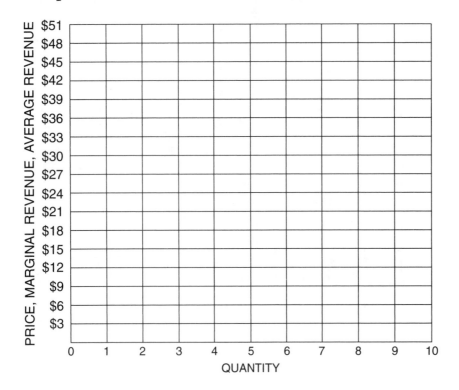

Figure 3-6.2

Marginal Revenue, Average Revenue, and Demand Functions of a Perfectly Competitive Firm

11. Does the demand curve D represent the firm's demand for something, such as inputs?

12. Why is the demand function horizontal?

13. What would happen to the quantity demanded of the firm's product if it increased the price above the market price of $17? What does this tell you about the price elasticity of demand for the firm's product?

14. Would you recommend that this firm lower its price below the market price of $17? Why?

15. What do you note about the relationship between price and marginal revenue for a perfectly competitive firm? What about between price and average revenue?

Part B: Cost Measures of a Perfectly Competitive Firm

The short-run cost curves of a perfectly competitive firm give you values of the various cost measures at different output levels.

16. Complete Table 3-6.2, which has the seven cost measures of a typical firm in this market. Put the MC values at the new output level. For example, when the firm increases output from four to five units, its total cost increases by $4, so put "+$4" in the MC column for Q = 5. Some of the cost values are provided for you.

Table 3-6.2
Cost Measures of a Perfectly Competitive Firm

(1) Output (Q) [boxes]	(2) Total fixed cost (TFC)	(3) Total variable cost (TVC)	(4) Total cost (TC)	(5) Marginal cost (MC) = ΔTC/ΔQ	(6) Average fixed cost (AFC) = TFC/Q	(7) Average variable cost (AVC) = TVC/Q	(8) Average total cost (ATC) = TC/Q
0			$40.00	–	–	–	–
1		$10.00					
2	$40.00			+$6.00			
3						$7.00	
4							$16.50
5		$30.00		+$4.00			
6						$6.00	
7			$85.50		$5.71		
8	$40.00						$12.00
9		$72.00					
10				+$18.00			

17. What happens to the value of AFC as Q rises? Why?

18. What happens to the value of AVC as Q increases? Why?

19. What happens to the value of MC as Q increases? Is this trend related to the marginal physical productivity of the firm's variable resources? Explain.

20. Is the value of MC the same whether it is computed as a change in TC or as a change in TVC? Why?

21. Why does the value of TVC continue to get larger as the firm produces more Q?

22. The slope of the TC curve is $\Delta TC/\Delta Q$. Do you recognize this ratio as the expression of some other important economic function?

23. Plot the firm's TC, TVC, and TFC data in Figure 3-6.3.

Figure 3-6.3

TC, TVC, and TFC Functions of a Perfectly Competitive Firm

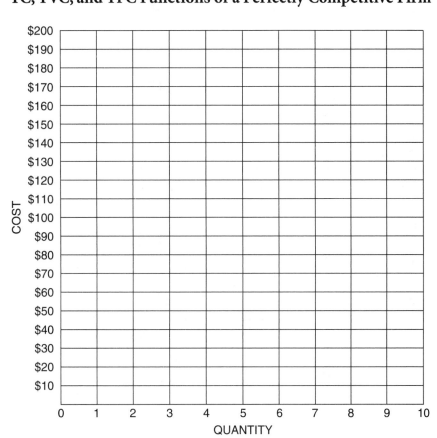

24. What does the vertical gap between the TC and TVC represent? What happens to the size of this gap as the firm increases its level of production?

25. Why does the TC cost curve not begin at the origin?

26. Why does the TVC curve have the same slope as the TC curve?

27. Plot the firm's ATC, AVC, AFC, and MC data in Figure 3-6.4. Connect the MC values with a dotted line in your graph.

Figure 3-6.4

ATC, AVC, AFC, and MC Functions of a Perfectly Competitive Firm

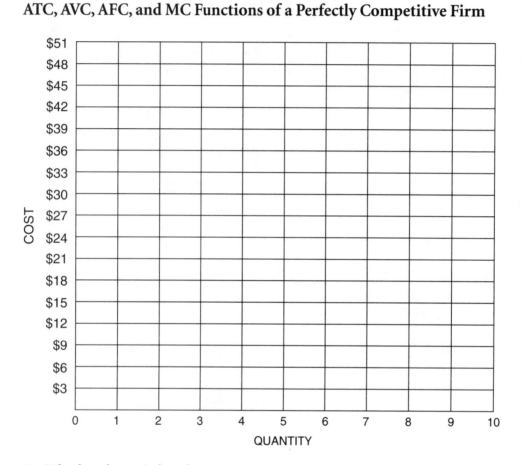

28. Why does the vertical gap between the ATC and AVC curves get smaller as the firm increases its Q?

29. At what unique point does the MC curve intersect both the AVC curve and the ATC curve? Why?

30. Between Q = 6 and Q = 8, AVC is rising while ATC is falling. How can this be?

Part C: Profit Maximization by a Perfectly Competitive Firm

Now that you have mastered the revenue and cost terms for a perfectly competitive firm, you can bring them together to determine how many units of output the firm should produce to maximize its total profit.

31. Complete Table 3-6.3 using your data from Tables 3-6.1 and 3-6.2. Some data have been entered for you.

Table 3-6.3
A Perfectly Competitive Firm Maximizes Total Profit

Q	TR	TC	TΠ	MR	MC	MΠ
0		$40.00	−$40.00	–	–	–
1					+$10.00	
2	$34.00			+$17.00		
3			−$10.00			+$12.00
4		$66.00			+$5.00	
5				+$17.00		
6	$102.00					+$11.00
7			$33.50			
8		$96.00			+$10.50	
9				+$17.00		+$1.00
10	$170.00					

32. The value of TΠ is greatest at Q = _____ units. The maximum TΠ = $_____.

33. The firm should produce each unit for which MR > MC. The last unit with MR > MC is the _____ unit, which has MΠ = $_____.

34. Should the firm produce the tenth unit of Q? Why?

35. MΠ has its greatest value at Q = _____ units. Should this be the Q level the firm decides to produce? Why?

36. Go back to Figure 3-6.3 and draw the firm's TR function. (You can get it from Figure 3-6.1). Label the function "TR."

37. What do we call the vertical gap between the TR and TC curves?

38. We saw in Table 3-6.3 that this firm should produce Q = _____ units to maximize its TΠ. Indicate the part of Figure 3-6.3 that represents this maximum TΠ.

39. Go back to Figure 3-6.4 and draw the firm's D, MR, and AR functions at the current market price of $17. (You can get these from Figure 3-6.2). Label the functions.

40. The last unit of output for which MR > MC is the _____ unit. This is the last unit the firm should produce in order to maximize its TΠ.

41. What does the vertical gap between the MR and MC curves represent?

Part D: When Is a Firm's Best Just Not Good Enough?

You proved this firm can earn a positive total profit if the market price is $17. But what if the market price drops? Since a perfectly competitive firm is a price taker, it will have to sell its product at the lower market price, which will reduce its total profit.

42. Assuming all its costs are unchanged, what will happen to the perfectly competitive firm if the market price drops to $10? In Figure 3-6.4, draw a new "$D_1 = MR_1$" line at the price of $10.

    (A) Based on a comparison of MR and MC, the firm's optimal Q level is _____ units.

    (B) Its TR will be (*greater than / equal to / less than*) its TC at this Q level.

    (C) Its TR will be (*greater than / equal to / less than*) its TVC.

    (D) What should the firm do? Choose one of these decisions:

        (1) It should produce its optimal Q even though it will make a loss.

        (2) It should shut down and produce no Q this period.

43. Assuming all its costs are unchanged, what will happen to the perfectly competitive firm if the market price drops to $5? In Figure 3-6.4, draw a new "$D_2 = MR_2$" line at the price of $5.

    (A) Based on a comparison of MR and MC, the firm's optimal Q level is _____ units.

    (B) Its TR will be (*greater than / equal to / less than*) its TC at this Q level.

    (C) Its TR will be (*greater than / equal to / less than*) its TVC.

    (D) What should the firm do? Choose one of these decisions:

        (1) It should produce its optimal Q even though it will make a loss.

        (2) It should shut down and produce no Q this period.

Note: Even though economists chant, "Produce where MR = MC," in a discrete case with a limited number of Q levels being considered, there might not be a level of Q where MR = MC. In such a case, the firm should produce units for which MR > MC and stop before it produces units for which MR < MC. That's what you did in this example.

44. A puzzle for you! Economists say a perfectly competitive firm can sell at the Q it wants at the going market price. So why doesn't a single firm decide to produce all the Q that is demanded in the market?

Short-Run Equilibrium and Short-Run Supply in Perfect Competition

The word "equilibrium" refers to being in a state of rest or balance. You know the meaning of this term in the context of a competitive market: the equilibrium price is the one at which the quantity demanded is equal to the quantity supplied. Neither the buyers nor the sellers have reason to move from this spot, unless factors cause the demand or supply curve to shift.

Part A: Short-Run Equilibrium for a Perfectly Competitive Firm

A perfectly competitive firm is in a *short-run equilibrium* position when it produces the output level Q^* at which marginal revenue (MR) is equal to marginal cost (MC). The firm will stay at this output level unless something causes a change in its MR curve or MC curve. In its short-run equilibrium position, the firm could be in any of four profit scenarios as shown in Table 3-7.1.

1. In the last column, circle what you feel the firm should do in each of these cases—produce or shut down.

 Table 3-7.1

Four Possible Total Profit Positions of a Firm in Short-Run Equilibrium

Total profit (TΠ) at Q* where MR = MC	Total revenue (TR) compared to total cost (TC) and total variable cost (TVC) at Q*	What should the firm do?
1. TΠ > $0	TR > TC	*Produce Q* / shut down*
2. TΠ = $0	TR = TC	*Produce Q* / shut down*
3. TΠ < $0	TVC < TR < TC	*Produce Q* / shut down*
4. TΠ < $0	TR < TVC < TC	*Produce Q* / shut down*

Note: You will see in Activity 3-8 how a perfectly competitive firm moves from a position of short-run equilibrium to one of long-run equilibrium where it must break even (total profit = $0).

Part B: Short-Run Supply Curve of a Perfectly Competitive Firm

A market supply curve tells you how many units of a good or service producers will provide at different prices, other things being constant. The typical market supply curve is upward sloping because producers will put more units on the market at a higher price. A perfectly competitive firm also has a supply curve that is upward sloping. The basis of its short-run supply curve is its marginal cost curve as shown in the following exercise. Table 3-7.2 has information about some of the daily cost functions of the Fiasco Company, which sells its product in a perfectly competitive market.

2. Fill in the missing cost values in Table 3-7.2.

 Table 3-7.2
Cost Functions of a Perfectly Competitive Firm

Q	TC	TVC	MC	Average total cost (ATC)	Average variable cost (AVC)
0	$12.00		–	–	–
1		$4.00		$16.00	
2			+$3.00	$9.50	$3.50
3	$21.00				
4		$12.00			
5					$3.60
6			+$9.00		
7	$49.00				
8		$49.00	+$12.00		$6.13
9	$75.00			$8.33	
10				$9.10	

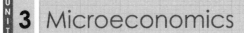
3. In Figure 3-7.1, plot and label the ATC, AVC, and MC curves of the firm. Plot the MC values at the higher of the two output levels. For example, when the firm increases output from 5 units to 6 units, its TC increases by $9, so plot the MC = $9 value at Q = 6. Use a dotted line to draw the MC curve.

 Figure 3-7.1
Cost Curves of the Fiasco Company

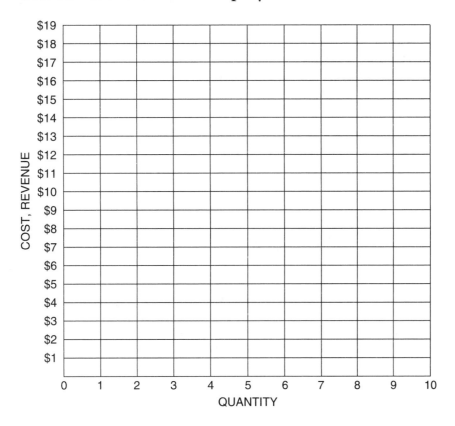

How many units of Q should the firm produce to maximize its total profit? Given its cost functions, the answer depends on the market price that the perfectly competitive firm must charge for its product. Consider these four possible market prices: $15.00, $11.00, $5.50, and $2.50.

4. In Figure 3-7.1, draw the appropriate marginal revenue curve for each of these prices (P) and label them as follows: MR_1 (for P = $15.00), MR_2 (for P = $11.00), MR_3 (for P = $5.50), and MR_4 (for P = $2.50).

5. Using Figure 3-7.1 and Table 3-7.2, complete Table 3-7.3 and determine how many units of Q the firm should produce at each of the four market prices.

Table 3-7.3

Optimal Output Level for the Fiasco Firm at Different Market Prices

(1) P	(2) Q* (units)	(3) TR	(4) TVC	(5) TFC	(6) TΠ
$15.00					
$11.00					
$5.50					
$2.50					

6. What rule did you use to determine the Q level that would maximize the firm's TΠ if P were $15.00? Why?

7. Did you use this same rule to find the profit-maximizing Q level at P of $11.00? Why?

8. Should the firm shut down if P is $5.50? What if P is $2.50? Explain.

9. Complete Table 3-7.4, which is the supply schedule for the Fiasco Firm. It shows how many units the firm will provide to the market at different prices.

Table 3-7.4

Supply Schedule for the Fiasco Firm

P	Q supplied (units)
$15.00	
$11.00	
$5.50	
$2.50	

Advanced Placement Economics Microeconomics: Student Resource Manual © Council for Economic Education, New York, N.Y.

10. Plot the supply curve of the Fiasco Firm in Figure 3-7.2. Label the curve as "S."

Figure 3-7.2
Supply Curve of the Fiasco Firm

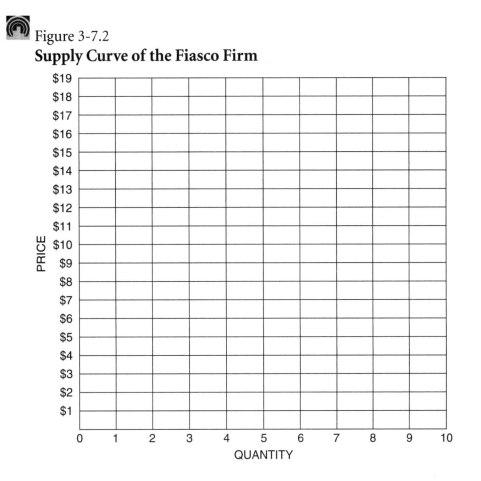

11. To create the supply curve of this perfectly competitive firm, you used two important rules of profit maximization:

    (A) The firm's optimal Q level is the one where _____ = _____.

    (B) The firm should shut down if at its best Q level, _____ < _____.

12. In general, the supply curve of a perfectly competitive firm is that part of its _____ cost curve that lies above its _____ cost curve. Refer back to Figure 3-7.1 to see where you went at each of the four prices to find the best Q level for the firm.

13. What is the connection between a perfectly competitive firm having diminishing marginal productivity and its short-run supply curve being upward sloping?

Part C : Short-Run Supply Curve of a Perfectly Competitive Industry

The industry (or market) supply curve tells you how many units will be supplied by all firms at each possible price. To get the industry supply, you add the quantity supplied by each firm at each price. Economists call this *adding horizontally* because you add the quantity supplied (measured on the horizontal axis) at each price. Assume the Fiasco Firm is a typical firm in a perfectly competitive industry with 800 firms.

14. Complete Table 3-7.5. Refer to Table 3-7.4 for how many units a typical firm supplies at each price.

 Table 3-7.5

Supply Schedule for the Industry (800 firms)

P	Q supplied (units)
$15.00	
$11.00	
$5.50	
$2.50	

15. Plot the data from Table 3-7.5 in Figure 3-7.3. Is the market supply curve upward sloping? Why?

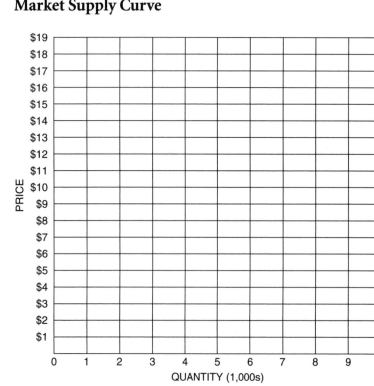 Figure 3-7.3

Market Supply Curve

Long-Run Equilibrium and Long-Run Supply in Perfect Competition

A firm is in a *short-run equilibrium (SRE)* position when it maximizes its total profit by producing the output level where marginal revenue equals marginal cost: MR = MC. When firms in short-run equilibrium in a perfectly competitive market are earning positive total profits, other firms will enter the market. If firms are making a loss in their short-run equilibrium position, over time some of the firms will exit the market. Eventually the perfectly competitive market reaches a *long-run equilibrium* (LRE) where all of the firms in the industry are earning zero total profits, based on the current market demand. Firms in other industries thus have no incentive to enter this market. And firms in this market have no incentive to leave it because they are earning their normal profit. An industry's *long-run supply* (LRS) curve is the set of LREs where each LRE is based on a different level of market demand. The shape of the LRS curve depends on how the production costs of firms change as the industry expands. The three cases to consider are *constant-cost, increasing-cost,* and *decreasing-cost industries.*

Part A: Movement from Short-Run Equilibrium to Long-Run Equilibrium

Table 3-8.1 presents some cost data for a typical firm in the perfectly competitive market for bricks. These cost data are shown in Figure 3-8.1.

Table 3-8.1

Cost Data for a Typical Perfectly Competitive Firm

Output (Q) (tons)	Average total cost (ATC)	Average variable cost (AVC)	MC
0	–	–	–
1	$50.00	$40.00	+$40.00
2	$40.00	$35.00	+$30.00
3	$33.33	$30.00	+$20.00
4	$32.50	$30.00	+$30.00
5	$34.00	$32.00	+$40.00
6	$36.67	$35.00	+$50.00
7	$40.00	$38.57	+$60.00
8	$43.75	$42.50	+$70.00

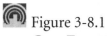
 Figure 3-8.1

Cost Functions of a Typical Firm

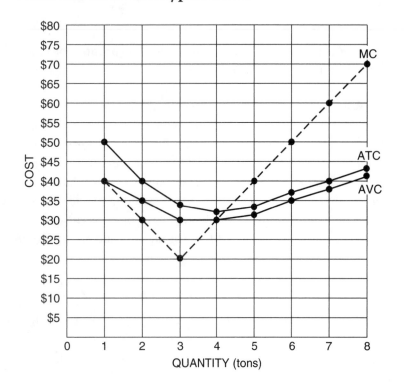

1. Complete Table 3-8.2, which shows how many units a firm will make available at different prices. Assume a firm cannot produce fractions of a unit.

 Table 3-8.2

Supply Schedule of a Typical Firm

Price (P)	Quantity supplied (Q_s) (tons)
$70	
$60	
$50	
$40	
$30	
$20	
$10	

2. Assume there are 1,000 firms in the brick industry. Complete Table 3-8.3, which shows the market supply schedule. Information about the market demand schedule is included in Table 3-8.3.

Table 3-8.3
Market Supply and Demand Schedules

P	Q_s (tons)	Quantity demanded (Q_d) (tons)
$70		2,000
$60		3,000
$50		4,000
$40		5,000
$30		6,000
$20		7,000
$10		8,000

3. Figure 3-8.2 shows the market demand curve D_1. Draw the market supply curve S_1 from Table 3-8.3. What is the equilibrium price of bricks? What is the equilibrium quantity? Label the SRE intersection of D_1 and S_1 as "SRE."

Figure 3-8.2
The Market for Bricks

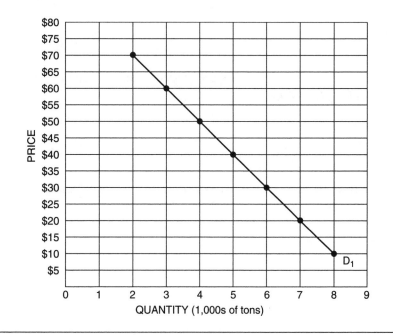

4. In Figure 3-8.1, draw the marginal revenue (MR_1), average revenue (AR_1), and demand (D_1) curves of a firm at the equilibrium price. How many units will the firm produce to maximize its total profit? (Assume the firm cannot produce fractions of a unit.) Does this number agree with your work in Table 3-8.2?

5. What is the value of the firm's average profit? What is the value of its total profit? In Figure 3-8.1, shade in the area representing its total profit.

6. Is the industry in a position of LRE? How do you know?

7. Why will other firms want to enter this industry? Assume the cost curves of a typical firm in the industry do not change as new firms enter.

8. As more firms enter the industry, the market supply curve shifts to the (*right / left*), which makes the market price (*increase / decrease*).

9. The industry is in a position of LRE when all firms break even based on the current level of market demand D_1. What is the LRE price? Why?

10. In Figure 3-8.2, draw the new market S curve (label it S_2) that will result in this LRE price. Do not change the existing market demand curve D_1. Label the LRE point as "LRE."

11. In Figure 3-8.1, draw the firm's MR_2, AR_2, and D_2 curves at the LRE price. How many units will the typical firm produce at this price? What is the total profit of a firm in this LRE position?

12. If all firms in the market earn $0 in economic profit, will other firms still want to enter the market? Will some firms want to exit the market? Why?

Part B: Long-Run Equilibrium for a Perfectly Competitive Firm

Let's leave the brick market and move to some other perfectly competitive market. Figure 3-8.3 shows a perfectly competitive firm in LRE, selling 640 units at a price of $18.

Figure 3-8.3
A Perfectly Competitive Firm in Long-Run Equilibrium

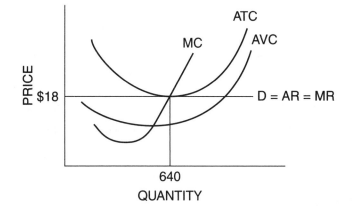

13. What does it mean for a firm to be productively efficient? Is this firm productively efficient? How do you know?

14. What does it mean for a firm to be allocatively efficient? Is this firm allocatively efficient? How do you know?

Part C: Long-Run Supply for a Perfectly Competitive Industry

The industry shown in Figure 3-8.4 is in LRE at point A with supply curve S_1 and demand curve D_1. The market price is $20, and the equilibrium quantity is 500 units. Now the demand for the industry's product increases to D_2. The price increases to $27 and quantity increases to 620 units. Because this boost in the market price results in positive total profits for firms in the industry, point B is considered a *short-run equilibrium (SRE)*. How the industry moves to its new LRE in response to this increase in demand depends on whether it is a constant-cost, increasing-cost, or decreasing-cost industry.

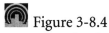 Figure 3-8.4
A Perfectly Competitive Industry

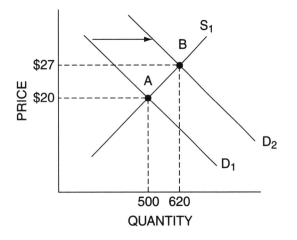

15. Assume the industry is a constant-cost industry. Explain how the industry moves to its new LRE. Show changes in supply and/or demand in Figure 3-8.4 and indicate the new LRE as point C.

16. Is the new LRE price greater than, equal to, or less than $20? Why?

17. The industry's LRS curve is the collection of LREs where each LRE is based on a different market demand curve. Draw a line connecting point A and point C, and label this line as "LRS." Is the LRS curve of a constant-cost industry upward sloping, horizontal, or downward sloping? What does this tell you about how price and quantity change as the industry expands in response to increases in demand?

18. Now assume the industry is an increasing-cost industry. In Figure 3-8.5, the industry is in LRE at point A. When demand increases to D_2, the industry moves to SRE at point B, where firms enjoy positive total profit. Explain how the industry moves to its new LRE. Show changes in supply and/or demand in Figure 3-8.5 and indicate the new LRE as point C.

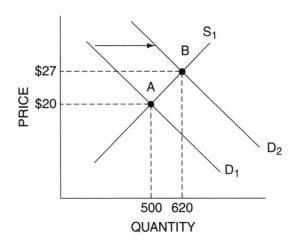

Figure 3-8.5
A Perfectly Competitive Industry

19. Is the new LRE price greater than, equal to, or less than $20? Why?

20. Draw a line connecting point A and point C, and label this line as "LRS" for long-run supply. Is the LRS curve of an increasing-cost industry upward sloping, horizontal, or downward sloping? What does this tell you about how price and quantity change as the industry expands in response to increases in demand?

21. If the industry were a decreasing-cost industry, what would happen to the market price and quantity as the industry expanded? What would be the shape of the industry LRS curve?

Graphing Perfect Competition

Figures 3-9.1 through 3-9.6 show side-by-side graphs of perfectly competitive industries and firms. Each pair of graphs illustrates the specific situation that is given.

(A) For the industry's graph, draw the supply (S) and demand (D) curves. Indicate by P* and Q* the equilibrium price and quantity.

(B) For the firm's graph, draw the average total cost (ATC), average variable cost (AVC), average revenue (AR), and demand (D) curves. Indicate by P* and Q* the firm's optimal price and output.

(C) Explain the reasoning for your graphs in each situation.

1. A firm earning positive total profit in the short run.

Figure 3-9.1
Short-Run Economic Profit

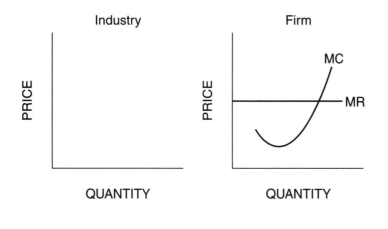

Explanation:

2. A firm operating with an economic loss but not wanting to shut down in the short run.

 Figure 3-9.2
Short-Run Economic Loss but Not Shutting Down

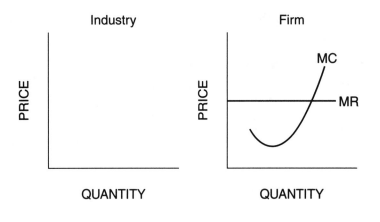

Explanation:

3. A firm in a classic shutdown position in the short run.

 Figure 3-9.3
Classic Shutdown Position

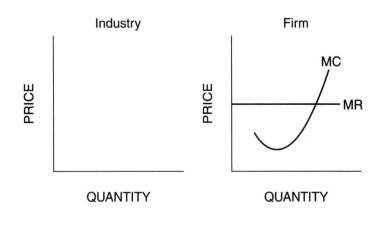

Explanation:

4. LRE for a firm and the industry.

Figure 3-9.4
Long-Run Equilibrium

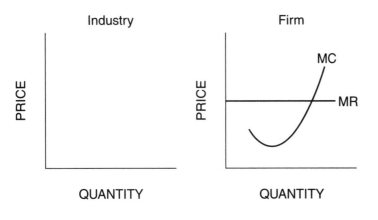

Explanation:

5. Illustrate how economic profits will disappear in the long run.

Figure 3-9.5
From Short-Run Profit to Long-Run Equilibrium

Explanation:

6. Illustrate how economic losses will disappear in the long run.

Figure 3-9.6

From Short-Run Loss to Long-Run Equilibrium

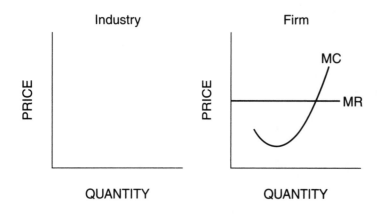

Explanation:

The Revenue Functions of a Monopoly

At the opposite end of the market spectrum from perfect competition is monopoly. A monopoly exists when only one firm sells the good or service. This means the monopolist faces the market demand curve since it has no competition from other firms. If the monopolist wants to sell more of its product, it will have to lower its price. As a result, the price (P) at which an extra unit of output (Q) is sold will be greater than the marginal revenue (MR) from that unit.

Student Alert: P is greater than MR for a monopolist.

1. Table 3-10.1 has information about the demand and revenue functions of the Moonglow Monopoly Company. Complete the table. Assume the monopoly charges each buyer the same P (i.e., there is no price discrimination). Enter the MR values at the higher of the two Q levels. For example, since total revenue (TR) increases by $37.50 when the firm increases Q from two to three units, put "+$37.50" in the MR column for Q = 3.

Table 3-10.1
The Moonglow Monopoly Company

Q	P	TR	MR	Average revenue (AR)
0	$100.00		–	–
1				$87.50
2		$150.00		
3	$62.50		+$37.50	
4				$50.00
5		$187.50		
6	$25.00			
7			–$62.50	
8		$0.00		

2. Draw the demand (D), AR, and MR curves in Figure 3-10.1. Plot the MR values at the higher of the two Q levels.

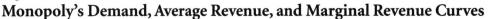
Figure 3-10.1
Monopoly's Demand, Average Revenue, and Marginal Revenue Curves

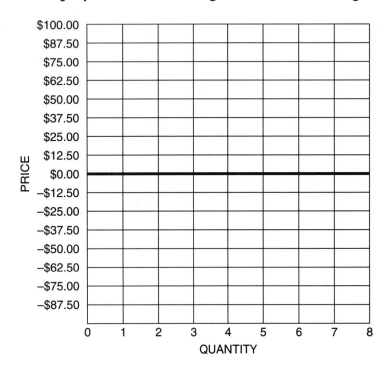

3. Plot the firm's TR curve in Figure 3-10.2.

Figure 3-10.2
Monopoly's Total Revenue Curve

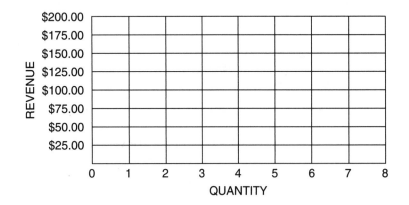

4. We see in Table 3-10.1 that the price at which the firm can sell three units is $62.50. Yet the MR from the third unit is only $37.50. How do you explain this difference?

5. Why does the vertical gap between the firm's D curve and MR curve get larger as the firm sells more output?

Table 3-10.1 is an example of a *discrete* case because it has a small number of observations (output varies from zero to eight units). Figure 3-10.3 is an example of a *continuous* case because it is based on a large number of observations. Answer Questions 6–8 based on Figure 3-10.3.

 Figure 3-10.3

A Continuous Example of a Monopoly's Revenue Curves

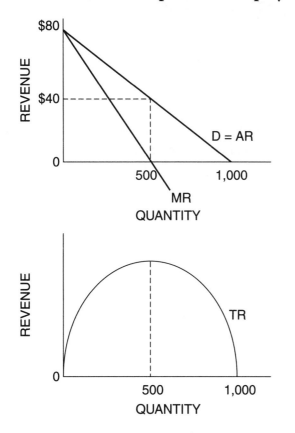

6. Indicate clearly in the top graph of Figure 3-10.3 the elastic, unitary elastic, and inelastic portions of the D curve. Explain your answer.

7. Marginal revenue is found using the ratio MR = ΔTR/ΔQ. This is also the formula for the slope of the TR curve. Thus, MR = slope of the TR curve.

   (A) Over what range of output is the slope of the TR curve positive? Over what range of output is the firm's MR positive?

   (B) Over what range of output is the firm's MR negative? Over what range of output is the slope of the TR curve negative?

   (C) Over what range of output is the slope of the TR curve equal to zero? Over what range of output is the firm's MR equal to zero?

8. What is the maximum dollar value of TR this firm can receive?

Bonus Question!

9. When the Galaxy Firm lowers its price from $60 to $57, the number of units it sells increases from 36 to 39. What is the value of MR? How should you interpret this value?

Profit Maximization by a Monopoly

The profit-maximizing monopolist works with the same key rules as any firm:

1. The optimal output level (Q*) is the one where marginal revenue equals marginal cost (MR = MC).

2. The optimal price (P*) is found on the demand curve at output Q*.

3. The firm should shut down if at Q* it finds its total revenue is less than its total variable cost (TR < TVC).

Because price (P) and MR were equal for a perfectly competitive firm, that firm could also find its Q* by setting P = MC. But that is not the case for a monopoly since P and MR will be different. The monopolist will find its profit-maximizing output (Q) where MR = MC, not where P = MC. This activity shows how a monopolist finds the output at which it will maximize its total profit and the price it should charge for that output.

Part A: Determining the Optimal Output and Price for a Monopoly

Table 3-11.1 provides some revenue, cost, and profit data for a monopoly.

1. Complete Table 3-11.1. Enter the MR and MC values at the higher of the two output levels. For example, the MR value of $300 is placed at Q = 4 rather than at Q = 3.

   Be sure to distinguish between total profit (TΠ), average profit (AΠ), and marginal profit (MΠ):

   (A) $T\Pi = TR - TC = (Q)(A\Pi)$

   (B) $A\Pi = AR - ATC = T\Pi/Q$

   (C) $M\Pi = MR - MC = \Delta T\Pi/\Delta Q$

Table 3-11.1
Revenue, Cost, and Profit Values for a Monopoly

Q	P	TR	TC	TΠ	AR	ATC	AΠ	MR	MC	MΠ
0	$1,350		$100		–	–	–	–	–	–
1				$300	$1,200	$900			+$800	
2		$2,100	$1,600				$250			+$200
3	$900			$600						
4					$750		$150	+$300		
5	$600		$2,800							–$400
6		$2,700				$600			+$800	

2. In Figure 3-11.1, draw the monopolist's D, AR, MR, ATC, and AVC curves using the data from Table 3-11.1. Plot the MR and MC values at the higher of the two output levels rather than at the midpoint between the two levels. Use dotted lines for the MR and MC curves in your graph. Label each curve.

Figure 3-11.1

Revenue and Cost Curves of a Monopolist

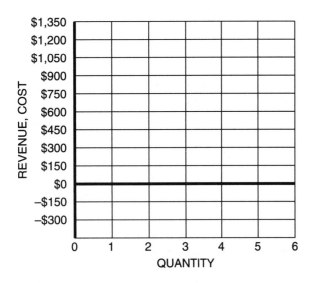

3. To maximize its total profit, this monopolist should produce _____ units.

4. What price should the monopolist charge for each of these units?

5. What is the total profit this firm will earn? _____ Shade in the total profit area in Figure 3-11.1.

Part B: Other Monopoly Examples

6. Suppose a monopolist can sell an extra unit of its good at a price of $50 and the MR of that unit is $44. If the MC of producing the extra unit is $46, the firm's total profit would (*increase / decrease*) by _____ if the firm sells that unit. Should the firm produce this additional unit of output? Explain your answer.

7. Figure 3-11.2 shows the MR and MC curves of a monopolist. Economists claim that the firm will maximize its total profit by producing 800 units where MR = MC. Show your understanding of this rule by circling the correct answer in each cell of Table 3-11.2.

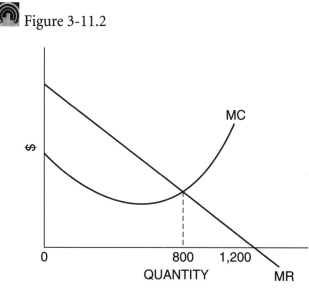

Figure 3-11.2

Table 3-11.2

The Logic behind the "MR = MC" Rule

Units of Q	For each extra unit of output in this range:		
1–799	MR is *(> / = / <)* MC.	MΠ is *(> / = / <)* $0.	TΠ will (*rise / fall / not change*).
800	MR is *(> / = / <)* MC.	MΠ is *(> / = / <)* $0.	TΠ will (*rise / fall / not change*).
801–1200	MR is *(> / = / <)* MC.	MΠ is *(> / = / <)* $0.	TΠ will (*rise / fall / not change*).

8. The firm illustrated in Figure 3-11.2 will maximize its total revenue if it produces 1,200 units. So why does it not want to produce those units between 800 and 1,200?

9. The monopolist's profit-maximizing output level will be in the (*elastic / unitary elastic / inelastic*) range of its demand curve. Explain.

Equilibrium in a Monopolistic Market

Part A: Equilibrium in a Perfectly Competitive Market

Consider Figure 3-12.1, which shows a perfectly competitive market. The market supply curve S is the horizontal summation of the marginal cost (MC) curves of all the firms in the market. Use Figure 3-12.1 to answer the questions that follow the graph.

 Figure 3-12.1
Equilibrium in a Perfectly Competitive Market

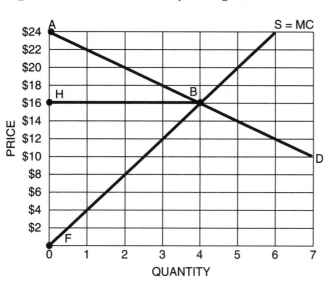

1. What is the equilibrium quantity in the market?

2. What is the equilibrium price?

3. What area of the graph represents consumer surplus in the market? Calculate the dollar value of consumer surplus.

4. What area of the graph represents producer surplus in the market? Calculate the dollar value of producer surplus.

5. What area of the graph represents total surplus (also called social welfare or total welfare)? Calculate the dollar value of total surplus.

Part B: Equilibrium in a Monopolistic Market

Now consider the same demand and cost curves, but assume the market is a monopoly. Because the monopoly faces the downward sloping market demand curve, it must reduce its price to sell more output, which means price will be greater than marginal revenue (MR). We add the firm's MR curve below its demand curve in Figure 3-12.2, as well as the monopolist's MC curve. Use Figure 3-12.2 to answer the questions that follow the graph.

Figure 3-12.2
Equilibrium in a Monopolistic Market

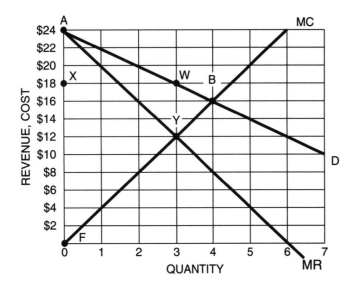

6. What output level will the monopolist produce? Why?

7. What price will the monopolist charge for this output? Why?

8. What area of the graph represents consumer surplus in the market? Calculate the dollar value of consumer surplus.

9. What area of the graph represents producer surplus? Calculate the dollar value of producer surplus.

10. What area of the graph represents total surplus? Calculate the dollar value of total surplus.

Part C: Comparing Equilibrium in the Two Markets

11. How do the price and output of a monopolist differ from those in the perfectly competitive market?

12. What is the dollar value of the portion of consumer surplus in the competitive market that is transferred to the firm's producer surplus in the monopoly situation?

13. How does a monopoly affect consumer surplus? Is this good or bad from the perspective of consumers?

14. What area of Figure 3-12.2 represents the deadweight loss resulting from the market being a monopoly? Calculate the dollar value of the deadweight loss.

Price Discrimination

When producers have market power and sell a good or service that cannot be resold, the possibility of price discrimination arises. *Price discrimination* exists when a producer charges different prices to different customers for the same item, for reasons other than differences in cost. The seller needs to be able to divide the total market for the good into separate submarkets, each with a different demand for the good. There also must be no possibility of resale of the product between the submarkets; otherwise the different submarkets will collapse into a single market.

Part A: Regular Monopoly with No Price Discrimination

Pat's Patriotic Tattoos is the only tattoo parlor in town. Pat provides only one tattoo—the American flag. There are 10 consumers in town who are willing to buy one tattoo, and they vary in their willingness to pay. One consumer is willing to pay $20 for a tattoo, another is willing to pay $18, and so forth, down to the tenth consumer who is willing to pay only $2. Table 3-13.1 shows the demand schedule for Pat's flag tattoo.

1. Complete Table 3-13.1 assuming the firm can only charge one price for its service. (There is no price discrimination yet.) If Pat wants to sell three units, she will sell all three units at a price of $16, so her TR is $48. Put each MR value at the higher of the two output levels.

Table 3-13.1
Demand Schedule for Pat's Tattoo

Price	Quantity	Total revenue (TR)	Marginal revenue (MR)
$20	1		+$20
$18	2		
$16	3	$48	
$14	4		
$12	5		+$4
$10	6		
$8	7		
$6	8		
$4	9	$36	−$12
$2	10		

2. What is the total consumer surplus if Pat sells three units at a price of $16?

3. What is the total consumer surplus if she sells five units at a price of $12?

4. In Figure 3-13.1, draw the demand curve for Pat's tattoos.

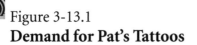
 Figure 3-13.1
Demand for Pat's Tattoos

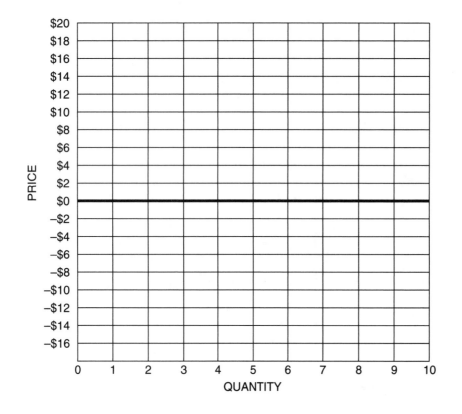

Part B: Perfect Price Discrimination (Also Called First-Degree Price Discrimination)

Perfect price discrimination is a monopolist's dream because it means that the firm can charge each individual consumer the highest price that he or she is willing to pay for the firm's product. As we will see in this activity, perfect price discrimination eliminates all consumer surplus and increases the monopolist's total profit above what it would if the firm sold all output at one price. For the questions in this section, assume that Pat's average total cost and marginal cost are constant and equal to $8 (ATC = MC = $8).

5. In Figure 3-13.1, draw the firm's ATC=MC curves as a horizontal line at $8.

6. If this were a perfectly competitive market, the MC curve would represent the supply of the product. If Pat produces the perfectly competitive quantity and charges the perfectly competitive price:

(A) How many tattoos will she supply? Why?

(B) What price will she charge for each tattoo? Why?

(C) What is the amount of consumer surplus? Why?

7. If Pat produces the monopoly quantity and charges the monopoly price:

(A) Draw her marginal revenue (MR) curve in Figure 3-13.1.

(B) How many tattoos will she supply? Why?

(C) What price will she charge for each tattoo? Why?

(D) What is the amount of consumer surplus? Why?

8. Now assume Pat knows the tastes and preferences of all consumers and the conditions necessary for first-degree price discrimination apply.

(A) Does the MR curve for the non-discriminating monopolist still apply? Why?

(B) How many tattoos will she supply? Why?

(C) Complete Table 3-13.2, which shows what price she will charge each individual consumer for her/his tattoo.

Table 3-13.2
Prices Charged by a Perfectly Discriminating Monopsonist

Consumer	1st	2nd	3rd	4th	5th	6th	7th	8th	9th	10th
Price										

(D) What is the amount of consumer surplus?

9. In Table 3-13.3, show Pat's total profit under each of the three market structures. Remember our assumption that ATC = MC = $8.

Table 3-13.3
Profit in Each Market Structure

Type of market	Pat's total profit
Perfect competition	
Regular monopoly	
Perfect price discrimination monopoly	

10. How does the total profit of the perfectly discriminating monopolist compare to the consumer surplus that existed in the perfectly competitive market? [See Question 6 (C).] Why?

11. Is the total profit for a regular monopolist different from the total profit of a monopolist that is able to practice perfect price discrimination? Why?

12. Is the output the same for perfect competition and perfect price discrimination? Why?

13. Is there a deadweight loss resulting from the non-discriminating monopolist? What about from the monopolist with first-degree price discrimination?

14. If an orange sells in Nebraska for $1.00 and the same quality orange sells in Florida for only $0.50, is this clear evidence of price discrimination? Why?

15. What is an example of price discrimination that works in favor of students?

Regulating a Monopoly

There are some firms that have decreasing marginal costs over a large range of output. As long as marginal cost (MC) is below average total cost (ATC), the firm also will experience decreasing ATC. Such firms are called *natural monopolies* and are often regulated by a governmental agency that allows the firm to be the only provider of the service. This is an attempt to take advantage of the low average total cost of the firm. This activity lets you explore several regulation plans and their effects on the firm and the market.

Suppose you are the manager of a local natural monopoly. Figure 3-14.1 illustrates the revenue and cost functions of your monopoly.

Figure 3-14.1
Revenue and Cost Functions

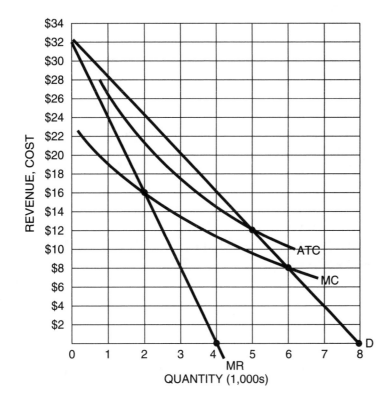

1. Complete Table 3-14.1, which examines three possible pricing plans for the monopoly.

Table 3-14.1
Three Pricing Regulation Plans

	Output (Q)	Price (P)	Total revenue (TR)	Total cost (TC)	Average profit (AΠ)	Total profit (TΠ)
Unregulated monopoly						
Fair return pricing						
Socially optimal pricing						

2. In Figure 3-14.1, shade in the area representing your firm's total profit under each of the three regulation plans.

3. As the manager of this firm, which of the three regulation plans would you prefer? Why?

4. As the manager of the firm, which plan would you totally oppose? Why? What could the government do to make this plan acceptable to you?

5. Which plan would society like to see the government agency apply to your firm? Why?

6. Under the fair return pricing plan, does your firm earn an economic profit? Does it earn a normal profit?

7. Each of the three plans has its own rule for deciding how many units of output your firm will provide. State those rules.

Comparing Perfect Competition and Monopoly

The productivity and cost curves of a firm are the same regardless of the degree of competition the firm faces in the product market. The shapes of the productivity and cost curves depend on the productivity of resources and the prices the firm pays to acquire those resources. It is on the revenue side of the firm that we find the impact of the type of product market in which the firm sells its good or service.

Part A: A Comparison of Firms

Answer the following questions based on Figure 3-15.1, which shows the revenue and cost functions of a monopoly and a perfectly competitive firm. Assume the monopoly will charge only one price for output (i.e., it does not price discriminate).

Figure 3-15.1
Revenue and Cost Functions for a Monopoly and a Perfectly Competitive Firm

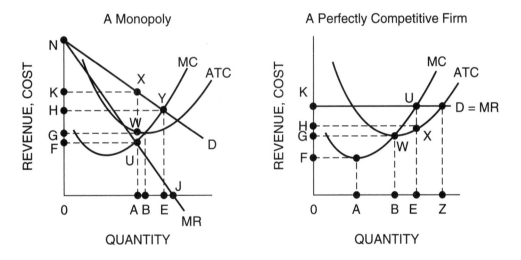

Note: The values of coordinates are not the same in both graphs. For example, the value of 0K is greater in the monopoly graph than is the value of 0K in the graph of the competitive firm.

1. The monopoly will maximize its total profit by producing _____ units of output.

   (A) 0A   (B) 0B   (C) 0E   (D) 0J

2. The perfectly competitive firm will maximize its total profit by producing _____ units of output.

   (A) 0A   (B) 0B   (C) 0E   (D) 0Z

3. The profit-maximizing price for the monopoly is

   (A) 0F.   (B) 0G.   (C) 0H.   (D) 0K.

---

4. The profit-maximizing price for the perfectly competitive firm is

    (A) 0F. (B) 0G. (C) 0H. (D) 0K.

5. The maximum total profit of the monopoly is shown by the coordinates

    (A) AX. (B) UX. (C) GWXK. (D) 0AXK.

6. The maximum total profit of the perfectly competitive firm is shown by the coordinates

    (A) EU. (B) UX. (C) 0EUK. (D) HXUK.

7. The maximum average profit of the perfectly competitive firm is at output

    (A) 0A. (B) 0B. (C) 0E. (D) 0Z.

8. The marginal profit of the monopoly is $0 at output

    (A) 0A. (B) 0B. (C) 0E. (D) 0J.

9. The marginal profit of the perfectly competitive firm is $0 at output

    (A) 0A. (B) 0B. (C) 0E. (D) 0Z.

10. The marginal profit of the perfectly competitive firm is maximized at output

    (A) 0A. (B) 0B. (C) 0E. (D) 0Z.

11. At output 0A, the total cost of the monopoly is shown by the coordinates

    (A) AU. (B) AW. (C) 0AUF. (D) 0AWG.

12. The monopolist will maximize its total revenue at output

    (A) 0A. (B) 0B. (C) 0E. (D) 0J.

13. What price will the perfectly competitive firm charge when it is in long-run equilibrium?

    (A) 0F (B) 0G (C) 0H (D) 0K

14. What area represents consumer surplus when the monopoly maximizes its total profit?

    (A) KXN (B) 0AXN (C) GWXN (D) HYN

15. The profit-maximizing output of the monopoly is _____ the output society would like the firm to produce.

    (A) greater than (B) equal to (C) less than

16. The profit-maximizing output of the perfectly competitive firm is _____ the output society would like the firm to produce.

    (A) greater than (B) equal to (C) less than

17. Is the perfectly competitive firm in a position of long-run equilibrium?

    (A) Yes (B) No (C) We need more information.

18. Which firm will operate at the minimum point of its ATC curve in long-run equilibrium?

(A) Only the perfectly competitive firm

(B) Only the monopolistic firm

(C) Both firms

(D) Neither firm

Part B: A Comparison of Markets

Figure 3-15.2 shows a perfectly competitive market with demand curve D and supply curve S. The equilibrium output is Q_2, and the equilibrium price is 0F. If the market were to become a monopoly, the firm would restrict output to some smaller output such as Q_1. Answer the questions below Figure 3-15.2.

Figure 3-15.2
Comparing Perfect Competition and Monopoly

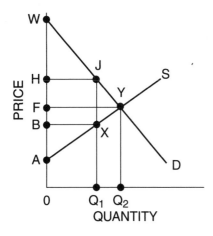

19. Complete Table 3-15.1 with the coordinates of the variables under each type of market.

Table 3-15.1
Comparing Perfect Competition and Monopoly

Market type	Consumer surplus	Producer surplus	Total surplus*
Perfect competition	FYW		
Monopoly			
*Total surplus is also called total welfare and social welfare.			

20. Explain what the triangle JXY represents.   dead weight loss

Monopolistic Competition

Monopolistic competition is an appropriate name for this important market structure. There is competition because there is a large number of firms producing similar but not identical products. Each firm has some monopoly power over price because its product is different from others with which it is competing. Each monopolistically competitive firm faces a downward sloping demand (D) curve so it has to reduce its price to have consumers buy more of its product. This means it has a downward sloping marginal revenue (MR) curve that lies below its D curve. In fact, the revenue graph of a monopolistically competitive firm looks like the revenue graph of a monopoly.

A monopolistically competitive firm is similar to a perfectly competitive firm because while it can earn a positive total profit in its short-run equilibrium, it will break even in its long-run equilibrium. It is different from a monopoly in this regard because a monopoly can maintain a positive total profit in the long run as long as it has barriers to entry that prevent other firms from coming into the market.

Part A: Short-Run Equilibrium of a Monopolistically Competitive Firm

A monopolistically competitive firm is in short-run equilibrium when it produces the output where marginal revenue equals marginal cost (MR = MC). Its optimal price is found on its demand curve at this output level. Like other firms, the firm will shut down if at its best output level, its total revenue is less than its total variable cost. Figure 3-16.1 shows a monopolistically competitive firm in short-run equilibrium with an output of 600 units per period. Answer the questions that follow the graph.

Figure 3-16.1
A Monopolistically Competitive Firm in Short-Run Equilibrium

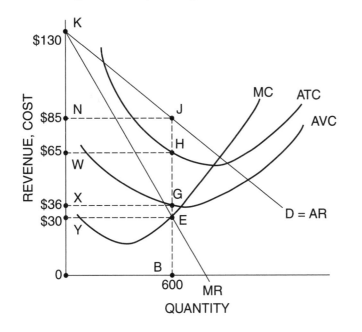

1. What price will the firm charge for its profit-maximizing output?

2. What are the dollar values and coordinates of these items at the output of 600 units?

    (A) Total revenue

    (B) Total cost

    (C) Total profit

    (D) Average profit

    (E) Marginal profit

3. What is the value of the firm's total fixed cost at 600 units? What is the value of its total fixed cost at 0 units?

4. Should this firm shut down? Why?

5. On the horizontal axis, indicate by Q_1 the output level society would like this firm to produce. Why does the firm not want to produce Q_1?

6. On the horizontal axis, indicate by Q_2 the output level at which this firm would maximize its total revenue. Why does the firm not want to produce Q_2?

7. What are the dollar value and the coordinates of consumer surplus when the firm maximizes its total profit?

Part B: Movement from Short-Run Equilibrium to Long-Run Equilibrium

If firms in a monopolistically competitive market are earning positive economic profits, other firms have an incentive to enter this market. As they do so, each firm's share of the total market demand gets smaller and smaller. This means the demand curve facing a monopolistically competitive firm shifts to the left. This process continues until all firms remaining in the industry break even. Outside firms then will no longer have an incentive to enter the market, and existing firms will have no reason to leave because they are receiving their normal profit. Figure 3-16.2 shows the demand and average total cost curves for a typical firm in the monopolistically competitive market for sport shirts.

 Figure 3-16.2
Movement of a Monopolistically Competitive Firm to Long-Run Equilibrium

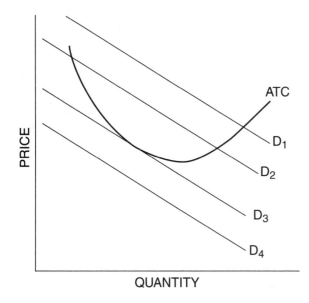

8. If the demand curve for this firm is D_1, is the firm earning positive total profit? If so, will other firms enter the market? What will this do to this firm's share of the market demand?

9. If this firm's demand decreases from D_1 to D_2, will the firm earn a positive total profit? What will happen to this firm's share of the market demand?

10. Assume the demand facing the firm drops from D_2 to D_4. Will it earn a positive total profit? If some other firms in the industry are in a similar situation, what will happen to the number of firms in the industry? What will happen to this firm's share of the market demand?

11. Suppose this firm's demand shifts from D_4 to D_3. Is this firm making a positive total profit or a loss? If this is the condition for other firms as well, will firms enter or leave the market?

Part C: Evaluation of a Monopolistically Competitive Firm in Long-Run Equilibrium

When a monopolistically competitive firm is in long-run equilibrium, it will break even or earn $0 in total economic profit. Because it is receiving its normal profit, it is doing as well with its resources here as it would in its best alternative. Thus, the firm has no incentive to leave the industry. Figure 3-16.3 illustrates a monopolistically competitive firm in long-run equilibrium with quantity Q* and price P*.

Figure 3-16.3

A Monopolistically Competitive Firm in Long-Run Equilibrium

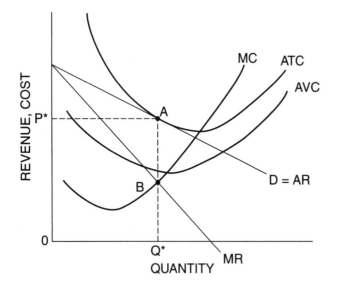

12. If you were asked to draw a graph of a monopolistically competitive firm in a position of long-run equilibrium, there are two conditions you must show with your graph at the profit-maximizing output.

(A) At Q*, the firm's average revenue (or price) must be (*greater than / equal to / less than*) its average total cost. This is shown by drawing the demand curve tangent to the ATC curve at point A.

(B) At Q*, the firm's marginal revenue must be (*greater than / equal to / less than*) its marginal cost. This is shown by drawing your MR curve through the MC curve at Q* at point B.

13. Is a monopolistically competitive firm productively efficient when it is in long-run equilibrium? Explain.

14. Is a monopolistically competitive firm allocatively efficient when it is in long-run equilibrium? Explain.

15. Is the demand curve facing a monopolistically competitive firm more or less elastic than the demand curve facing a monopoly? Why?

16. What are the characteristics of a monopolistically competitive market? What are two examples of such a market?

Game Theory

Strategic thinking is the art of outdoing an adversary, knowing that the adversary is trying to do the same to you.   Dixit and Nalebuff[*]

Game theory is used to explain how two or more players make decisions or choose actions when their actions (or strategies) affect each participant. Each player determines his or her best response to the possible actions of every other player. According to game theory, a player's choice of strategy depends on the strategy the player thinks other players will choose. In some cases, these strategies reinforce each other, but in other cases they do not. When the chosen strategies reinforce each other, the game achieves what is called a *Nash Equilibrium*. The Nash Equilibrium is named after John F. Nash, Jr., who was co-winner of the 1994 Nobel Prize in Economics for his work in this area and the subject of the 2001 movie, *A Beautiful Mind*.

Game theory provides insights into how business and government decisions are made and has numerous real-world applications. For example, game theory has helped economists analyze antitrust policy, tariff wars, and auctioning behavior. This lesson is an introduction to the basic elements of game theory. As you do the math, think about the implications of the results.

Part A: The Basic Elements of Game Theory

The three basic elements of a game are

(A) the players,

(B) the strategies available to each player,

(C) the payoffs each player receives.

These three elements are summarized in a table called a *payoff matrix*. A payoff matrix describes the payoffs to each player for combinations of given strategies. Here is an example of a payoff matrix:

		Coke	
		Advertise	Don't Advertise
Pepsi	Advertise	80, 80	120, 45
	Don't Advertise	45, 120	100, 100

The first number in each square refers to the payoff for the row (horizontal) player, here Pepsi. The second number in each square refers to the payoff for the column (vertical) player, here Coke. The numbers represent the profit (in $ millions) for Pepsi and Coke.

---

[*]Avinash K. Dixit and Barry J. Nalebuff, *Thinking Strategically: The Competitive Edge in Business, Politics, and Everyday Life* (New York: W.W. Norton, 1991), p. 409.

In this game:

    (A) The players are Pepsi and Coke.

    (B) Here are the strategies available to each player:

        ■ Pepsi, as the row player, can choose either Advertise or Don't Advertise.

        ■ Coke, as the column player, can choose either Advertise or Don't Advertise.

    (C) The payoffs each player receives:

        ■ If Pepsi chooses Advertise and Coke chooses Advertise, Pepsi earns 80 and Coke earns 80.

        ■ If Pepsi chooses Advertise and Coke chooses Don't Advertise, Pepsi earns 120 and Coke earns 45.

        ■ If Pepsi chooses Don't Advertise and Coke chooses Advertise, Pepsi earns 45 and Coke earns 120.

        ■ If Pepsi chooses Don't Advertise and Coke chooses Don't Advertise, Pepsi earns 100 and Coke earns 100.

In some games, one or more players can have a *dominant strategy*. A dominant strategy is the best strategy for a player regardless of the strategy chosen by the other player.

1. To see if Pepsi has a dominant strategy, answer these questions based on the information in the payoff matrix.

    (A) If Coke decides to advertise, Pepsi's best strategy would be (*Advertise / Don't Advertise*).

    (B) If Coke decides not to advertise, Pepsi's best strategy would be (*Advertise / Don't Advertise*).

    (C) Is Pepsi's best strategy the same regardless of whether Coke advertises or doesn't advertise? Does this mean Pepsi has a dominant strategy?

2. To see if Coke has a dominant strategy, answer these questions based on the information in the payoff matrix.

    (A) If Pepsi decides to advertise, Coke's best strategy would be (*Advertise / Don't Advertise*).

    (B) If Pepsi decides not to advertise, Coke's best strategy would be (*Advertise / Don't Advertise*).

    (C) Is Coke's best strategy the same regardless of whether Pepsi advertises or doesn't advertise? Does this mean Coke has a dominant strategy?

3. Do the profit values in the payoff matrix make sense? Why would Pepsi's profit be much higher than Coke's profit when Pepsi advertises and Coke does not? Why could both companies' profit be higher if they both don't advertise compared to if they both do advertise?

A *dominated strategy* yields a lower payoff than at least one other strategy. In this game, the dominated strategy for Pepsi is Don't Advertise; it is dominated by Advertise. Regardless of the strategy selected by Coke, Pepsi gains more by choosing Advertise. If Pepsi chooses Don't Advertise, the payoff is 45, while a strategy of Advertise has a payoff of 80. Since 45 is less than 80, the dominated strategy is Don't Advertise.

The dominated strategy for Coke is Don't Advertise; it is dominated by Advertise. If Coke chooses Don't Advertise, Coke receives 45 if Pepsi chooses Advertise and 100 if Pepsi chooses Don't Advertise. Since 45 is less than 100, the dominated strategy for Coke is Don't Advertise.

A *Nash Equilibrium* exists when each player is doing his/her best, given what the other player is doing. It is a combination of strategies for each player, such that each chooses his/her best response to the other's strategy choice. In this game, the Nash Equilibrium is both players deciding to Advertise. Although in this example both Coke and Pepsi select the same strategy, in a Nash Equilibrium the players do not have to select the same strategy.

A Nash Equilibrium is similar to a market equilibrium in that there is no incentive for producers and consumers to change from the equilibrium price. Thus a Nash Equilibrium is an "enforceable" equilibrium because the firms do not have an incentive to cheat as they might in a cartel.

Other economic examples of game-theory applications are decisions by firms about what price to charge, whether to enter a market, where to locate, and what kind of product or quality level to produce; decisions by a central bank on monetary policy actions; and decisions by a nation on the optimal tariff policy.

Part B: The Prisoner's Dilemma Game

One classic application of game theory is the *prisoner's dilemma game*. Prisoner's dilemma games are games in which each player has a dominant strategy; and when both players play the dominant strategy, the payoffs are smaller than if each player played the dominated strategy. The dilemma is how to avoid this bad outcome.

The basics of the prisoner's dilemma game are as follows: two prisoners, Charles and Frances, have the option to confess or not confess to a crime they committed. The prosecutor has only enough information to convict both criminals of a minor offense and is, therefore, relying on a confession. The minor offense carries one year in jail. The prisoners are questioned in different cells, without the ability to communicate. They are told that if one prisoner confesses while the other remains silent, the prisoner confessing will go free and the prisoner remaining silent will serve 20 years in jail. If both prisoners confess, both prisoners will serve three years in jail.

If a player goes free, the payoff is 0. If a player serves one year in jail, the payoff is −1. If a player spends 20 years in jail, the payoff is −20. Use these numbers in your payoff matrix. Note that the negative numbers come from losing years of freedom.

4. Determine the three basic elements of the game.

   (A) The players

   (B) The strategies for each player

   (C) The payoffs for each player

5. Create a payoff matrix for the prisoner's dilemma game.

6. Are there dominant strategies? Explain.

7. Identify any dominated strategies. Explain.

8. Is there a Nash Equilibrium? Explain.

Part C: Variation of the Prisoner's Dilemma Game

You are in a class with one other student. It is the end of the semester, and final exams are in a week. Your teacher has said the final exam will be graded so that anyone who scores the class average on the final exam will receive a "B" in the class. Anyone who scores above the average will receive an "A" in the class, and anyone who scores below the average will fail the class. You would certainly score higher on the exam than the other student. You and the other student have made an agreement not to take the final exam so that the class average is zero and you both receive "B" grades.

9. Determine the three basic elements of the game.

(A) The players

(B) The strategies for each player

(C) The payoffs for each player

10. Create a payoff matrix for this game.

11. Do you have a dominant strategy? Explain.

12. Using a four-point scale (A = 4, B = 3, C = 2, and D = 1), which choice results in the highest class GPA?

If you finished Parts B and C correctly, you will realize that when each player chooses his or her dominant strategy, the result is unattractive to the group.

The key to avoiding the prisoner's dilemma outcome of lower payoffs for both players is to find a way for players to credibly commit to playing a dominated strategy. Merely having both prisoners agree to Not Confess or both students to Not Take the Exam will not work. This results because it is always optimal for Prisoner 1 (or Prisoner 2) to still play the Confess strategy, and it is always optimal for the better student to play the Take the Exam strategy. One possible way to have credible commitment in the prisoner's dilemma game would be to have both prisoners reveal another past crime they committed, thus ensuring that if they confess to this crime, the other prisoner will have additional information to punish the prisoner who cheats on an agreement to not confess.

One way to do this is to form a *cartel*. A cartel is a coalition of firms that coordinate their decisions to reach a more optimal solution for all members of the group by finding ways to credibly commit players to play their dominated strategies. Cartels, however, are not always successful in maintaining their agreements because there may be an incentive for a member to cheat on the cartel.

Part D: What Should These Firms Do?

There are two firms that produce fiberglass canoes. Both River Queen and Ace Current must decide whether to market a Premium canoe or a Regular canoe. The profit of a firm depends on the type of canoe produced by the other firm. In this chart, the first value is the profit of River Queen, and the second value is the profit of Ace Current. The firms make their decisions simultaneously in a one-period situation. (The values in the chart are thousands of dollars.)

		Ace Current	
		Premium	Regular
River Queen	Premium	$400, $100	$450, $200
	Regular	$150, $400	$200, $150

13. Does River Queen have a dominant strategy? What decision will River Queen make?

Yes, premium. Produce premium canoes.

14. Does Ace Current have a dominant strategy? What decision will Ace Current make?

NO. They are dependent on what the other firm does

15. Is there a Nash Equilibrium?

Yes

River Queen   Ace Current
premium dominant - bestplay regular

Part E: Questions

16. Is the Coke and Pepsi advertising game a prisoner's dilemma game? Explain why or why not.

17. Interpret "standing at a concert" in terms of the prisoner's dilemma game.

18. Explain at least one way the optimal outcome for players, which would be for all players to play the dominated strategy, can be reached in Question 17. What are the possible commitment problems?

19. A rivalry exists between the U.S. jet producer Boeing and the European jet producer Airbus. Each government has the opportunity to subsidize its jet producer to give it a competitive edge in the global market. Using game theory, explain what you would expect to observe in practice.

Circle the letter of each correct answer.

1. True statements about the theory of the firm in the short run and long run include which of the following?

   I. All input quantities are fixed in the short run.

   II. All input quantities are variable in the long run.

   III. At least one input quantity is fixed in the short run.

   (A) I only
   (B) II only
   (C) III only
   (D) I and II only
   (E) II and III only

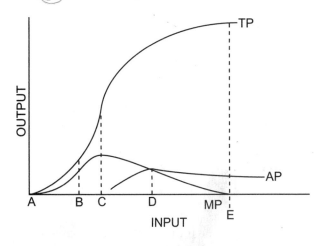

2. On the graph above, the onset of diminishing marginal returns occurs beyond

   (A) Point A.
   (B) Point B.
   (C) Point C.
   (D) Point D.
   (E) Point E.

3. Which of the following statements about a firm's production function are true?

   I. When total product is at its maximum, marginal product is zero.

   II. When total product rises, marginal product is rising.

   III. When marginal product is greater than average product, average product is rising.

   IV. When marginal product is less than average product, average product is falling.

   (A) I and II only
   (B) II and III only
   (C) II and IV only
   (D) I, III, and IV only
   (E) I, II, III, and IV

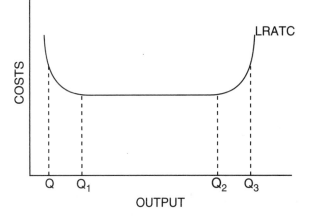

4. According to the graph above, if the firm is producing any quantity greater than Q_2, the firm is experiencing

   (A) economies of scale.
   (B) minimum efficient scale.
   (C) diseconomies of scale.
   (D) constant returns.
   (E) increasing returns.

5. For a perfectly competitive firm, if the market price is $8, then

   (A) marginal revenue is greater than $8.

   (B) marginal revenue is less than $8.

   (C) marginal revenue is equal to $8.

   (D) average revenue is greater than $8.

   (E) average revenue is less than $8.

6. A firm's short-run marginal cost curve will eventually increase because of

   (A) more efficient production.

   (B) economies of scale.

   (C) diseconomies of scale.

   (D) diminishing marginal returns.

   (E) increasing marginal returns.

7. Assume that in the short run at the profit-maximizing output, the price is lower than average variable cost. The perfectly competitive firm should

   (A) increase its price.

   (B) decrease its price.

   (C) increase its output.

   (D) decrease its output.

   (E) shut down.

8. Assume that a perfectly competitive firm is operating where marginal revenue is greater than marginal costs. To increase total profits, the firm should

   (A) increase production.

   (B) decrease production.

   (C) increase price.

   (D) decrease price.

   (E) do nothing.

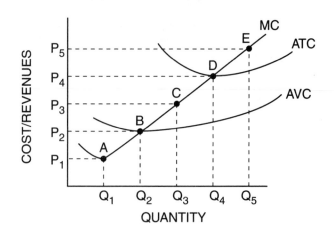

Use the graph above to answer Questions 9, 10, and 11.

9. If the firm is in short-run equilibrium at a price of P_5, a perfectly competitive firm will maximize total profits by producing at which of the following levels of output?

   (A) Q_1 (D) Q_4

   (B) Q_2 (E) Q_5

   (C) Q_3

10. At which price will this perfectly competitive firm make an economic profit?

    (A) P_1 (D) P_4

    (B) P_2 (E) P_5

    (C) P_3

11. Which price-quantity combination represents long-run equilibrium for this perfectly competitive firm?

    (A) Point A   (D) Point D

    (B) Point B   (E) Point E

    (C) Point C

750 - 500

12. If the average variable cost of producing five units of a product is $100 and the average variable cost of producing six units is $125, then the marginal cost of producing the sixth unit is

$5 \times 100 = 500$
$6 \times 125 = 750$

$MC \quad \dfrac{\triangle cost1}{\triangle cost2}$

(A) $25.   (D) $500.

(B) $125.   (E) $750.

(C) $250.

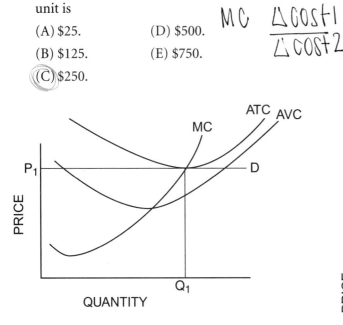

13. According to the graph above, if the firm is producing at Q_1, the firm is

(A) losing money because the firm is operating at the shutdown point.

(B) losing money because the price does not cover average fixed cost.

(C) making profits because the price is above average variable cost.

(D) making normal profits because the price just covers average total cost.

(E) making normal profits because the price is above average variable cost.

14. Which of the following represents the correct relationship between the demand curve for a perfectly competitive industry and the demand curve for a perfectly competitive firm?

	PC industry demand	PC firm demand
(A)	Downward slope to the right	Downward slope to the right
(B)	Downward slope to the right	Perfectly elastic
(C)	Perfectly elastic	Downward slope to the right
(D)	Perfectly elastic	Perfectly elastic
(E)	Perfectly inelastic	Perfectly elastic

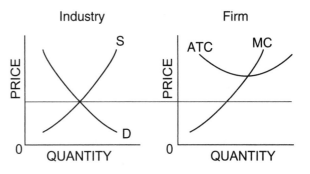

15. According to the graphs above, in which of the following ways are the industry supply curve and the equilibrium price most likely to change in the long run?

	Industry supply	Equilibrium price
(A)	Decrease	Decrease
(B)	Decrease	Increase
(C)	Increase	Decrease
(D)	Increase	Increase
(E)	Not change	Decrease

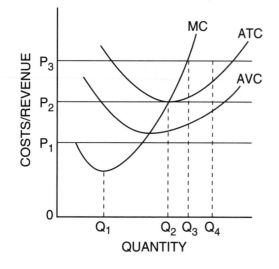

Use the graph above to answer Question 16.

16. If price is P_3, the firm will

    (A) produce Q_2 units and earn only a normal profit.

    (B) produce Q_1 units and earn an economic profit.

    (C) produce Q_3 units and earn an economic profit.

    (D) produce Q_4 units and earn an economic profit.

    (E) shut down.

17. Which of the following is true of a pure monopolist's demand curve?

    (A) It is perfectly inelastic.

    (B) It is perfectly elastic.

    (C) It coincides with its marginal revenue curve.

    (D) It lies below its marginal revenue curve.

    (E) It lies above its marginal revenue curve.

18. Average fixed cost is shown as the vertical distance between

    (A) marginal cost and average variable cost.

    (B) marginal cost and average total cost.

    (C) average variable cost and average total cost.

    (D) average total cost and the horizontal axis.

    (E) marginal cost and the horizontal axis.

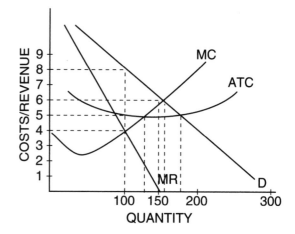

Use the graph above to answer Questions 19, 20, and 21.

19. Assume that the firm in the graph above is an unregulated monopolist. It will produce

    (A) 175 units at a price of $7.00.

    (B) 100 units at a price of $6.00.

    (C) 100 units at a price of $8.00.

    (D) 150 units at a price of about $5.00.

    (E) about 210 units at a price of about $4.00.

20. Assume that the firm in the graph is an unregulated monopolist. It will earn long-run profits of

    (A) $0.   (D) $500.

    (B) $300.   (E) $900.

    (C) $400.

21. At 100 units of output, the firm's average revenue is

    (A) $0. (D) $8.
    (B) $4. (E) $800.
    (C) $6.

25. Total revenue will be maximized when price is equal to

    (A) P_1. (D) P_4.
    (B) P_2. (E) P_5.
    (C) P_3.

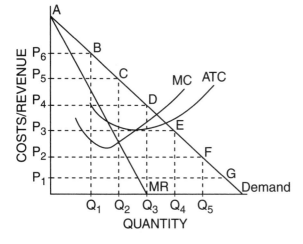

Use the graph above to answer Questions 22 through 25.

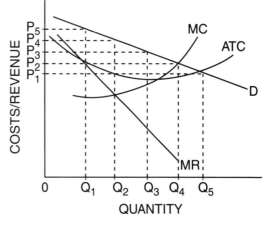

Questions 26, 27, and 28 are based on the graph above of cost and revenue curves for a monopoly firm.

22. For the firm in the graph—an unregulated monopolist—the price elasticity of demand is unit elastic at a price and an output of

    (A) P_6 and Q_1. (D) P_3 and Q_4.
    (B) P_5 and Q_2. (E) P_3 and Q_4.
    (C) P_4 and Q_3.

23. Consumer surplus for this profit-maximizing monopolist will be represented by area

    (A) ABP_6. (D) AEP_3.
    (B) ACP_5. (E) AGP_1.
    (C) ADP_4.

24. The profit-maximizing price for this firm is

    (A) P_2. (D) P_5.
    (B) P_3. (E) P_6.
    (C) P_4.

26. To maximize total profit, this monopolist should produce at which of the following levels of output?

    (A) Q_1 (D) Q_4
    (B) Q_2 (E) Q_5
    (C) Q_3

27. The price the monopolist charges at the profit-maximizing level of output will be

    (A) P_1. (D) P_4.
    (B) P_2. (E) P_5.
    (C) P_3.

28. When the firm maximizes total profit, the profit per unit will be

    (A) $P_2 - P_1$. (D) $P_4 - P_1$.
    (B) $P_3 - P_2$. (E) $P_1 - 0$.
    (C) $P_4 - 0$.

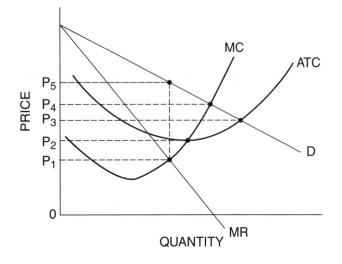

Use the graph above to answer Questions 29 and 30.

29. If this monopoly is regulated so as to have it produce the socially optimal output level, what price should the firm charge?

   (A) P$_1$ (D) P$_4$

   (B) P$_2$ (E) P$_5$

   (C) P$_3$

30. If a regulating agency requires this monopoly to charge a price that allows the firm to have a fair return (where all costs are covered, including a normal profit), the price would be

   (A) P$_1$.   (D) P$_4$.

   (B) P$_2$.   (E) P$_5$.

   (C) P$_3$.

31. What happens to a monopolist's price, profits, and output if its total fixed costs decrease?

	Price	Profits	Output
(A)	Decrease	Increase	Decrease
(B)	Decrease	Decrease	Decrease
(C)	No change	Increase	No change
(D)	Increase	Increase	Increase
(E)	Decrease	No change	Increase

32. The presence of both allocative and productive efficiency is possible in which of the following market structures?

   I.   Perfectly competitive

   II. Monopolistic

   III. Oligopolistic

   IV. Monopolistically competitive

   (A) I only

   (B) II only

   (C) III only

   (D) I and IV only

   (E) II and IV only

33. Which of the following is true of monopolists that practice price discrimination?

   (A) They charge all customers the same price.

   (B) They earn a smaller profit than those that do not practice price discrimination.

   (C) They charge customers different prices according to different elasticities of demand.

   (D) They produce lower quantities than pure monopolists.

   (E) They produce the same quantity of output as pure monopolists.

34. Characteristics of an oligopolistic market include which of the following?

   I.   Easy entry and exit of firms

   II. Few firms

   III. Interdependence among firms

   (A) I only

   (B) II only

   (C) III only

   (D) II and III only

   (E) I, II, and III

35. In the long run, a monopolistically competitive firm will make

    (A) more economic profit than a perfectly competitive firm.

    (B) less economic profit than a perfectly competitive firm.

    (C) more economic profit than a monopoly.

    (D) more economic profit than an oligopolist.

    (E) zero economic profit.

36. If all of the firms in an oligopoly could, without any additional cost, form an industry-wide cartel to jointly maximize profits, the demand curve facing the cartel would be

    (A) less elastic than the industry demand curve.

    (B) the same as the industry demand curve.

    (C) more elastic than the industry demand curve.

    (D) perfectly inelastic.

    (E) horizontal at the market-clearing price.

37. Characteristics of an oligopoly include which of the following?

    I.   Collusion can increase oligopolists' profits.

    II. Oligopolistic firms are interdependent.

    III. Independent price decision making leads to lower returns.

    (A) I only

    (B) II only

    (C) III only

    (D) I and II only

    (E) I, II, and III

38. The shapes of the marginal product curve and the total product curve are best explained by the

    (A) law of demand.

    (B) law of supply.

    (C) principle of diminishing marginal utility.

    (D) least-cost rule.

    (E) law of diminishing marginal returns.

Royal's Burgers and Fries

		Concentrate on fries	Concentrate on burgers
Brewer's Fries and Burgers	Concentrate on fries	120, 85	150, 120
	Concentrate on burgers	65, 100	50, 80

Use the payoff matrix above and the information below to answer Questions 39 and 40.

Two competing fast-food restaurants in a small town, Royal's Burgers and Fries and Brewer's Fries and Burgers, realize that each must consider the method of attracting customers that the other is using. The payoff matrix above illustrates the firms' possible strategies and the profits to each restaurant under each possible outcome. (The first number in each box represents the payoff to Brewer's; the second the payoff to Royal's.)

39. Based on the payoffs above, which of the following statements is true?

   (A) Brewer's has a dominant strategy to concentrate on fries.

   (B) Brewer's has a dominant strategy to concentrate on burgers.

   (C) Royal's has a dominant strategy to concentrate on fries.

   (D) Royal's has a dominant strategy to concentrate on burgers.

   (E) Neither restaurant has a dominant strategy.

40. What is the Nash Equilibrium in this game?

   (A) Both fast-food restaurants should choose to concentrate on fries.

   (B) Both fast-food restaurants should choose to concentrate on burgers.

   (C) Brewer's should choose to concentrate on fries, and Royal's should choose to concentrate on burgers.

   (D) Brewer's should choose to concentrate on burgers, and Royal's should choose to concentrate on fries.

   (E) There is no Nash Equilibrium in this game.

41. Which of the following is true of a cartel?

   (A) A cartel is a coalition of firms that seek to coordinate their decisions so all firms can earn a higher economic profit.

   (B) A cartel is a way for firms to earn more by playing their dominant strategies.

   (C) A cartel is considered stable.

   (D) A cartel seeks to maximize total revenue of its members.

   (E) A cartel sets price and output of its members in the same way that a price discriminating monopolist would.

42. Which of the following best characterizes the firms in an oligopoly industry?

   (A) Firms can easily enter the industry when profits are high.

   (B) There are more firms than in a monopolistically competitive industry.

   (C) They are independent.

   (D) They always collude to increase profits.

   (E) They use strategic decision making.

Acme

		Advertise	Don't advertise
AAA	Advertise	Acme: 150 AAA: 150	Acme: −100 AAA: 400
	Don't advertise	Acme: 400 AAA: −100	Acme: 0 AAA: 0

Use the payoff matrix above and the information below to answer Questions 43, 44, and 45.

Acme and AAA are the two major firms in the industry. Each must decide whether to conduct a television advertising campaign. The returns from each firm's decision depend on the decision of the other. The profits resulting from each possible combination of the firms' decisions are given in the payoff matrix above.

43. If AAA advertises and Acme does not, Acme's profits will change by
    (A) −$100.   (D) $300.
    (B) $0.   (E) $400.
    (C) $150.

44. If AAA advertises, Acme will
    (A) decide not to advertise because this is its dominant strategy.
    (B) advertise because this is its dominant strategy.
    (C) not have a dominant strategy.
    (D) lose money.
    (E) increase its profit by $400 if it advertises.

45. Which of the following statements is true?
    (A) If AAA advertises, Acme's dominant strategy is to advertise.
    (B) If Acme advertises, AAA's dominant strategy is NOT to advertise.
    (C) The two firms are in a prisoner's dilemma game.
    (D) The two firms would be better off to agree to save their money and NOT advertise.
    (E) A collusive agreement to advertise would benefit both firms.

MICROECONOMICS

Factor Markets

Unit 4

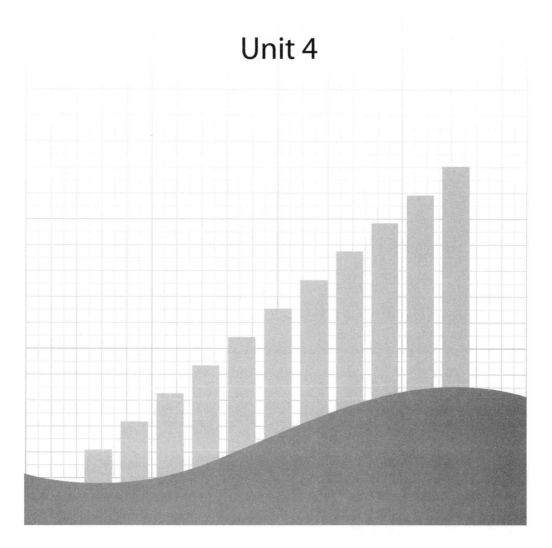

■ Firms are sellers in product markets and buyers in factor (resource) markets.

■ The demand for any resource is derived from the demand for the products that the resource can produce. Thus, resource demand depends on the price of the good or service that the resource produces and on the resource's productivity in producing the good or service.

■ The demand curve for a resource in the short run is downward sloping because the marginal physical product (MPP) of additional inputs of a resource will decrease as a result of the law of diminishing marginal returns. In some textbooks, marginal physical product is called marginal product.

■ A firm will continue to hire factors of production as long as its marginal revenue product (MRP) exceeds its marginal resource cost (MRC). A firm will not hire more resources once MRC exceeds MRP.

■ The marginal revenue product curve for a firm selling its product in an imperfectly competitive market will be steeper than the marginal revenue product curve for a firm selling in a perfectly competitive market. The steeper slope results from both a decrease in the marginal physical product and a decrease in the product price required to permit the firm to sell a larger output.

■ A firm maximizes total profits where a factor's marginal revenue product equals the factor's marginal resource cost. A firm maximizes total profit where MRP = MRC.

■ In a perfectly competitive labor market, a firm can hire all the workers it wants at the current market wage. The firm will hire workers until the last worker's wage (MRC) equals the marginal revenue product of that last worker hired.

■ When a combination of resources is employed in producing a good or service, the profit-maximizing rule is

$$\frac{MRP_a}{MRC_a} = \frac{MRP_b}{MRC_b} = \frac{MRP_n}{MRC_n} = 1.$$

■ When a firm produces the profit-maximizing level of output, it must utilize a least-cost combination of resources. The rule for a least-cost combination of resources is

$$\frac{MPP_a}{MRC_a} = \frac{MPP_b}{MRC_b} = \frac{MPP_n}{MRC_n}.$$

■ For a firm facing a perfectly competitive resource market, resource supply is perfectly elastic and equal to marginal resource cost at a market-determined price (wage) for the resource. Under monopsony or other imperfect conditions of employment, both resource supply and marginal resource cost are positively sloped curves with the marginal resource cost being a value greater than the price (wage) for all units beyond the first unit of the resource employed.

■ Given a downward-sloping marginal revenue product curve and the differences existing between supply and marginal resource cost in perfect competition and monopsony, a monopsonistic employer will pay a lower price (wage) and hire fewer units of a resource than a perfect competitor.

■ Economic rent is any payment to the supplier of a resource that is greater than the minimum amount required to employ the desired quantity of the resource.

■ The equilibrium real interest rate influences the level of investment and helps allocate financial and physical capital to specific firms and industries.

- Profits are the return to entrepreneurs for assuming risk and for organizing and directing economic resources.

- Profits allocate resources according to the demands of consumers.

How Many Workers Should a Firm Hire?

You are the president of Acme Yo-Yo Company, a small manufacturing firm that produces Supersonic Yo-Yos, a popular toy that makes a "supersonic" noise when used.

■ Acme yo-yos are produced by workers operating with two yo-yo-making machines. You have estimated how many yo-yos can be made using different numbers of workers and you must decide how many workers to hire to maximize your firm's total profit.

■ Acme is a perfect competitor in the product market. This means your firm can sell as many yo-yos as you want at the market price of a yo-yo.

■ Acme also is a perfect competitor in the labor resource market. This means you can hire as many workers as you want at the market wage.

■ You will hire each worker who adds more to your firm's total revenue than he/she adds to your total cost. You will not hire a worker who adds less to total revenue than to total cost.

■ Marginal physical product (MPP) is the change in your firm's total output (Q) from adding an extra worker: $MPP = \Delta Q / \Delta L$, where L stands for labor.

■ Marginal revenue product (MRP) is the change in your firm's total revenue (TR) from adding an extra worker: $MRP = \Delta TR / \Delta L$. Because you can sell all the yo-yos you want at the market price (P), $MRP = (MPP)(P \text{ of a yo-yo})$.

■ Marginal resource cost (MRC) is the change in your firm's total cost (TC) from adding an extra worker: $MRC = \Delta TC / \Delta L$. Because you can hire all the workers you want at the market wage, $MRC = \text{Wage}$.

■ The profit-maximizing rule for an employer is to hire the number of workers at which $MRP = MRC$. This means the employer hires those workers with $MRP > MRC$ and stops before hiring workers with $MRP < MRC$. (If this rule sounds familiar, it uses the same logic as the $MR = MC$ rule a firm uses to find its profit-maximizing amount of output.)

🛈 *Student Alert:* **Some textbooks use marginal factor cost (MFC) or marginal labor cost (MLC) instead of marginal resource cost (MRC).**

Part A: Creating the Firm's Demand for Labor

Table 4-1.1
Productivity and Revenue Data for Yo-Yo Workers

L (workers per day)	Q (yo-yos per day)	MPP	P	TR	MRP
0	0	–		$0	–
1	20				
2	50	+30			+$150
3	70		$5		
4	85			$425	
5	95	+10			
6	100				

1. Complete Table 4-1.1. Assume the market price of a yo-yo is $5.

2. Why does the number of extra yo-yos produced by an additional worker decrease as more workers are added? Is it because the additional workers are less motivated and less talented than previous workers?

3. Plot the MRP values in Figure 4-1.1. Connect those values and label the curve as "MRP." Plot each MRP value on the higher of the two L values, not at the midpoint. For example, plot the MRP value of $150 at L = 2 rather than at L = 1.5.

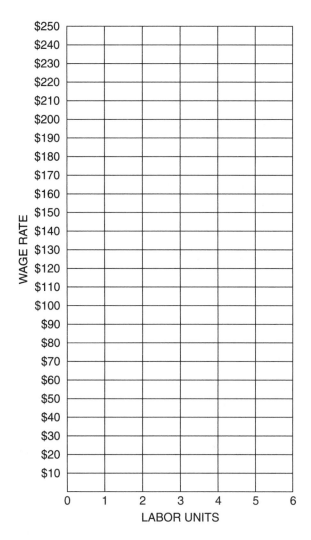

Figure 4-1.1

The Acme Firm's Demand for Labor and Supply of Labor

4. If the market wage is $100 per worker per day, your firm can hire all the workers it wants at that wage. This means the supply of labor to your firm can be shown as a horizontal line at the wage of $100. Draw a horizontal line in Figure 4-1.1 at $100 and label the line as "$S_1 = MRC_1$." The MRC to the firm of each extra worker is equal to the wage of $100.

5. At a wage of $100, how many workers should your firm hire? Why?

6. Now assume the market wage drops to $75. Draw a new horizontal line at that wage and label it as "$S_2 = MRC_2$." How many workers will be hired at the wage of $75?

7. Finally, assume the market wage is $50. Draw another horizontal line at that wage and label it as "$S_3 = MRC_3$." How many units of labor will be hired at the wage of $50?

8. The firm's demand for labor shows how many workers it will hire at different wages. Complete Table 4-1.2 based on your work above.

 Table 4-1.2

Acme's Demand for Labor

Wage	Number of workers hired
$100	
$75	
$50	

9. If a firm hires labor in a perfectly competitive factor market, then the downward sloping portion of its MRP curve is its demand (D) curve for labor. If the wage is equal to the MRC, then by going to its MRP curve at a given wage, the firm finds the amount of labor where MRP = MCL. Go back to Figure 4-1.1 and label the MRP curve as "MRP = D."

10. Is the law of demand evident in Table 4-1.2? Why does a firm hire more workers when the wage decreases?

Part B: The Derived Demand for Labor

We saw in Part A that if a firm operates in perfectly competitive resource markets, its demand for labor is its MRP curve. So what can increase the firm's demand for labor? Remember how we calculate MRP if the product market is perfectly competitive: MRP = (MPP)(price of the good). An increase in the MPP of labor or an increase in the price of the good will increase the MRP of labor, thus increasing the firm's demand for labor.

A decrease in the marginal physical product or a decrease in the good's price will reduce the demand for labor.

11. In Table 4-1.3, indicate for each situation whether the product or labor market is being affected, whether the MPP of labor or the price (P) of the good will change, and whether the demand for labor will increase or decrease.

Table 4-1.3

Factors Changing a Firm's Demand for Labor

Situation	Which market?	Change in MPP?	Change in P?	Change in demand for labor
(A) A new yo-yo machine increases productivity of labor.	Product / Labor	Yes / No	Yes / No	Increase / Decrease
(B) The price of yo-yos increases.	Product / Labor	Yes / No	Yes / No	Increase / Decrease
(C) New government safety regulation reduces worker productivity.	Product / Labor	Yes / No	Yes / No	Increase / Decrease
(D) The demand for yo-yos decreases.	Product / Labor	Yes / No	Yes / No	Increase / Decrease
(E) New technology increases output of yo-yos.	Product / Labor	Yes / No	Yes / No	Increase / Decrease
(F) Consumers become tired of yo-yos.	Product / Labor	Yes / No	Yes / No	Increase / Decrease

The demand for any resource is called a *derived demand* because it is derived from the demand for the good or service that is produced by the resource. It is important that you understand the relationship between demand in the factor market and demand in the product market. (Even if you are a charming individual, unless you produce a good or service that is in demand, you will find it hard to land a good job.)

12. Assume that yo-yos become a hot fad and the increased demand for them drives the market price of a yo-yo up to $8. Complete Table 4-1.4, which has the same productivity data as Table 4-1.1.

Table 4-1.4
Productivity and Revenue Data for Yo-Yo Workers

L (workers per day)	Q (yo-yos per day)	MPP	P	TR	MRP
0	0	–		$0	–
1	20				
2	50	+30			+$240
3	70		$8		
4	85			$680	
5	95	+10			
6	100				

13. Plot the new MRP data in Figure 4-1.1 and label it as "$D_2 = MRP_2$." Does this represent an increase in Acme's demand for labor? What caused it?

14. Based on your new MRP_2 curve in Figure 4-1.1, fill in Table 4-1.5.

Table 4-1.5
Acme's New Demand for Labor

Wage	Number of workers hired
$100	
$75	
$50	

Part C: How Many Workers to Hire?

Figure 4-1.2 shows the MRP curve and the MRC curve for a company that sells its product in a perfectly competitive goods market and hires its labor in a perfectly competitive resource market.

15. You tell your friend that this firm should hire 760 units of labor because that is where MRP = MRC. Your friend is confused and asks how this firm can maximize total profit with 760 labor units since the marginal profit from the 760th labor unit appears to be $0. Can you help your friend understand the logic of the MRP = MRC rule?

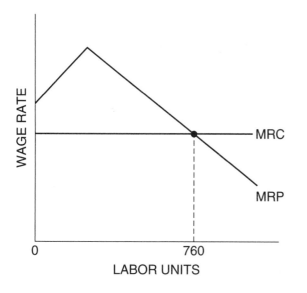

Figure 4-1.2

Logic of the MRP = MRC Rule

The Optimal Combination of Resources

In Activity 4-1, we assumed the Acme Yo-Yo Company was operating in the short run with a fixed amount of capital (equipment) and with labor as its variable resource. Let's now consider a long-run example where the firm can change its capital as well as its labor. What combination of labor (L) and capital (K) should the firm employ?

Part A: The Least-Cost Combination of Resources

What should a firm do if it wants to produce the most output possible from a given resource budget? What should it do if it wants to produce a given level of output at the lowest total cost? The approach to both of these problems is similar. The firm should allocate its resource budget between units of labor and units of capital in such a way that the following condition is satisfied, where marginal physical product is MPP and marginal resource cost is MRC:

$$\frac{MPP_L}{MRC_L} = \frac{MPP_K}{MRC_K}.$$

If the resource markets are perfectly competitive, the price the firm pays for an extra unit of a resource is equal to its MRC. In that case the condition can be written as

$$\frac{MPP_L}{P_L} = \frac{MPP_K}{P_K}.$$

where P_L is the price of a unit of labor and P_K is the price of a unit of capital.

Another way of stating this condition for *economic efficiency* is that the firm should get the same extra output from the last dollar spent on each type of resource.

Assume a firm has allocated its given resource budget between labor and capital and finds the marginal physical product for the resources to be 200 units from labor and 400 units from capital. That means the last unit of labor increased total output by 200 units while the last unit of capital increased output by 400 units. At first glance, you might think the firm should move some money away from labor and over to capital. But that would totally ignore the prices of the two resources. Assume the prices of labor and capital in competitive resource markets are $10 and $40, respectively.

1. Calculate the "MPP per $1" for each resource.

2. Based on your work in Question 1, is the firm getting the most output possible from its given resource budget? If so, explain why. If not, how should it reallocate its budget between labor and capital?

3. Suppose the MPP values are as given in Question 1, but that the prices of labor and capital are $10 and $20, respectively. Is the firm now getting the most output possible from its resource budget? Explain.

4. A different firm has allocated its resource budget between labor and capital and is producing a given output level at the lowest possible total cost. The MPP of labor is 25 units, and the MPP of capital is 20 units. If the price of a unit of labor is $100, what is the price of a unit of capital?

Part B: The Profit-Maximizing Combination of Resources

The economic efficiency condition in Part A is what economists call a "necessary but not sufficient" condition for profit maximization. In other words, if a firm is not using an economically efficient (least-cost) combination of resources, then it cannot possibly be maximizing its total profit. If it is using an economically efficient combination, then it might be profit maximizing, but an additional condition must be satisfied to guarantee that is the case.

Here is the profit-maximizing condition for a combination of two resources:

$$\frac{MRP_L}{MRC_L} = \frac{MRP_K}{MRC_K} = 1.$$

If the resource markets are perfectly competitive, the condition can be written as

$$\frac{MRP_L}{P_L} = \frac{MRP_K}{P_K} = 1.$$

While this condition looks similar to the one in Part A, there are two significant differences.

1. The firm is comparing MRP, not MPP, to MRC.

2. The two ratios must both be equal to 1.

The second difference means the MRP from the last unit of each resource must be equal to its MRC. If the MRP of a unit of labor is greater than its MRC, the firm should hire more labor. If the MRP of a unit of capital is less than its MRC, the firm should get rid of some capital. (This is the rule we used in Activity 4-1 to find the profit-maximizing amount of labor in the short run when capital was fixed: Hire the amount of labor where MRP = MCL.)

5. Suppose the Ebbets Company produces 1,000 units of output with a combination of labor and capital such that the MRP of labor is $30 and the MRP of capital is $40. If this firm is maximizing its total profit at this output, what are the prices of units of labor and capital? (Assume the firm buys resources in perfectly competitive markets.)

6. The Shibe Company produces 800 units of output per period. The MRP of labor is $60, and the MRP of capital is $40. The market prices of units of labor and capital are $12 and $8, respectively. Is this firm maximizing its total profit? Explain.

7. The Honus Company currently produces Q_1 units of output each period. It sells its good in a perfectly competitive product market and buys its resources in perfectly competitive factor markets. The MPP of labor is 50 units, and the MPP of capital is 80 units. The prices it pays for units of labor and capital are $100 and $160, respectively.

   (A) Is the company operating in an economically efficient manner? Explain.

   (B) What would the market price of its good have to be for the firm to be maximizing its total profit?

   The least-cost and profit-maximization conditions also apply to a firm with more than two resources (W, X, and Y).

   Least-cost combination: $\dfrac{MPP_W}{MRC_W} = \dfrac{MPP_X}{MRC_X} = \dfrac{MPP_Y}{MRC_Y}.$

   Profit-maximization combination: $\dfrac{MRP_W}{MRC_W} = \dfrac{MRP_X}{MRC_X} = \dfrac{MRP_Y}{MRC_Y} = 1.$

The Only Game in Town

In Activity 4-1, we assumed the Acme Yo-Yo Company sold its product in a perfectly competitive market. Acme could sell all the yo-yos it wanted at the price determined in the market. Now, let's suppose that Acme is a monopolist and controls the yo-yo market. Because it still hires its workers in a perfectly competitive labor market, we will continue to treat its marginal revenue product (MRP) curve as its demand for labor (L). It can hire all the workers it wants at the market wage rate.

What is different in our analysis if Acme is a monopolist in the product market rather than a perfectly competitive seller of yo-yos? The difference is that now the firm must lower its price to sell more yo-yos. That will create a wedge between its price and the marginal revenue it receives from an extra sold unit. And it will make the workers' MRP decrease faster than it did when the firm was perfectly competitive. Now there are two reasons why MRP decreases as more workers are hired: diminishing marginal productivity and diminishing marginal revenue.

Part A: Creating the Monopolist's Demand for Labor

1. Complete Table 4-3.1, which shows the prices at which the Acme monopolist can sell the different quantities of yo-yos it is producing. You can see that the firm must lower the price to sell more of its product. The productivity data are the same as they were in Activity 4-1; the fact that the firm now has no competition in the product market does not affect the productivity of workers.

Student Alert: **You cannot find the MRP of a worker by multiplying the marginal physical product (MPP) by the price (P). That worked in Activity 4-1 because the firm sold its output (Q) at the market price. But now the firm is a monopolist and must lower price to sell more output. MRP is found here as the change in total revenue (TR) when the firm adds an extra worker.**

Table 4-3.1
Productivity and Revenue Data for Yo-Yo Workers

L (workers per day)	Q (yo-yos per day)	MPP	P	TR	MRP
0	0	–	$8.00	$0	–
1	20		$7.25		
2	50	+30	$6.00		+$155.00
3	70		$5.25		
4	85		$4.70	$399.50	
5	95	+10	$4.30		+$9.00
6	100		$4.00		

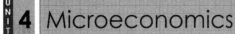
2. Plot the firm's MRP data in Figure 4-3.1. Connect the MRP values and label the curve as "D = MRP." Plot the MRP values at the new labor amount rather than at the midpoint.

Figure 4-3.1
The Acme Firm's Demand for Labor and Supply of Labor

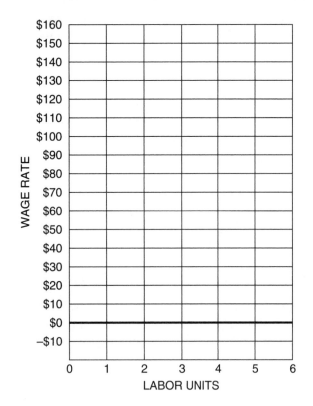

3. Draw three horizontal labor supply curves in Figure 4-3.1 at wages of $120, $60, and $30. Label them as "$S_1 = MRC_1$," "$S_2 = MRC_2$," and "$S_3 = MRC_3$."

4. Complete Table 4-3.2, which shows how many workers the firm will hire at each of these wages.

Table 4-3.2
Acme's Demand for Labor

Wage	Number of workers hired
$120	
$60	
$30	

5. Does the law of demand apply to this firm, which is a monopolist in the product market?

6. Why can we consider the firm's MRP curve as its labor demand curve? Is it important that the labor market is perfectly competitive? Is it important that the product market is not perfectly competitive?

7. Other things being equal, would Acme's demand curve for labor be steeper or flatter now than it was when it was in a perfectly competitive goods market? Why?

Factor Market Pricing

A perfectly competitive labor market determines the equilibrium wage and employment in that market. Firms that buy labor in this market will pay the market wage and can hire all the workers they want at this wage. This activity demonstrates how the market wage is set and how a firm interacts with the labor market.

Part A: Labor Demand for the Perfectly Competitive Firm

The Awesome Belt Company (ABC) is a price taker in both the input and output markets. It hires labor in a perfectly competitive resource market and sells its belts in a perfectly competitive product market. The total revenue (TR) the firm receives from each amount of labor is found by multiplying output (Q) by the price (P) at which that level of output can be sold. The marginal revenue product (MRP) of an extra unit of labor is the change in TR resulting from the firm adding the extra labor unit.

1. Complete Table 4-4.1 based on two different possible prices for ABC's belts.

 Table 4-4.1
ABC's Productivity and Revenue Data

Labor (L)	Output (Q)	Marginal physical product (MPP) ($\Delta Q/\Delta L$)	Price = $2.00		Price = $3.00	
			TR	MRP	TR	MRP
0	0	–	$0	–		–
1	10	+10		+$20		
2	30	+20	$60			
3	70				$210	
4	105					+$105
5	135		$270	+$60		
6	160				$480	
7	180	+20		+$40		+$60
8	195		$390		$585	
9	205	+10				+$30
10	205	+0				+$0
11	195		$390	–$20		

2. Now complete Table 4-4.2 and Table 4-4.3, which show ABC's demand for labor at two different prices of belts. The demand schedules indicate the highest wage the firm will pay for a given number of workers, based on the MRP of workers in Table 4-4.1.

 Table 4-4.2
ABC's Demand for Labor if the Price of Belts Is $2.00

Wage	Quantity of labor demanded
$20	
$30	
$40	
$50	
$60	
$70	
$80	

Table 4-4.3
ABC's Demand for Labor if the Price of Belts Is $3.00

Wage	Quantity of labor demanded
$30	
$45	
$60	
$75	
$90	
$105	
$120	

Part B: The Perfectly Competitive Labor Market

3. Assuming there are 1,000 firms identical to ABC in the belt industry, complete Table 4-4.4, based on the market price of belts being $2.00. Since the firms are identical, you can simply multiply the quantity of labor demanded by ABC at the different wages by 1,000 to derive the market demand for labor. Table 4-4.4 also has information about the number of workers willing to supply their labor at the different wages. Comparing the quantity of workers demanded and the quantity supplied, indicate whether there is a shortage or a surplus of labor at each wage. One wage is the equilibrium wage in the market.

Table 4-4.4
The Labor Market Based on the Price of Belts Being $2.00

Wage	Quantity of labor demanded	Quantity of labor supplied	State of the labor market
$20		3,000	Shortage / Equilibrium / Surplus
$30		4,000	Shortage / Equilibrium / Surplus
$40		5,000	Shortage / Equilibrium / Surplus
$50		6,000	Shortage / Equilibrium / Surplus
$60		7,000	Shortage / Equilibrium / Surplus
$70		8,000	Shortage / Equilibrium / Surplus
$80		9,000	Shortage / Equilibrium / Surplus

4. In Figure 4-4.1, plot the market demand and supply curves for labor from Table 4-4.4. Label the demand curve as "$D_{\$2.00}$" and the supply curve as "S".

Figure 4-4.1
The Labor Market

5. Why is the market demand curve for labor downward sloping? Why is the market supply curve of labor upward sloping?

6. Assume the wage is at some level greater than the equilibrium wage. Is there a shortage or surplus of labor? What adjustments take place in the market to move the wage to the equilibrium wage?

7. Assume the wage is at some level less than the equilibrium wage. Is there a shortage or surplus of labor? What adjustments take place in the market to move the wage to the equilibrium wage?

8. Assuming there are 1,000 firms identical to ABC in the belt industry, complete Table 4-4.5, based on the market price of belts being $3.00.

 Table 4-4.5
The Labor Market Based on the Price of Belts Being $3.00

Wage	Quantity of labor demanded	Quantity of labor supplied*	State of the labor market
$30		4,000	Shortage / Equilibrium / Surplus
$45		4,500	Shortage / Equilibrium / Surplus
$60		7,000	Shortage / Equilibrium / Surplus
$75		8,000	Shortage / Equilibrium / Surplus
$90		10,000	Shortage / Equilibrium / Surplus
$105		11,500	Shortage / Equilibrium / Surplus
$120		13,000	Shortage / Equilibrium / Surplus
*Some of the quantity supplied figures are interpolated from the supply data in Table 4-4.4.			

9. In Figure 4-4.1, plot the market demand curve for labor from Table 4-4.5. Label the demand curve as "D$_{\$3.00.}$" (The supply curve is the same as in Table 4-4.4.)

10. Why did the market demand curve for labor shift to the right when the price of belts increased from $2.00 to $3.00?

11. What happened to the equilibrium wage and the equilibrium quantity of labor when the labor demand curve shifted to the right?

Part C: The Perfectly Competitive Labor Market and a Firm's Demand for Labor

A perfectly competitive employer takes the market wage and can hire all the labor it wants at that wage. The firm does not have to raise its wage to attract more workers. The labor supply curve for the firm is horizontal at the market wage. This supply curve is perfectly elastic. If the firm drops its wage below the equilibrium wage, it will not be able to hire any workers.

Figure 4-4.2

The Labor Market and a Typical Firm in That Market

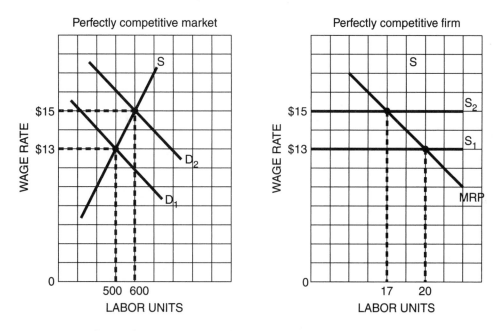

Figure 4-4.2 shows the competitive labor market and a typical firm that buys labor in that market. Answer the following questions based on this graph.

12. If the market demand for labor is D_1, the equilibrium wage will be $_____ and the equilibrium quantity of labor will be _____ workers.

13. How many workers will the firm hire at this market wage? _____

14. If the market demand for labor increases to D_2, the market wage will increase to $_____ and the equilibrium number of workers will increase to _____.

15. How many workers will the firm hire at this new market wage? _____

16. When the market wage increased, did the firm hire more or fewer workers? Why?

17. Is the firm's MRP curve also its demand curve for labor? Explain.

18. Are the workers in this market demanded exclusively by firms that produce the identical good, or are they hired by firms that make a variety of different goods?

How Wages Are Determined in Labor Markets

This activity examines how wages and employment are determined in two types of labor markets. A *perfectly competitive labor market* is one in which all buyers and sellers are so small that no one can act alone and affect the market wage. The interaction of market demand (D) and supply (S) determines the wage and the level of employment. A *monopsony* exists if there is only one buyer of labor in the resource market. The monopsonist pays as low a wage as possible to attract the number of workers needed.

Student Alert: If the monopsonist needs more workers, the wage will have to be raised.

Part A: A Perfectly Competitive Labor Market

Figure 4-5.1
A Perfectly Competitive Labor Market

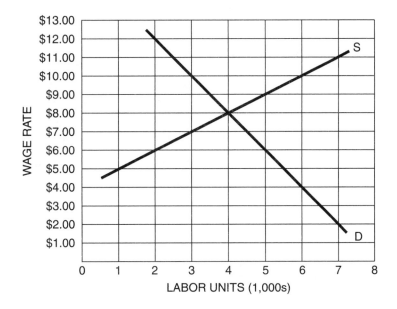

Figure 4-5.1 illustrates a perfectly competitive labor market. Labor is measured in thousands of labor hours. Answer the following questions based on this graph.

1. What are the equilibrium wage and number of labor hours in this labor market?

2. Why is the demand for labor downward sloping?

3. Why is the supply of labor upward sloping?

Part B: A Minimum Wage

4. Why does the government create a minimum wage in a labor market?

5. If the government sets a minimum wage of $10.00 in the labor market shown in Figure 4-5.1, will there be a shortage or surplus of labor? How large is this shortage or surplus? Indicate this on the graph at the wage of $10.00.

6. Are some workers made better off because of the minimum wage? Are some workers made worse off because of it? Explain.

7. Would skilled or unskilled workers be more likely to lose their jobs because of a minimum wage law?

8. If the demand for labor were more inelastic, would more or fewer workers lose their jobs because of the minimum wage? Explain.

Advanced Placement Economics Microeconomics: Student Resource Manual © Council for Economic Education, New York, N.Y.

Part C: A Monopsonistic Labor Market

Assume the Ross Textile Company is a monopsony in a small town. Because it faces the upward sloping market supply of labor, Ross must raise its wage if it wants to increase the quantity supplied of workers. The company pays the same wage to all its employees, so if it increases the wage to attract another worker, the marginal resource cost of that worker is greater than the wage paid to the worker: MRC > Wage.

Student Alert: If the wage is raised to hire another worker, then MRC > Wage.

9. Table 4-5.1 shows the supply of labor to Ross. Complete the table.

 Table 4-5.1
Labor Supply Schedule

Workers	Wage	Total labor cost	Marginal resource cost
1	$5.00	$5.00	
2	$5.50	$11.00	$6.00
3	$6.00		
4	$6.50		
5	$7.00		$9.00
6	$7.50	$45.00	

10. Plot the Ross Company's labor supply (S) curve and MRC curve in Figure 4-5.2. The firm's marginal revenue product (MRP) curve is already in the graph.

Figure 4-5.2
A Monopsonistic Labor Market

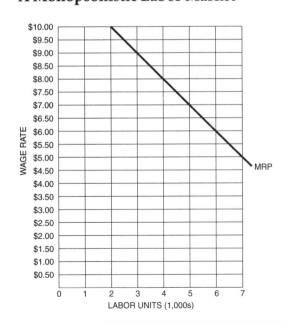

11. Why is the MRC curve above the S curve?

12. What is more important to Ross as it considers hiring another worker—the wage paid to the worker or the worker's MRC? Why?

13. How many workers will Ross hire? What wage will it pay to each of these workers?

14. Is the MRP curve the firm's D curve for labor?

15. What would be the equilibrium wage and employment if this were a perfectly competitive market? How do these values compare with those of the monopsonist?

16. If any firm hires the amount of labor at which MRP = MRC, is it also true that the firm is producing the output level at which MR = MC? Does the answer depend on whether the firm is perfectly competitive or monopolistic in the goods market, or whether it is perfectly competitive or monopsonistic in the labor market?

Wages and Employment in Competitive and Monopsonistic Labor Markets

This activity asks you to show how changes in economic conditions, government policy, and union activity affect different types of labor markets. The impact of such changes depends on the degree of competition on the demand and supply sides of the labor market. The symbols W_C, L_C, W_M, and L_M refer to the wages and labor in the competitive and monopsonistic labor markets. You are to consider the short-run effects in the specified labor market.

Part A: Perfect Competition and Monopsony

Figure 4-6.1

Perfectly Competitive and Monopsonistic Labor Markets

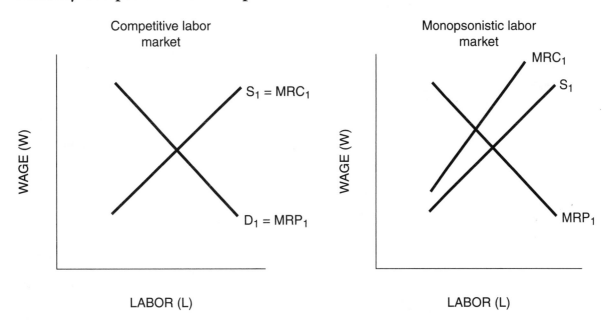

Figure 4-6.1 presents the basic setup of a perfectly competitive labor market and a monopsonistic labor market. Answer the following questions based on this figure.

1. Why is the marginal revenue product (MRP) curve equal to the market demand (D) curve for labor in the perfectly competitive labor market?

2. Why is the MRP curve not equal to the market D curve for labor in the monopsonistic labor market?

3. Why is the marginal resource cost (MRC) curve equal to the market labor supply (S) curve in the perfectly competitive labor market?

4. Why is the MRC curve not equal to the market labor S curve in the monopsonistic labor market?

5. In the appropriate graph, indicate by W_{C1} and L_{C1}, or W_{M1} and L_{M1}, the market wage and quantity of labor.

Part B: Analyzing Changes in the Labor Market

For each of the following scenarios, analyze the short-run effect of the specified event on each labor market. In the perfectly competitive labor market graph, indicate by W_{C1} and W_{C2} the market wage before and after the event. Indicate by L_{C1} and L_{C2} the equilibrium quantity of labor before and after the event. In the monopsonistic labor market graph, indicate by W_{M1} and W_{M2} the market wage before and after the event. Indicate by L_{M1} and L_{M2} the equilibrium quantity of labor before and after the event. State whether the event increases, decreases, or does not change the market wage and labor. Be sure to shift the curves that are affected by the events, leading to the changes in wage and labor.

6. Event: The state passes legislation requiring new teachers to pass a competency test in order to be employed by any school in the state. (The graphs refer to the labor market for teachers.)

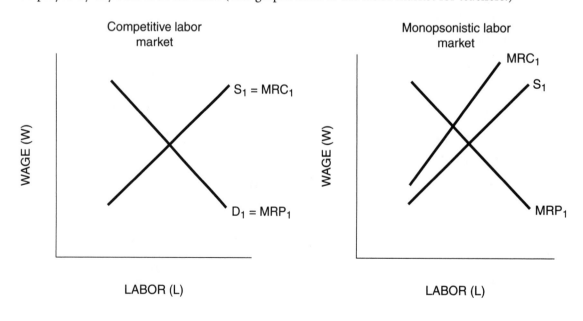

7. Event: New training methods increase the productivity of workers in the automobile industry. (The graphs refer to the labor market for automobile workers.)

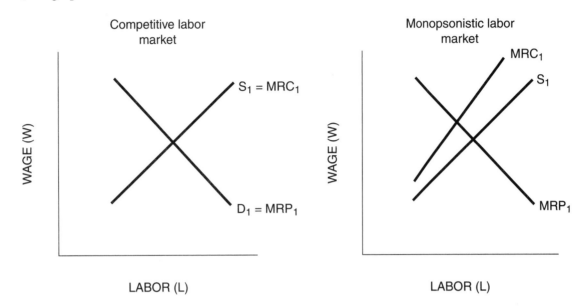

Competitive labor market

$S_1 = MRC_1$

$D_1 = MRP_1$

WAGE (W)

LABOR (L)

Monopsonistic labor market

MRC_1

S_1

MRP_1

WAGE (W)

LABOR (L)

8. Event: The U.S. government relaxes a tough immigration law, making it easier for construction workers from other countries to enter the United States. (The graphs refer to the American labor market for construction workers.)

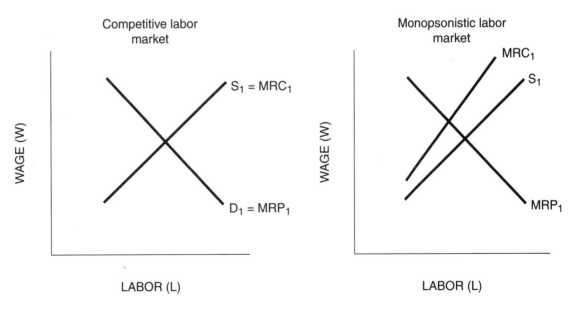

Competitive labor market

$S_1 = MRC_1$

$D_1 = MRP_1$

WAGE (W)

LABOR (L)

Monopsonistic labor market

MRC_1

S_1

MRP_1

WAGE (W)

LABOR (L)

9. Event: The German government lowers tariffs on shoes imported into Germany. (The graphs refer to the labor market for shoe workers in Germany.)

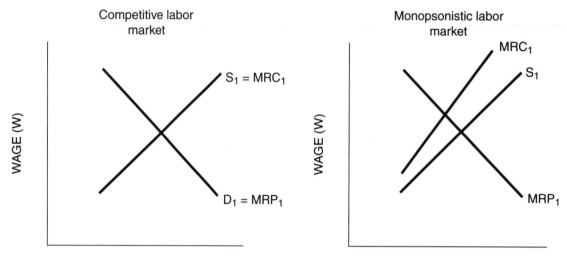

10. Event: Labor unions conduct a successful advertising campaign urging people to buy goods and services produced by American workers. (The graphs refer to the labor market for all American workers.)

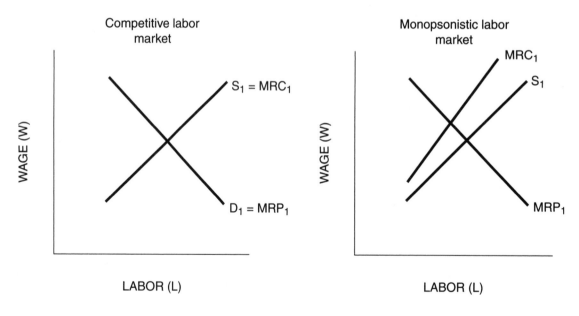

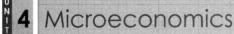
Part B: Monopsony and a Minimum Wage

Figure 4-6.2 illustrates the labor market in which there is only one employer. This monopsonist sells its good in a perfectly competitive product market.

Figure 4-6.2

A Monopsonistic Labor Market

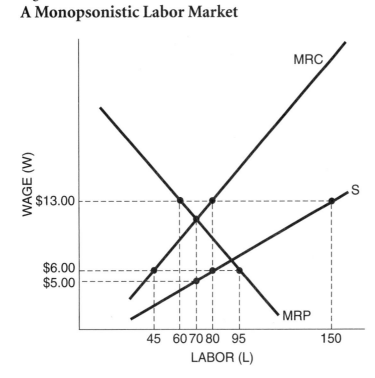

1. What is the profit-maximizing amount of labor for this monopsonistic firm? Why?

2. What wage will it pay each unit of labor? Why?

3. If the government sets a minimum wage of $13.00, how many units of labor would be hired? How many units of labor will be unemployed with this minimum wage? Explain.

4. If the government sets a minimum wage of $6.00, how many units of labor would be hired? How many units of labor will be unemployed with this minimum wage? Explain.

Problems Dealing with Factor Markets

Part A: Factor Market Questions

Answer the questions and briefly explain your answers. Feel free to use diagrams to illustrate your points.

1. Why are some basketball players paid more than brain surgeons? Explain using the concept of marginal revenue product.

2. True, false, or uncertain, and explain why? "If it were not for unions pushing up wages, we'd all be working 60 hours a week for $100 a month just like people did a century ago."

3. Use a graph to explain why a firm that wants to maximize its total profits uses a resource until the marginal revenue product of this resource equals the marginal resource cost.

4. True, false, or uncertain, and explain why? "American workers who are paid $10 an hour cannot possibly compete with workers who are paid $1 an hour in developing countries."

5. Why might a university pay a Nobel Prize-winning faculty member more than its president? Does this make sense economically for the university? Support your answer.

6. What are the effects of a minimum wage that is above the equilibrium wage in a perfectly competitive market? What about in a market in which the employer is a monopsonist? Give an example of a relatively competitive labor market and a less competitive labor market.

7. The National Collegiate Athletic Association (NCAA) regulates all college athletics in the United States. It sets the amount of scholarships, the number of scholarships granted, and the regulations for recruiting athletes. The NCAA has hundreds of rules regulating intercollegiate athletics.

(A) What effect do these regulations have on who receives the economic rent from college athletics?

(B) Which colleges have greater incentives to cheat? Why?

(C) Who would gain if the NCAA could no longer set rules for college athletics? Why?

(D) Who would lose if the NCAA could no longer control college athletics? Why?

(E) True, false, or uncertain, and why? "The NCAA is a champion for amateur athletics, and its rules protect the rights of college athletes."

Part B: How Many Workers to Hire?

Table 4-7.1 gives you information about a firm operating in a perfectly competitive product market. Consider all factors of production fixed, with the exception of labor. The other factors of production cost the firm $50 a day, which may be thought of as the firm's total fixed cost. Assume the firm is a profit maximizer.

 Table 4-7.1

Firm Operating in a Competitive Product Market

Labor (L) (workers per day)	Output (Q) (units per day)	Marginal physical product (MPP)	Total revenue (TR)	Marginal revenue product (MRP)
0	0	–	$0	–
1	22			
2	40	+18	$120	+$54
3	56			
4	70			
5	82	+12		+$36
6	92		$276	
7	100	+8	$300	
8	106	+6	$318	+$18

Fill in the answer blanks or underline the correct words in parentheses.

8. Assume the firm sells its output at $3 per unit. Complete Table 4-7.1.

   (A) If the equilibrium market wage is $36 per day, the firm will hire _____ workers per day and produce _____ units of output.

   (B) Given your answer to the preceding question, the firm will have total revenue of _____ per day and total cost of _____ per day.

   (C) The above will result in a (*profit / loss*) of _____ per day.

9. Suppose you work for a firm that sells its output in a monopolistic market. Answer the following questions.

   (A) If you hire an additional worker, output goes up from 75 to 125 units per day. If you want to sell the additional 50 units, you must lower your price from $3 per unit to $2 per unit. What is the highest wage you would be willing to pay the additional worker?

   (B) Assume that you hired the additional worker and output now stands at 125 units per day. If you hire another worker, output rises to 165 units per day. Given the demand curve for your product, you know that to sell the additional output, price will have to be dropped from $2 per unit to $1 per unit. What is the maximum wage you would be willing to pay *this* additional worker? Would you hire this additional worker? Why or why not?

10. Use a graph to explain why monopsonists will always hire fewer workers and pay lower wages than firms operating in competitive labor markets. (Assume that the monopsonistic and competitive firms have the same costs.)

Circle the letter of each correct answer.

1. Derived demand is
   (A) demand for an input used to produce a product.
   (B) demand derived from the satisfaction of a buyer for the product.
   (C) caused by monopoly control of the inputs.
   (D) derived from government policy.
   (E) dependent on the demand for a substitute or a complementary input.

Use the following information to answer Questions 2, 3, and 4.

Number of chefs	Number of pizzas that can be made in an hour
0	0
1	10
2	18
3	24
4	28
5	30
6	29

2. The law of diminishing marginal returns occurs with the hiring of which chef?
   (A) First   (D) Fourth
   (B) Second   (E) Fifth
   (C) Third

3. The marginal productivity of the third chef is
   (A) 24 pizzas   (D) 8 pizzas
   (B) 18 pizzas   (E) 6 pizzas
   (C) 10 pizzas

4. If the price per pizza is $10 and if each chef receives $20 an hour, how many chefs will the owner hire to maximize total profits?
   (A) 2   (D) 5
   (B) 3   (E) 6
   (C) 4

5. Which of the following would determine the marginal revenue product of an input used in a perfectly competitive output market?

   I. Dividing the change in total revenue by the change in the input
   II. Dividing the change in marginal revenue by the change in the output
   III. Multiplying the marginal product by the price of the output
   IV. Multiplying marginal revenue by the price of the output

   (A) I only   (D) I and III only
   (B) II only   (E) II and IV only
   (C) III only

6. Which of the following explains why the marginal revenue product of an input in a perfectly competitive product market decreases as a firm increases the quantity of an input used?
   (A) Diminishing marginal productivity from labor
   (B) Diminishing marginal utility
   (C) The homogeneity of the product
   (D) The free mobility of resources
   (E) Diminishing marginal revenue from output

7. A profit-maximizing firm should hire an input as long as the

   (A) firm can increase its total revenue.

   (B) price of the input doesn't exceed the price of the other inputs used in the firm's production.

   (C) marginal revenue product of the input is less than the cost of hiring the input.

   (D) marginal revenue product of the input is greater than the marginal revenue products of other inputs the firm is using.

   (E) marginal revenue product of the input is at least as much as the marginal cost of hiring the input.

8. The demand for labor will decrease in response to which of the following?

   (A) Increased productivity of labor

   (B) Better training of all laborers

   (C) A decrease in the supply of labor

   (D) An increase in the supply of labor

   (E) Decreased demand for goods and services produced by labor

9. A firm hiring inputs in a perfectly competitive market will hire up to the point where

   (A) marginal physical product of the input is at a minimum.

   (B) marginal physical product of the input is at a maximum.

   (C) the price of the input equals the price of the output.

   (D) the price of the input equals the marginal physical product of the input.

   (E) the price of the input equals the marginal revenue product of the input.

10. A firm is a competitive seller of output at a market price of $3. The only resource it requires to create its product is labor, which it purchases competitively at a wage rate of $8 per hour. The last worker it employs increases total output from 36 to 40 units per hour. What is the marginal revenue product for this worker?

    (A) $3   (D) $12

    (B) $4   (E) $24

    (C) $8

Use the following information to answer Questions 11, 12, and 13.

Units of workers	Total product	Product price
0	0	$5.00
1	10	$4.50
2	19	$4.00
3	27	$3.50
4	34	$3.00
5	40	$2.50

11. The marginal revenue product of the third worker is equal to

    (A) $3.50   (D) $28.00

    (B) $10.50   (E) $94.50

    (C) $18.50

12. Which of the following is true according to the information in the table?

    (A) The firm is selling its product in a purely competitive market.

    (B) The firm is selling its product in an imperfectly competitive market.

    (C) There is no level of output at which this firm can earn a profit.

    (D) The law of diminishing returns is not applicable to this firm.

    (E) The firm is hiring its workers in an imperfectly competitive labor market.

13. If the wage rate is constant and equal to $21, how many workers will the profit-maximizing firm hire?

(A) 1 (D) 4

(B) 2 (E) 5

(C) 3

14. Which of the following will cause an increase in the demand for labor?

I. Increase in the price of the output
II. Increase in worker productivity
III. Increase in wages
IV. Increase in the supply of workers

(A) I only (D) I and II only

(B) II only (E) III and IV only

(C) III only

15. A firm requires labor and capital to produce a given output. Labor costs $8 per hour, and capital costs $12 per hour. At the current output level, the marginal physical product of labor is 40 units, and the marginal physical product of capital is 60 units. To minimize its production costs at the current level of output, in which of

the following ways should the firm change the amount of labor and capital?

	Labor	Capital
(A)	Increase	Increase
(B)	Increase	Decrease
(C)	Decrease	Increase
(D)	Decrease	No change
(E)	No change	No change

16. In a competitive industry, suppose the marginal revenue product of the last donut baker hired is $35 and the marginal revenue product of the last bagel maker hired is $15. A bakery must pay donut bakers $40 a day and bagel makers $10 a day. Which of the following should the bakery hire to maximize profits?

(A) More donut bakers and fewer bagel makers

(B) Fewer donut bakers and more bagel makers

(C) Fewer of both donut bakers and bagel makers

(D) More of both donut bakers and bagel makers

(E) Neither more nor fewer donut bakers or bagel makers

Use the graph below to answer Questions 17, 18, and 19.

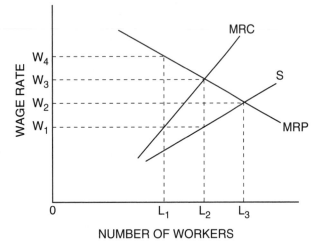

17. Under perfectly competitive conditions in the product and labor markets, the wage rate will be

    (A) W_1, and L_2 workers will be hired.

    (B) W_2, and L_2 workers will be hired.

    (C) W_3, and L_2 workers will be hired.

    (D) W_2, and L_3 workers will be hired.

    (E) W_4, and L_2 workers will be hired.

18. Now suppose that through an employers' association, firms in this industry establish a monopsony in the hiring of labor. In this case, the wage rate will be

    (A) W_1, and L_2 workers will be hired.

    (B) W_2, and L_2 workers will be hired.

    (C) W_3, and L_2 workers will be hired.

    (D) W_3, and L_3 workers will be hired.

    (E) W_4, and L_1 workers will be hired.

19. Now assume that workers react to the formation of this monopsony by establishing a union. To what level can this union increase the

wage rate without causing the number of jobs to decline below that which the monopsony would otherwise provide?

(A) W_1 (B) W_2 (C) W_3 (D) W_4

(E) Unions can never increase real wage rates.

20. If the wage paid to labor, the only variable input, is $20, and the marginal physical product of labor is four units per hour, the marginal cost of a unit of output is

    (A) $20.   (D) $10.

    (B) $16.   (E) $5.

    (C) $12.

21. Pure economic rent refers to the

    (A) capital gains received from the sale of property.

    (B) payment to any resource over and above what is required to keep the resource in supply at its current level in the long run.

    (C) difference between the return to owners of land and the market rate of interest.

    (D) implicit value of owner-occupied housing in the long run.

    (E) price paid for a resource that has a perfectly elastic supply.

22. One reason why the supply of carpenters is greater than the supply of physicians is that

    (A) carpenters demand less income.

    (B) physicians do not belong to a union.

    (C) physicians must make a greater investment in human capital.

    (D) carpenters belong to unions.

    (E) carpenters are in greater demand than are doctors.

23. Under what conditions is a firm's marginal revenue product of labor curve the same thing as its demand curve for labor?

    (A) If the firm sells its output in a perfectly competitive product market

    (B) If the firm sells its output in an imperfectly competitive product market

    (C) If the firm hires labor in a perfectly competitive resource market

    (D) If the firm hires labor in an imperfectly competitive resource market

    (E) The marginal revenue product curve is never the same thing as a firm's demand curve for labor.

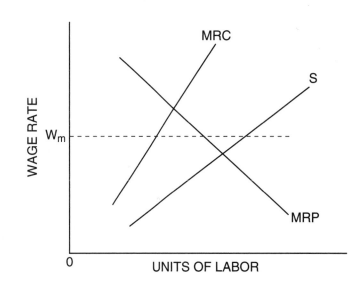

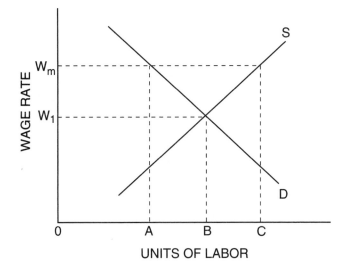

24. The competitive labor market shown above is initially in equilibrium. If a minimum wage level is set at W_m, employment will

    (A) increase from A to B.

    (B) increase from B to C.

    (C) decrease from B to A.

    (D) decrease from C to A.

    (E) decrease from C to B.

25. The monopsonistic labor market shown above is initially in equilibrium. If a minimum wage is set at W_M, the level of employment will

    (A) decrease.

    (B) increase.

    (C) stay the same.

    (D) increase or decrease depending on how the supply curve shifts as a result of the change in the wage rate.

    (E) be indeterminant under monopsonistic labor markets.

MICROECONOMICS

The Role of Government

Unit 5

- The economic functions of government include enforcing laws and contracts, maintaining competition, redistributing income, providing public goods, correcting allocations for externalities, and stabilizing the economy.

- Government must provide public goods because a private market will not provide them. Pure public goods must meet the criteria of nonrivalrous (shared consumption) and nonexclusion.

- Even a perfectly competitive market sometimes produces too little of some goods and too much of others; economists call this situation a market failure.

- The market overproduces goods that create negative externalities. A negative externality is created when part of the cost of a transaction is borne by third parties who are not directly involved in the transaction. Negative externalities include pollution and harmful effects of pesticides and smoking. Negative externalities are sometimes called spillover costs.

- The market underproduces goods that create positive externalities. A positive externality is created when benefits of a transaction or activity are received by third parties who are not directly involved in the transaction. Positive externalities include education, vaccinations against diseases, and flood control. Positive externalities are sometimes called spillover benefits.

- Government tries to discourage the production of goods that involve negative externalities and encourage the production of goods that involve positive externalities.

- Cleaning up the environment would be efficient if it were cleaned up to the point where the marginal social benefits of the cleanup were equal to the marginal social costs, and the cleanup were done at the least possible cost.

- Most economists believe the environment can be cleaned up at a lower cost by substituting market incentives for command and control policies.

- Sometimes buyers and sellers do not have perfect information, so the market outcome is not efficient. In these cases, it may be necessary for government to intervene in the market.

- The theory of public choice uses economic analysis to evaluate government operation and policies.

- Public-choice theorists believe politicians and government officials are as self-interested as business people. However, instead of trying to maximize profits, "political entrepreneurs" seek to maximize power, salaries, prestige, and votes. This behavior results in government waste and inefficiency.

- Governments tax to raise revenue. Some taxes are based on the ability-to-pay theory, while others are based on the benefits-received theory.

- Tax rates can be progressive, proportional, or regressive.

- Government taxing and spending policies can change a society's distribution of income.

- The incidence of a tax can be shifted from the person paying the government to someone else. This is accomplished through changes in prices, income, and outputs.

Private or Public? Public Goods and Services

Our Economic System

An economic system is the way in which people and societies organize economic life to answer three basic questions: *What* goods and services will be produced? *How* will they be produced? *For whom* will they be produced?

In many countries, most production decisions—what, how, and for whom to produce—are made in the marketplace through interactions of buyers and sellers. This is called the *private sector* of the economy. Other decisions are made by different levels of government. This is called the *public sector* of the economy. Many economic systems are called *mixed* systems since they produce a combination of private and public goods and services.

What Goods and Services Should Governments Provide?

While many goods and services can be provided by the private or the public sector, a few can be provided effectively only by governments. Generally, governments try to provide the goods and services that are necessary but that individual consumers might not purchase directly on their own. There are two criteria that can be used in judging whether something should be provided by governments: *nonexclusion* and *nonrivalrous* (*shared consumption*).

Nonexclusion

In some situations people cannot be excluded from the benefits of a good or service even if they do not pay for it. If only some of the people paid for national defense, for example, others could not be excluded from the benefits of national defense if it is provided. The nonpurchasers of national defense would be protected just as much as the purchasers. People who receive the benefit of a good but don't pay for it are called *free riders*.

Nonrivalrous (Shared Consumption or Joint Use)

In some situations one person's use or consumption of a good or service does not reduce its usefulness to others. The security one person receives from a street light is not diminished by a neighbor receiving the same security. The protection the street light provides is not reduced by additional people using it.

Private businesses will not produce things that people are not willing to buy, and individual consumers are reluctant to pay for goods and services from which others who do not pay will reap the benefits: "Why should I be the one to buy the street light if everyone else also is getting the benefits?" Governments therefore must provide some goods and services such as national defense, flood control, and judicial and legal systems that are characterized by shared consumption and are necessarily or should be nonexclusive. Public goods are goods that are provided by government and will not be provided by the private sector.

Private and Public Goods

Pure private goods are subject to exclusion and rivalry. Nonbuyers cannot consume the good, and if one person consumes a unit of the good, someone else cannot consume that unit. They are purchased directly in the marketplace. *Pure public goods* are subject to nonexclusion and shared consumption. They are purchased indirectly through tax dollars.

Some goods have elements of both private goods and public goods. Fishing in the ocean, for example, is generally not subject to exclusion; but once one person catches a fish, it is not available to others. Likewise, it is sometimes possible to exclude people from theaters, national parks, or even roads by charging admission fees or tolls. But one person camping in a park or driving on a highway usually does not reduce the usefulness of these places to others. Controversy often arises over how these *mixed goods*—sometimes called *common-pool resources* and *toll goods*—should be provided and who should pay for them. Some goods do not fall into neat boxes, but show degrees of nonexclusion and shared consumption.

Table 5-1.1
Combinations of Exclusion and Shared Consumption

		Shared consumption	
		No	Yes
Exclusion	Yes	Pure private goods: haircuts, bread, ice cream	Toll goods: theaters, cable TV, parks, toll roads
	No	Common-pool resources: fish taken from the ocean, irrigation water taken from a river, congested roads	Pure public goods: national defense, flood control, street lights, mosquito abatement, judicial and legal system

1. What is the difference between the private and public sectors of our economy?

2. What are the characteristics of a pure private good?

3. What are the characteristics of a pure public good?

4. Place each of the goods and services in the list below into one of the four boxes in Table 5-1.2.

Circle the box that contains pure private goods. Then draw two circles around the box that contains pure public goods.

(A) A college education

(B) Electric power

(C) A haircut

(D) National defense

(E) A private amusement park

(F) Spraying for mosquitoes

(G) Cable television

(H) Canine rabies shots

(I) Street lights

(J) The Panama Canal

(K) Public toll roads and bridges

(L) Police and fire protection

(M) Health care

(N) National forest campgrounds

(O) Potato chips

(P) Auto airbags

Table 5-1.2

Determining Combinations of Exclusion and Shared Consumption

		Shared consumption	
		No	Yes
Exclusion	Yes		
	No		

5. What is a free rider? Select three goods from the list in Question 4 that could have free riders.

Externalities

A *market externality* refers to a situation where some of the costs or benefits from an activity fall on someone other than the people directly involved in the activity. Externalities may be either positive (the activity provides a benefit to someone else) or negative (the activity places a cost on someone else). Costs that fall on someone else are called *external costs*, and benefits that fall on someone else are called *external benefits*. These external effects of an activity are also called *social spillover costs* and *social spillover benefits*, or *third-party costs* and *third-party benefits*.

The demand curve for a good or service shows the *marginal private benefit (MPB)* to those individuals who are consuming the product. It shows how many units will be demanded by consumers at different prices. The demand curve also shows the highest prices consumers will pay for different quantities of the product. The supply curve of a good or service shows the *marginal private cost (MPC)* to those individuals who are producing the product. It shows how many units will be supplied by producers at different prices. The supply curve also shows the lowest prices producers will accept for different quantities of the product.

If there are no positive externalities associated with the activity, then the marginal private benefit from an additional unit will be equal to the *marginal social benefit (MSB)*. The marginal social benefit shows the benefit to society from an extra unit of the activity. If no one other than the person associated with the activity receives any benefit from the extra unit, then MPB = MSB.

If there are no negative externalities associated with the activity, then the marginal private cost from an additional unit will be equal to the *marginal social cost (MSC)*. The marginal social cost shows the cost to society from an extra unit of the activity. If no one other than the person associated with the activity incurs any cost from the extra unit, then MPC = MSC.

Consumers of a product buy according to their marginal private benefits as shown by the demand curve, and producers of the item produce according to their marginal private costs as shown by the supply curve. The equilibrium quantity of the product in a perfectly competitive market will be the quantity where MPB = MPC. This is where the market demand curve intersects the market supply curve. *If there are no externalities, the competitive market output is the socially optimal (efficient) quantity because it is where MSB = MSC.* Society feels the market is producing exactly the right amount of the product. Given the marginal benefit society is receiving from the last unit, it feels the correct amount of its scarce resources is being allocated to the provision of that unit.

The competitive market results in *market failures*, however, if there are positive or negative externalities associated with the consumption or production of the good or service. These spillover benefits or costs, if not corrected, will result in the market producing either too much or too little of the activity from society's perspective. The externalities drive a wedge between the MSB and the MPB, or between the MSC and the MPC. Because the market will produce the output where MPB = MPC, these differences yield a quantity of the product at which MSB is not equal to MSC. We often turn to the government to attempt to correct these market failures.

To understand how externalities can result in market failures, it is important that you know these relationships:

■ Marginal Social Benefit = Marginal Private Benefit + Marginal External Benefit

$$MSB = MPB + MEB$$

■ Marginal Social Cost = Marginal Private Cost + Marginal External Cost

$$MSC = MPC + MEC$$

Summary of key points:

■ Society wants a market to produce the quantity where MSB = MSC.

■ Private decision makers want to have the quantity where MPB = MPC.

■ As long as MEB and MEC are zero (no externalities), the market quantity will be the socially optimal (efficient) quantity.

■ If MEB or MEC is not zero, we will have a market failure.

🛈 *Student Alert:* **Some textbooks use slightly different approaches to the topic of externalities. While the end results with regard to the effects of externalities are the same, be sure you understand the approach and terminology that are being used.**

Part A: How Much Music?

Figure 5-2.1
External Benefits

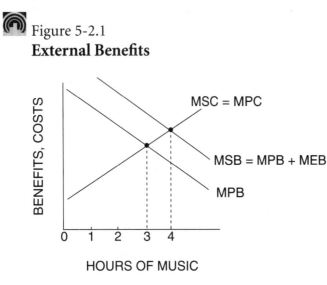

1. Margaret has Wendy as her roommate in a college residence hall. Wendy has brought an expensive stereo system to play in the room. Figure 5-2.1 shows Wendy's MPB and MPC curves for music played on the stereo system. Based on Figure 5-2.1, answer the following questions.

   (A) If Wendy considers only the MPB and MPC from playing music, how many hours of music will be played? Label the number of hours in Figure 5-2.1 as Q_p to indicate the private market quantity.

   (B) Assume that Wendy plays music only at times that do not disturb Margaret and plays only music that Margaret also enjoys. The "MSB = MPB + MEB" curve in Figure 5-2.1 shows the MSB from the music, including the MEB to Margaret. If Wendy considers the MSB from playing music rather than only the MPB, what happens to the quantity of music played? Label the number of hours as Q_s in Figure 5-2.1 to indicate the socially optimal quantity.

   (C) In Figure 5-2.1, what does the vertical gap between the MSB and MPB curves represent?

   (D) Assuming there are no external costs from the music, when Wendy does not consider the MEB from playing music, the number of hours played is (*greater than / equal to / less than*) the socially efficient number of hours.

Figure 5-2.2
External Costs

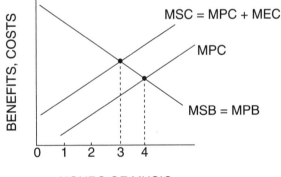

2. Again, Wendy has a new stereo system and Margaret is her roommate.

   (A) In Figure 5-2.2, assume Wendy only considers her MPB and MPC from music. How many hours of music will be played? Label the number of hours in Figure 5-2.2 as Q_p to indicate the private market quantity.

   (B) Now assume that Wendy plays music only at times that Margaret is trying to study and plays only music that Margaret hates. In Figure 5-2.2, the "MSC = MPC + MEC" curve shows the MSC from the music, including the MEC to Margaret. If Wendy considers the MSC from playing music rather than only the MPC, what happens to the quantity of music played? Label the number of hours as Q_s in Figure 5-2.2 to indicate the socially optimal quantity.

   (C) In Figure 5-2.2, what does the vertical gap between the MSC and MPC curves represent?

(D) Assuming there are no external benefits from the music, when Wendy does not consider the MEC from playing music, the number of hours played is (*greater than / equal to / less than*) the socially efficient number of hours.

3. How can government regulation (in this case, residence hall rules) assure the efficient quantity of music? Consider the circumstances under which prohibiting stereos or imposing daily "quiet hours" are efficient ways to regulate stereo use in the hall. Does economics suggest a more efficient approach to stereo regulation?

Part B: More Externalities Examples

4. For each of these activities, explain whether there is a positive or negative externality.

(A) Private high school education

(B) Smog from an electric power plant

(C) Your neighbor's yappy dog

(D) Pre-kindergarten measles vaccinations

Part C: Applying Your Knowledge of Externalities

The Women's National Basketball Association (WNBA) is considering awarding a new franchise to the city of Metropolis, but only if the team has a new arena in which to play. Proponents of the franchise argue that the team will generate new businesses, provide jobs, increase tax revenue, and promote tourism in Metropolis. Opponents argue that most of the money spent on basketball games will come from Metropolis-area residents who will simply reduce their spending on other activities. The opponents claim there will be few new jobs, little increase in tax revenue, and few new tourists coming to Metropolis. They also say the new arena will cause property values to fall in the area and create traffic congestion and noise pollution.

Voters have the following three proposals before them:

Proposal #1: No city money should be used to construct the arena. Team owners should pay the full cost of building the facility and include that cost in the price of game tickets.

Proposal #2: The city should place a tax on each ticket sold to pay the full cost of the arena.

Proposal #3: The city should build the arena and lease the right to play there to the basketball club at a subsidized rate.

For the analysis that follows, assume the output of the team is the number of tickets sold.

5. What assumption does Proposal #1 make about external costs and external benefits associated with the new franchise?

Figure 5-2.3 can be used to illustrate the position of opponents to the franchise. Answer the following questions based on this graph.

 Figure 5-2.3
Social Spillover Costs

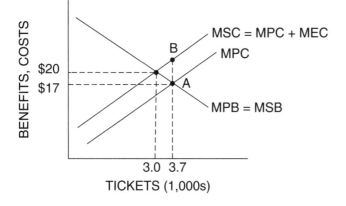

6. What assumption is made about social spillover benefits from the franchise? Explain.

7. What assumption is made about social spillover costs from the franchise? Explain.

8. How many tickets will be sold based on the MPB and MPC?

9. What is the socially optimal number of tickets?

10. What does the vertical gap "AB" represent?

11. What can the Metropolis city government do to make the market output be equal to the socially efficient output? Explain, using the graph to illustrate your answer.

Figure 5-2.4 can be used to illustrate the position of supporters of the franchise. Answer the following questions based on this graph.

 Figure 5-2.4
Social Spillover Benefits

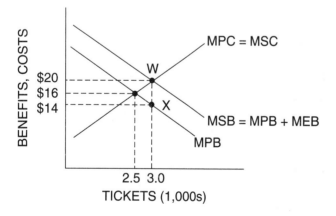

12. What assumption is made about social spillover benefits from the franchise? Explain.

13. What assumption is made about social spillover costs from the franchise? Explain.

14. How many tickets will be sold based on the MPB and MPC?

15. What is the socially optimal number of tickets?

16. What does the vertical gap "WX" represent?

17. What can the Metropolis city government do to make the market output be equal to the socially efficient output? Explain, using the graph to illustrate your answer.

Part D: Per Unit or Lump Sum? Which Type of Tax or Subsidy to Use?

🛈 *Student Alert:* **Which form of a tax or subsidy should the government use to correct the effects of an externality? Should it apply a per-unit or a lump-sum adjustment?**

Figure 5-2.5 shows the average total cost (ATC), average variable cost (AVC), marginal cost (MC), demand (D), marginal revenue (MR), and average revenue (AR) functions of a perfectly competitive firm. The firm is producing Q_1 units because that is where MR = MC. Assume there is a negative externality associated with the firm's product and the government would like to have the firm reduce its output.

Figure 5-2.5

A Profit-Maximizing Perfectly Competitive Firm

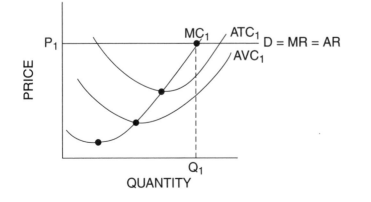

18. Suppose the government places a per-unit tax of "t" on the firm's product. Which cost measures will be affected by this per-unit tax: ATC, AVC, average fixed cost (AFC), or MC? Show in Figure 5-2.6 how the cost curves will look after the tax is imposed. What happens to the output level the firm wants to produce? Was the per-unit tax successful in having the firm reduce its quantity?

Figure 5-2.6
The Government Levies a Per-Unit Tax of "t"

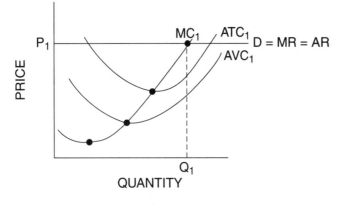

19. Suppose the government places a one-time, lump-sum tax of "T" on the firm's product. Which of these cost measures will be affected by this lump-sum tax: ATC, AVC, AFC, or MC? Show in Figure 5-2.7 how the graph will look after the tax is imposed. What happens to the output level the firm wants to produce? Was the lump-sum tax successful in having the firm reduce its quantity?

Figure 5-2.7
The Government Levies a Lump-Sum Tax of "T"

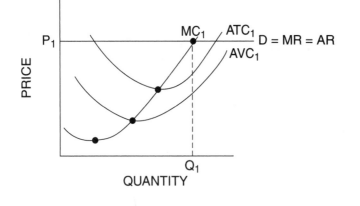

Advanced Placement Economics Microeconomics: Student Resource Manual © Council for Economic Education, New York, N.Y.

20. Assume a firm produces a product for which there is a positive externality. As an incentive to the firm to produce more of its product, should the government give the firm a per-unit subsidy or a lump-sum subsidy? Explain.

Part E: Summary

21. When positive externalities are involved, private markets produce (*more than / exactly / less than*) the socially optimal amount of the product.

22. When negative externalities are involved, private markets produce (*more than / exactly / less than*) the socially optimal amount of the product.

23. Why do economists say the presence of an externality results in a market failure?

24. How can a tax be used to remedy a negative externality?

25. How can a subsidy mitigate an inefficient output level in the presence of a positive externality?

Private or Public? The Coase Theorem

When an activity results in a negative externality (external cost), the market outcome will not be efficient. In these cases, the government may choose to intervene in the market and impose some form of regulation, for example, a legal restriction or a tax. If the external cost the activity creates is borne by those who conduct the activity, the market outcome will be efficient.

For example, if a firm dumps its waste into a river, it pollutes the river and creates a negative externality (external cost) for those downstream. The government may intervene to restrict dumping in the river, or it may impose an effluent tax (a tax on each unit of pollution released into the river). If the firm is forced to pay for the pollution it releases into the river, it will dump less. A sufficiently high tax will lead to the optimal reduction in river pollution from the firm. Thus, the firm has internalized the externality.

However, in some situations, it may not be necessary to regulate a market to achieve an efficient outcome. It may be possible for the parties affected by an externality to negotiate an efficient outcome on their own. For example, if people who use the river downstream can negotiate with the polluting firm, they may be willing to pay the firm to stop polluting. This idea is embodied in the *Coase Theorem*, which states that if those who are affected by an externality can negotiate, they may arrive at an efficient solution to the externality problem.

Two firms are involved in a dispute. Grunge, Inc., a manufacturing firm, pollutes a nearby river. The pollution travels downstream past White Water Expeditions, a company that provides river rafting trips. Dumping its waste into the river cuts Grunge's waste-disposal costs, while decreasing the number of people who want to raft on the river. The total profits of the two firms (both with and without waste dumping) are shown in Table 5-3.1.

Table 5-3.1
Total Profits per Month

	With dumping	Without dumping
Grunge, Inc.	$2,300	$2,000
White Water Expeditions	$1,500	$2,000

1. What are the total returns to both companies with and without dumping? Which situation (dumping or no dumping) is socially optimal—in other words, provides the highest combined returns?

2. If there is no government intervention in the market, and the two companies do not communicate, will Grunge dump waste into the river? Why or why not?

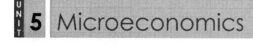
3. What is the cost to Grunge not to dump waste into the river?

4. What is the cost of the pollution to White Water each month? How much would White Water be willing to pay Grunge to stop dumping waste into the river?

5. If Grunge and White Water could negotiate, at no cost, could they come to an agreement that would eliminate the externality problem and result in the efficient outcome? If not, why not? If so, what would be the payment from White Water to Grunge?

6. Does it matter who has the property right: Grunge to dump or White Water to have clean water? Explain.

Economic Efficiency and the Optimum Amount of Pollution Cleanup

Student Alert: Does it make sound economic sense to clean up all pollution?

The human and environmental damage caused by industrial pollution often arouses public attention. Although it might be nice to restore our environment to its pristine state, pollution cleanup is costly and dollars used for cleanup might be spent elsewhere. It seems, then, that some sort of balance must be struck between undesirable pollution and its costly cleanup. Let's apply marginal analysis to determine an optimal amount of pollution and environmental cleanup.

The marginal social benefit (MSB) of cleaning up pollution tends to decline as additional units of pollution are cleaned up. The marginal social cost (MSC) of cleaning up pollution tends to increase as additional units of pollution are cleaned up. If society has accurate information about the total social (public and private) benefits and costs of various amounts of cleanup, society should be able to get close to the most efficient, or optimum, level of cleanup (and/or pollution) where the marginal social benefits equal the marginal social costs (MSB = MSC).

Imagine a community in which two firms emit foul sludge into two local lakes (one for each firm). Natural processes gradually break down the sludge, rendering it harmless. But as long as emissions continue, a certain equilibrium level of harmful sludge remains in the lake. If emissions are lowered, this equilibrium level will be reduced. The opposite occurs if emissions are increased. Currently each firm emits five units of sludge each week.

Given the information in Tables 5-4.1 and 5-4.2, you should be able to determine the optimal level of emissions for this community. Fill in the blanks in the tables, and use this information to answer Questions 1 through 4. Assume that benefits obtained and costs incurred for cleanup at one lake have no impact on costs and benefits at the other lake.

Table 5-4.1

Firm 1

Reduction of foul sludge emissions	Total social benefit of cleanup	Marginal social benefit of cleanup	Total social cost of cleanup	Marginal social cost of cleanup
0	$0	—	$0	—
1	$350	$350	$160	$160
2	$650		$370	
3	$900		$630	
4	$1,100		$940	
5	$1,250		$1,300	

1. Using the data from Table 5-4.1, fill in the blanks or underline the correct words in parentheses.

   (A) The marginal social benefit (MSB) of reducing emissions by the first unit of foul sludge is $_____, and the marginal social cost (MSC) of reducing pollution emissions by the first unit is $_____. The MSB is (*greater than / equal to / less than*) the MSC, so it (*would / would not*) be economically efficient from society's perspective to require Firm 1 to reduce pollution emission by the first unit.

   (B) The MSB of eliminating the last (fifth) unit of foul sludge is $_____, and the MSC of reducing pollution emissions by the last (fifth) unit is $_____. The MSB is (*greater than / equal to / less than*) the MSC, so it (*would / would not*) be economically efficient from society's perspective to require Firm 1 to reduce pollution emission by the fifth unit.

Table 5-4.2
Firm 2

Reduction of foul sludge emissions	Total social benefit of cleanup	Marginal social benefit of cleanup	Total social cost of cleanup	Marginal social cost of cleanup
0	$0	—	$0	—
1	$350	$350	$130	$130
2	$650		$280	
3	$900		$450	
4	$1,100		$640	
5	$1,250		$850	

2. Using the data from Table 5-4.2, fill in the blanks or underline the correct words in parentheses.

   (A) The MSB of eliminating the fourth unit of foul sludge is $_____, and the MSC of reducing pollution emissions by this fourth unit is $_____. The MSB is (*greater than / equal to / less than*) the MSC, so it (*would / would not*) be economically efficient from society's perspective to require Firm 2 to reduce pollution emissions by four units.

   (B) The MSB of eliminating the fifth (last) unit of foul sludge is $_____, and the MSC of reducing pollution emissions by this fifth (last) unit is $_____. The MSB is (*greater than / equal to / less than*) the MSC, so it (*would / would not*) be economically efficient from society's perspective to require Firm 2 to reduce pollution emissions by five units.

3. If this community decides to adopt a pollution control ordinance aimed at maximizing economic efficiency, how should it evaluate each of the following three proposals, all of which are based on the data presented above? Write a brief economic evaluation in the space provided after each of the proposals. Be sure to use the concepts of marginal social benefit and marginal social cost in your analysis.

Proposal A. "Foul sludge emissions should be reduced (by five units) to zero for each firm because we should eliminate all pollution from our lakes regardless of the cost."

This proposal (*would / would not*) maximize economic efficiency.

Proposal B. "Firm 2 should be forced to reduce emissions from five units to zero because the total social benefit of cleanup ($1,250) exceeds the total social cost of cleaning up ($850). But Firm 1 should not be forced to clean up at all, because the total social benefit of cleanup ($1,250) is less than the total social cost of reducing emissions to zero ($1,300)."

This proposal (*would / would not*) maximize economic efficiency.

Proposal C. "In the interest of equal treatment for all, each firm should be forced to clean up (reduce emissions) by three units."

This proposal (*would / would not*) maximize economic efficiency.

4. Using the data presented above, what do you think is the socially optimal level of emissions reduction for each firm? Explain why you chose these numbers.

   Firm 1: _____ units

   Firm 2: _____ units

5. What would you say to someone who makes the following statement? "Society should do all it can to eliminate all pollution."

What Is a Fair Tax?

Almost everyone is concerned about how much we pay in taxes. The best way to determine how much tax you pay is to state your tax as an *effective tax rate*. An effective tax rate is the percentage of your income you pay in taxes. This differs from a *nominal tax rate* or *legal tax rate*. For example, a sales tax rate may be 5 percent (the nominal rate), but this does not mean that all people pay 5 percent of their income in sales taxes. Outlays for rent, insurance, and medical bills, among other things, may not be subject to sales taxes. Neither, of course, are savings.

Let's look at the effective tax rate of Joanne Walters. If she made $30,000 a year and paid $6,000 in taxes, her effective tax rate would be 20 percent. You can figure this by dividing $6,000 by $30,000:

$$\frac{\$\ 6,000}{\$30,000} = 20\%.$$

There are three kinds of effective tax rates. If a tax is *progressive*, the effective tax rate increases as a person's income goes up. For example, a person who makes $30,000 a year may have an effective tax rate of 10 percent, while a person who makes $45,000 a year may have an effective rate of 18 percent.

If a tax is *proportional*, the effective tax rate stays the same regardless of income. In this case, a person making $30,000 a year and a person making $45,000 a year would both be taxed at an effective rate of, say, 10 percent. Of course, the person making $45,000 a year would pay more total dollars in taxes. A proportional tax is sometimes called a *flat tax*.

If a tax is *regressive*, the effective tax rate decreases as income goes up. For example, a person making $30,000 a year might pay an effective tax rate of 10 percent, while a person who makes $45,000 a year might pay an effective tax rate of 8 percent.

Now answer these questions to see if you understand progressive, proportional, and regressive tax rates.

1. A tax that requires each person to pay 3 percent of income regardless of the level of income is
   a _____ tax.

2. A tax levied at 1 percent on the first $1,000 of income, 2 percent on the next $1,000, and so on is
   a _____ tax.

3. A tax levied at 15 percent on the first $1,000 of income, 12 percent on the next $1,000, and so on is
   a _____ tax.

4. If it is true that a person with an income of $20,000 a year typically buys 10 gallons of gasoline per week and a person with an income of $40,000 typically buys 15 gallons of gasoline per week, this suggests that an excise tax of 40 cents per gallon would be a _____ tax. Explain.

5. Rick Morales has an income of $50,000 but spends only $40,000 on taxable goods. Chet Burton has an income of $25,000 and spends it all on taxable goods. Assuming an 8 percent sales tax, Mr. Morales will pay $_____ in sales taxes, which is _____ percent of his total income. On the other hand, Mr. Burton will pay $_____ in sales taxes, which is _____ percent of his total income. Therefore, we can conclude that the sales tax is (*progressive / proportional / regressive*).

6. Since the sales tax has the same nominal or legal rate based on sales, why is it regressive? What steps could be taken to make it less regressive?

7. Suppose that the government runs a pension fund to which all workers must contribute. The employee contribution rate is 6.2 percent on the first $84,900 of income. All income in excess of $84,900 is not taxed for pension purposes.

   (A) What is the effective pension tax rate for a person earning $20,000 a year? _____

   (B) What is the effective pension tax rate for a person earning $84,900? _____

   (C) What is the effective pension tax rate for a person earning $169,800? _____

   (D) Therefore, the pension tax is a (*progressive / proportional / regressive*) tax up to $84,900 of income. For incomes above $_____, the tax is (*progressive / proportional / regressive*).

   (E) In addition to the pension tax, assume people must pay 1.45 percent of their income for medical benefits. There is no income limit on the medical care tax. Does this make the total tax for pension and medical care more or less regressive? Why?

Advanced Placement Economics Microeconomics: Student Resource Manual © Council for Economic Education, New York, N.Y.

Who Pays the Income Tax?

Who actually pays the income tax? Do "the rich" escape paying their "fair" share of taxes? Is most of the income tax paid by middle-income people? Who are the rich? These questions are important for several reasons:

- Taxes can redistribute income. Like Robin Hood, government can tax the rich and redistribute this money to the poor. Instead of money, most tax revenue is redistributed in the form of college scholarships, food stamps, medical care, housing assistance, and other services for lower-income families. While the merits of these programs can be debated, almost no one would agree that a "Robin Hood in reverse" policy would be beneficial: taxing the poor and redistributing tax revenue to the wealthy.

- Some people think taxes should have *vertical equity*, that is, the tax burden should be distributed fairly across people according to their ability to pay. This argument for progressive taxation maintains that the rich have more ability to pay taxes, and therefore should bear a larger tax burden than low-income families.

- Some people think that income should be distributed more equally than it is today.

Part A: Examining the Tax Data

Tables 5-6.1 and 5-6.2 contain information regarding shares of income, taxes, and tax rates for federal income tax returns for 1997 and 2009. Use the tables to answer the questions that follow.

Table 5-6.1
Federal Income Tax Return Data: 2009

Percent of all taxpayers	Income range	Group's share of total income (adjusted gross income)	Group's share of total income taxes	Group's average tax rate
Top 1%	Above $343,927	16.9%	36.7%	24.0%
Top 5%	Above $154,643	31.7%	58.7%	20.5%
Top 10%	Above $112,124	43.2%	70.5%	18.1%
Top 25%	Above $66,193	65.8%	87.3%	14.7%
Top 50%	Above $32,396	86.5%	97.7%	12.5%
Bottom 50%	Below $32,396	13.5%	2.3%	1.8%
All taxpayers		100.0%	100.0%	11.1%

Source: Tax Foundation

 Table 5-6.2

Federal Income Tax Return Data: 1997

Percent of all taxpayers	Income range	Group's share of total income (adjusted gross income)	Group's share of total income taxes	Group's average tax rate
Top 1%	Above $250,736	17.4%	33.2%	27.6%
Top 5%	Above $108,048	31.8%	51.9%	23.6%
Top 10%	Above $79,212	42.8%	63.2%	21.4%
Top 25%	Above $48,173	65.0%	81.7%	18.2%
Top 50%	Above $24,393	86.2%	95.7%	16.1%
Bottom 50%	Below $24,393	13.8%	4.3%	4.5%
All taxpayers		100.0%	100.0%	14.5%

Source: Tax Foundation

1. Suppose you define "the rich" as the top 10 percent of all income earners. In 2009, what was the minimum income you had to earn to be "rich"?

2. What percentage of total income taxes did the top 1 percent of income earners pay in 2009?

3. In 2009, what percentage of total income taxes was paid by the bottom half of all income earners?

4. In 2009, the average U.S. taxpayer paid 11.1 percent of his/her income in taxes. Based on the information in the table, would you classify the U.S. income tax system as progressive, proportional, or regressive? Why?

5. Compare 1997 with 2009. What is the best description of what happened to the income tax burden in the United States over this 12-year period?

Part B: Equity Questions

Many people are concerned that "the rich are getting richer and the poor are getting poorer." Using the income tax data from Tables 5-6.1 and 5-6.2, answer the following questions.

6. Is there evidence that the rich got richer and the poor got poorer between 1997 and 2009? Explain.

7. Some politicians argue that the wealthy are not paying their "fair" share of taxes. Based on the data in the two tables, do you agree or disagree? Explain.

8. Would you argue that the U.S. income tax system promotes or hinders greater income equality? Why?

The Lorenz Curve and Gini Coefficient

The labor markets often fail to allocate income equally. Some households earn much income while many more earn little income. Differences in worker productivity, varying trade patterns, patterns of past discrimination, and tax policies are some of the reasons for what economists call *income inequality*. For example, increased demand for workers with at least bachelor's degrees and decreased demand for workers with only high school diplomas have resulted in income inequality as college-educated laborers' income has risen and high school-educated laborers' income has fallen.

Two important measures of income inequality are the Lorenz curve and the Gini coefficient. The *Lorenz curve* is a graph of income inequality that shows what percentage of a country's income is being earned by a percentage of the country's households.

Figure 5-7.1
Lorenz Curve #1

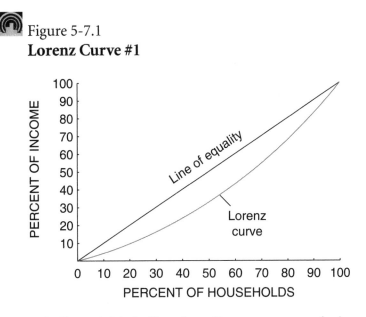

In Figure 5-7.1, the line of equality represents a perfectly even distribution of income. A perfectly even distribution means that 10 percent of the households earn 10 percent of the income, 20 percent of the households earn 20 percent of the income, and so on. The Lorenz curve shows the actual distribution of income. The closer the Lorenz curve is to the line of equality, the more evenly distributed is the income. The more the Lorenz curve sags away from the line of equality, then the more unevenly income is distributed. Figure 5-7.2 shows more income inequality than Figure 5-7.1.

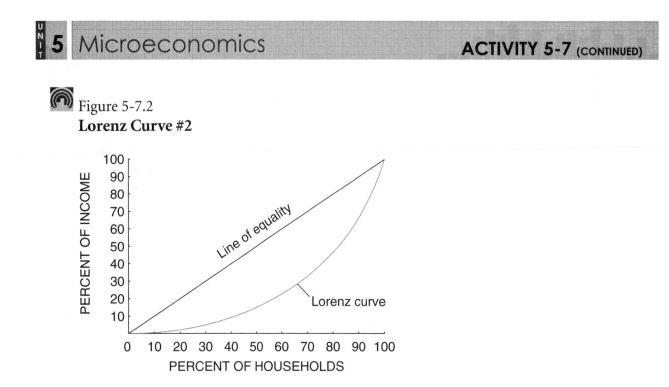
Figure 5-7.2
Lorenz Curve #2

1. In Figure 5-7.3, determine the amount of income that is being earned by 50 percent of the households in the country of Maxopia.

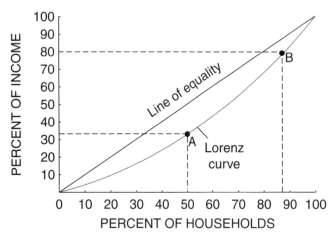

Figure 5-7.3
Lorenz Curve for the Country of Maxopia

2. Now, determine the percentage of income being earned by 88 percent of the households.

3. Using Figure 5-7.4, determine the percentage of income being earned by 50 percent of the households and then by 88 percent of the households in the country of Minopia. You may want to use a ruler to help you.

(A) 50 percent of households earn _____ of the income.

(B) 88 percent of households earn _____ of the income.

Figure 5-7.4
Lorenz Curve for the Country of Minopia

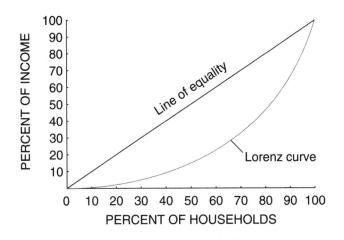

4. Compare your results from Questions 1 and 2 with your results from Questions 3A and 3B. Which country has more income equality—Maxopia or Minopia?

2. In Figure 3-11.1, draw the monopolist's D, AR, MR, and ATC curves using the data from Table 3-11.1. Plot the MR and MC values at the higher of the two output levels rather than at the midpoint between the two levels. Use dotted lines for the MR and MC curves in your graph. Label each curve.

Figure 3-11.1
Revenue and Cost Curves of a Monopolist

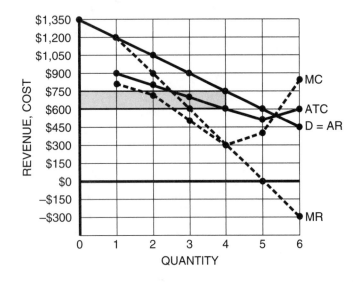

3. To maximize its total profit, this monopolist should produce __**4**__ units.
   The first three units have MR > MC. The fourth unit has MR = MC. Subsequent units have MR < MC and should not be produced.

4. What price should the monopolist charge for each of these units?
   The highest price the firm can charge for four units is $750. This price is found on the D curve.

5. What is the total profit this firm will earn? __**$600**__ Shade in the total profit area in Figure 3-11.1.
   The AΠ for four units is $150: AΠ = AR – ATC = $750 – $600.

   TΠ = (Q)(AΠ) = (4)($150) = $600.

Part B: Other Monopoly Examples

6. Suppose a monopolist can sell an extra unit of its good at a price of $50 and the MR of that unit is $44. If the MC of producing the extra unit is $46, the firm's total profit would (*increase* / ***decrease***) by __**$2**__ if the firm sells that unit. Should the firm produce this additional unit of output? Explain your answer.
   The firm should not produce the extra unit because its MR is less than its MC. This unit has a marginal profit of –$2 which means the firm's total profit would decrease by $2 if it sold that unit. The firm compares MR to MC, not P to MC, to decide if an extra unit should be produced.

Circle the letter of each correct answer.

1. Which of the following characterizes a public good?

    (A) People who do not pay for the good can be excluded from using it.

    (B) If one person uses the good, it does not prevent others from using it.

    (C) It is easy to determine who must pay for the good.

    (D) The good exhibits negative externalities.

    (E) The good exhibits positive externalities.

2. The free rider problem is associated with

    (A) all market goods.

    (B) goods that are exclusionary.

    (C) bus transportation.

    (D) the production of public goods.

    (E) the production of public transportation.

3. Which of the following best meets the criteria of a public good?

    (A) A phone card

    (B) An airline ticket

    (C) National defense

    (D) A college education

    (E) A restaurant

4. The market system fails to produce public goods because

    (A) there is no need or demand for such goods.

    (B) private firms cannot restrict the benefits of such goods only to consumers who are willing to pay for them.

    (C) public enterprises can produce such goods at lower cost than can private enterprises.

    (D) their production seriously distorts the distribution of income.

    (E) a person unwilling to pay can be excluded from the benefits that the product provides.

5. Which of the following are economic functions of government?

    I. Enforcing laws and contracts

    II. Providing public goods

    III. Correcting market failures *externalities*

    (A) I only

    (B) II only

    (C) III only

    (D) II and III only

    (E) I, II, and III

6. In a market economy, the distribution of income is

    (A) equitable because people who are willing to work earn income.

    (B) primarily determined by the prices of scarce resources people own.

    (C) primarily determined by the government through its power to tax.

    (D) based on need.

    (E) always more equal than in a command economy.

7. If the production of a good creates negative externalities, the private market will produce

    (A) too much of the good at too low a price.

    (B) too much of the good at too high a price.

    (C) too little of the good at too high a price.

    (D) too little of the good at too low a price.

    (E) the right amount of the good at the correct price.

8. If the production of a good creates positive externalities, the private market will produce

    (A) too much of the good at too high a price.

    (B) too much of the good at too low a price.

    (C) too little of the good at too low a price.

    (D) too little of the good at too high a price.

    (E) the right amount of the good at the correct price.

Use the supply and demand graph below to answer Questions 9, 10, and 11. In the graph, S_1 shows the marginal private cost to producers of the product, S_2 shows the marginal social cost, and D shows both the marginal private benefit and the marginal social benefit.

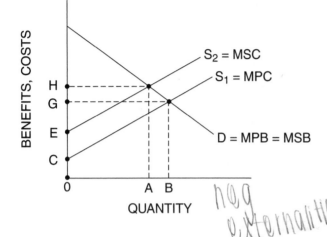

neg externalities

9. Based on the graph

   (A) the market will produce A units, which is the socially efficient quantity.

   (B) the market will produce B units, which is the socially efficient quantity.

   (C) the market will produce A units while the socially efficient quantity is B.

   (D) the market will produce B units while the socially efficient quantity is A.

   (E) we cannot determine the socially efficient quantity.

10. One solution to the externality problem in this market is to

    (A) give consumers a subsidy equal to H – G.

    (B) give producers a subsidy of the amount C – 0.

    (C) tax producers by the amount E – C.

    (D) tax producers by the amount H – G.

    (E) tax consumers by the amount H – C.

11. If the government corrects this externality problem with a tax so that all costs are included in the cost of producing the item, then the product price will be

    (A) C.   (D) H.

    (B) E.   (E) H – G.

    (C) G.

Use the supply and demand graph below to answer Questions 12 and 13. In the graph, D_1 shows the marginal private benefit to consumers of the product, D_2 shows the marginal social benefit, and S shows both the marginal private cost and the marginal social cost.

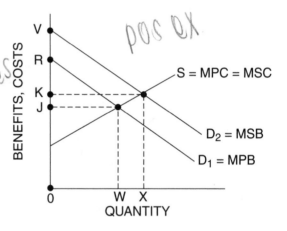

pos ex

12. Based on the graph

    (A) the market will produce W units, which is the socially efficient quantity.

    (B) the market will produce X units, which is the socially efficient quantity.

    (C) the market will produce W units while the socially efficient quantity is X.

    (D) the market will produce X units while the socially efficient quantity is W.

    (E) we cannot determine the socially efficient quantity.

13. One solution to the externality problem in this market is to

    (A) give consumers a subsidy equal to K – J.

    (B) give producers a subsidy of the amount V – R.

    (C) give producers a subsidy of the amount R – K.

    (D) tax producers by the amount R – J.

    (E) tax consumers by the amount J – 0.

14. Which of the following best summarizes most economists' position on allocating resources to control pollution?

    (A) All forms of air and water pollution should be eliminated.

    (B) Government policies to reduce pollution have zero opportunity costs.

    (C) Pollution should be reduced to the point where the marginal social cost of pollution control equals the marginal social benefit of pollution control.

    (D) Pollution should be reduced to the point where the total social cost of pollution control equals the total social benefit of pollution control.

    (E) Pollution should be reduced to the point where the average social cost of pollution control equals the average social benefit of pollution control.

15. Public-choice theory is based on the idea that

    (A) self-interest motivates participants only in the private sector of the economy.

    (B) self-interest motivates participants only in the public sector of the economy.

    (C) self-interest motivates participants in both the public and private sectors of the economy.

    (D) the interests of society are the main interest of participants in the public sector of the economy.

    (E) the interests of society are the main interest of participants in the private sector of the economy.

16. Government may attempt to reduce income inequality by doing which of the following?

    I.   Provide transfer payments to the poor

    II. Directly influence market prices, such as establishing a minimum wage

    III. Tax high-income earners at a higher rate than low-income earners

    (A) I only   (D) I and II only

    (B) II only   (E) I, II, and III

    (C) III only

17. Which of the following is the best example of a tax based on the ability-to-pay theory of taxation?

    (A) Sales tax

    (B) Property tax

    (C) Excise tax on gasoline

    (D) Federal income tax

    (E) Highway tolls

18. In which of the following taxes is the benefits-received principle of taxation most evident?

    (A) Corporation income tax

    (B) Personal income tax

    (C) Excise tax on gasoline

    (D) Inheritance taxes

    (E) Progressive tax rates

19. Which of the following taxes is considered regressive?

    (A) Sales tax

    (B) Personal income tax

    (C) Corporation income tax

    (D) Federal estate tax

    (E) Inheritance taxes

20. An excise tax will generate the most revenue for government if

    (A) demand is unit elastic.

    (B) demand is elastic.

    (C) demand is inelastic.

    (D) supply is inelastic.

    (E) supply is perfectly elastic.

21. "The President's proposal to increase the federal tax on gasoline is intended to reduce the amount of gasoline purchased and raise more revenue." The second goal would be best served (and the first goal least served) if the demand for gasoline were which of the following?

    (A) Unit elastic

    (B) Relatively elastic

    (C) Relatively inelastic

    (D) Perfectly inelastic

    (E) Decreased by the tax

22. A motel owner is upset that the scenic view provided by the neighboring wooded property will be destroyed because the property's owner plans to cut and sell the trees to a commercial lumber company. The Coase Theorem suggests that this dispute could be resolved by

    (A) a law passed by the government.

    (B) a zoning ordinance against commercial lumbering.

    (C) the owners themselves.

    (D) a government fine for cutting trees.

    (E) an environmental campaign against altering wildlife habitat.

23. If the government increases the amount of government insurance on bank deposits, this action would

    (A) increase the probability of adverse selection.

    (B) lessen the probability of adverse selection.

    (C) increase the probability of a moral hazard problem.

    (D) lessen the probability of a moral hazard problem.

    (E) eliminate the probability of adverse selection or moral hazard.

24. Which of these statements indicates that a country has a more equal distribution of income today than it did ten years ago?

    (A) Its Lorenz curve is closer to the 45-degree line and its Gini coefficient is larger.

    (B) Its Lorenz curve is closer to the 45-degree line and its Gini coefficient is smaller.

    (C) Its Lorenz curve is farther from the 45-degree line and its Gini coefficient is larger.

    (D) Its Lorenz curve is farther from the 45-degree line and its Gini coefficient is smaller.

    (E) Its Lorenz curve and Gini coefficient are unchanged.